SIMON & SCHUSTER
Rockefeller Center
1230 Avenue of the Americas
New York, New York 10020

10 9 8 7 6 5 4 3 2 1

Library of Congress Cataloging-in-Publication
Data

Stuart, Otis.
    Perpetual motion : the public and private lives
of Rudolf Nureyev / Otis Stuart.
        p.   cm.
Includes bibliographical references and index.
1. Nureyev, Rudolf, 1938–   .   2. Ballet dancers
—Russia
(Federation)—Biography.   I. Title.
GV1785.N8S78   1995
792.8'028'092—dc20
[B]   94-40874   CIP
ISBN 0-671-87539-6

Title page: Performing for Martha Graham in
Lucifer.
Photograph by Martha Swope.

OTIS STUART

SIMON & SCHUSTER

New York • London • Toronto
Sydney • Tokyo • Singapore

Perpetual Motion

THE PUBLIC AND PRIVATE LIVES OF RUDOLF NUREYEV

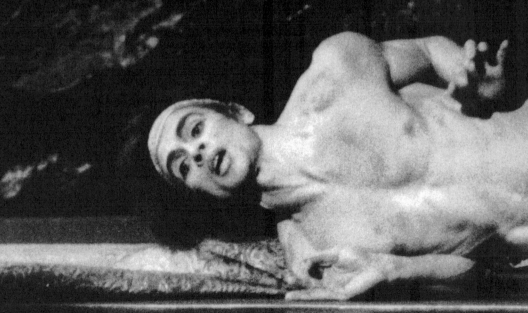

ACKNOWLEDGMENTS

The fact that *Perpetual Motion* exists at all is due to a quartet of associates who kept me moving forward. My generous friend Rick Whitaker introduced me to a crackerjack agent named Kim Witherspoon of Witherspoon & Associates in New York City. With her assistant Maria Massie, Kim kept me from being buried alive beneath an avalanche of press clips. Getting Simon & Schuster as a publisher and then Bob Bender as an editor were the final strokes of luck, and we were in business.

I could not begin to list the people who volunteered their time, their enthusiasm, and some great stories. I owe a special debt to the many press representatives who were willing to burrow through their files for obscure bits of Nureyeviana: Myra Armstrong and Kelly Ryan at American Ballet Theatre; Steve Scheller and Nina Berger of the Boston Ballet; Julia Drakr, Assis Carrero, and Sharon Vandailinde of the National Ballet of Canada; Ellen Jacobs of the Jacobs Agency in New York; Igor Stupnikov of the Kirov Ballet; Elizabeth Healy, L. Stephen Miller, and Geoffrey Peterson of New York City Ballet; Amanda Jones and Janine Limberg of the Royal Ballet in London; and Andrew Kessler of the Universal Ballet School in Washington, DC.

Particularly after the schedule finally had sunk in, friends and colleagues became more than that—they became a lifeline, especially my trio of Paris angels, Jacqueline Fynnaert, Josseline Le Bourhis, and, most of all, William Chatrier. Again, I can't name all of the people who went out of their way to help, but I would be seriously remiss without mentioning Carol Barance, Larry Becker, Christopher Brosius, Margaret Broussard, David Daniel, Don Daniels, Pamela Disimone, Richard Dworkin, Charles France, Leslie Getz, Merrill Goldin, Tobias Leibovitz, Jean-Yves Lormeau, Donald McDonagh, Patrick Merla, Sarah Pettit, Tim Scholl, Lee Smith, the gentlemen at *Ballet Review,* and the last gentleman scholar, Francis Mason. Neither would this book exist without a Nureyev follower named Joan Quatrano who allowed me a privileged glimpse at her insights on the ever elusive Rudi.

I would also like to thank two performing artists without whose work *Perpetual Motion* would have had a snowball's chance in hell of getting done. The first is Patti Lupone for her celestial account of "I Get a Kick Out of You" on the 1988 Broadway cast recording of *Anything Goes.* Who cares if the world is going down in flames when you've got the music of the spheres? I would also like to thank New York City Ballet soloist Ethan Stiefel for his performances during that company's recent winter season, about the time I realized that I had taken on the fantasy project from hell. Stiefel's exuberance and exactness and nerve in Jerome Robbins's *Interplay,* in Balanchine's *Harlequinade, Symphony in C,* and *Chaconne* were a regular reminder that ballet really can be the most fabulous goddamned thing there ever was.

And I would like to thank Rudolf Nureyev, for being exactly that —Rudolf Nureyev.

OTIS STUART
New York City
June 1994

In memory
of
PATRICK KELLY
1953–1993

CONTENTS

THREE: *Rudolf*

Prologue

The Throne
and the Wheelchair

"Great stars have great pride."
—NORMA DESMOND*

It was October 8, 1992, moments after the premiere of Rudolf Nureyev's version of the evening-length *La Bayadère* for the Paris Opéra Ballet. The final curtain call completed, the backstage scene was familiar enough. The scramble of activity filling the stage of the Opéra's Palais Garnier ought to have been standard-issue, regulation stuff—malingering *files* of dancers, wand-thin and too wound up from performance to head off for the dressing room; clusters of well-wishers working hard to freshen their compliments but breathless with the backstageness of it all; the inevitable impression that ballet makeup up close can look like something out of *The Cabinet of Dr. Caligari*. Tonight should have been indistinguishable from the backstage bustle after any first night. Another opening, another show.

Not this time.

Something else was going on. There was, of course, another event yet to transpire and everyone knew it, the reason everyone who was anyone in French dance, Parisian society, or

* *From* Sunset Boulevard.

both headed straight for the backstage area immediately after the last curtain. In a private, post-performance ceremony, Nureyev was to be awarded France's highest cultural honor, the rank of commander of arts and letters in the national Legion of Honor. Jack Lang, the endlessly visible French minister of culture, was on hand to make the presentation. The aura of importance the French live for embraced the anticipated proceedings—although the list Nureyev was joining includes Sylvester Stallone—but something more unnerving than anticipation was hovering over the stage.

Why, in the middle of the waves of motion that ripple across a stage in the wake of a final curtain call, was Nureyev of all people the only person seated? Why was Nureyev, Mr. Perpetual Motion himself, seated on an outsized piece of furniture that would have read as a throne from the back row of any theater on earth? And why was at least half the crowd surrounding him acutely, self-consciously aware of the fact that they were standing, and most of them uncomfortably? And why was the crowd openly staring at Nureyev, hard?

Being stared at, of course, was hardly an unusual event for Rudolf Nureyev; it was, in fact, the point of his life—or, more precisely, the point of half of his life, the public half Nureyev let the world see. Whatever they may claim about a right to privacy, performers live to be looked at. Some, like Nureyev, carry their own personal proscenium around with them. The off angle, the thing not quite standard in all the staring at the *Bayadère* premiere, began with the people doing the most intense staring— the Opéra dancers, most of them in extraordinary costumes and full stage makeup. Ballet dancers are not especially celebrated for their offstage powers of concentration. Tonight, every dancer in sight was lost in thought, so intent on Nureyev that they were blind to the banks of cameras recording the scene, oblivious to the easy opportunity for self-aggrandizement that the vaguest corps dancer could teach even actors about. Not one face looked into the cameras.

Out of everything off center about the scene, however,

Nureyev's own face was most wrong of all—this face of all faces, the one that everyone here had fixed on. Tonight, for once, Nureyev was not calling the shots. Simply by appearing in public, Nureyev was making his first open admission of the fact that the rumors about his health were not rumors. This was the face of AIDS. His features were still recognizable, in their outline, in their echoes. But they weren't the same either, and in a large, life-and-death way. Nureyev's cheeks were sunken, his skin translucent, his eyes uncertain. Within a matter of hours, the number of days Nureyev had left to live was the number one subject of speculation across Paris.

Leaning back into his throne, Nureyev had to have known what everyone was thinking. And he just continued to sit there, looking straight back at everyone.

Few performers, and surprisingly few ballet dancers, have ever mastered stillness on the scale achieved by Nureyev. When his powers were fully in play, no one could touch Nureyev in the art of the "caught" moment, the flash of revelation felt as a held breath on both sides of the footlights. It's his truest link to the legend of Nijinsky and, in a dancer of Nureyev's boundless energy and appetite, the type of paradox to spell Big Star. The man knew the value of the right pose in creating the impression that becomes a memory: suspension even figured in his moments of maximum physical intensity, those first unprecedented jetés that seemed to hang in midair and in the mind of anyone who saw them. Nureyev never had greater need for his capacity to intensify repose than he did in the backstage scene following the *Bayadère* premiere. He had rarely made more effective use of it.

Nureyev made what would prove his farewell public appearance from the exact point where he'd first appeared. Charles Garnier's Second Empire confection crowning the Avenue de l'Opéra—a rococo explosion viewed by the French old guard as Paris's street whore answer to the great lady Versailles—was the very frame in which Western audiences had first seen Nureyev dance, back during the tumultuous weeks in June 1961 when, on the first tour to Western Europe by Leningrad's Kirov Ballet,

Nureyev suddenly defected to the West at Paris's Le Bourget airport. By the *Bayadère* first night thirty years later, the Ian Fleming exhilaration of his first years in the West had evolved into a scene out of the Dostoyevsky novels Nureyev had cherished since adolescence. The sense of celebration that should have pervaded his last night at the Garnier took on ominous overtones instead. There wasn't a dry eye in the house.

Nureyev appeared at the Garnier for his *Bayadère* swathed in scarlet satin. During the performance, he reclined on a couch in a box overlooking the stage, visible to all and sipping champagne. This being a Nureyev evening, it was also not without that trademark touch of tension. Nureyev would not have had to look far to be reminded of rivalries past and present—and heated ones, too. The capacity crowd for the premiere included friends and colleagues from around the world as well as the highest strata of Parisian society. Titles were everywhere—les comtesses de Brantes and de Ribes and, de rigueur, la baronne Guy de Rothschild. At the dinner party he insisted on attending after the premiere, Nureyev chose a seat next to Pierre Bergé, the Opéra's president, so they could discuss plans for next year. The projects Nureyev proposed included a choreographic institute he wanted to establish in St. Petersburg.

Amid all the finery, that evening Nureyev could also find evidence of more than a few old scrapes. The *Bayadère* audience included his first real sparring partner and his last—two of the best, and toughest, both come, despite all, to pay tribute. One was Yuri Grigorovich, currently director of Moscow's Bolshoi Ballet, but the most promising young Soviet choreographer in the days when Nureyev was the Kirov's ranking problem child; when Grigorovich was preparing the ballet that confirmed his standing, *Legend of Love*, a work that remains a staple of the contemporary Russian repertory, clashes with Nureyev soon made Grigorovich the first person to give Nureyev the boot. And, in the tiniest of black dresses, the *Bayadère* audience also included Sylvie Guillem, the most popular French ballerina since Chauviré and a firecracker to rival Nureyev at his fieriest. Guillem had been the jewel in the crown of ballerinas cultivated by Nureyev during his stormy tenure as the Opéra's artistic director from 1983 to 1989. She finally had had to leave the Opéra for London's Royal Ballet because the banks of the Seine were just not big enough to hold the two of them.

Closer to home, the potential for some choice French fireworks had been simmering for days. Throughout his leadership of the Opéra, Nureyev had enjoyed a particularly public competition with Patrick Dupond, the danseur who was to succeed him as the Opéra's director. An electric audience favorite, Dupond was the closest the Opéra came to providing Nureyev with a rival for the attention of the Paris public and was nearly twenty-one years Nureyev's junior into the bargain. The tension between them became one of the hottest grapevine items of Nureyev's time as Opéra director. The hatchet ostensibly had been buried when the two performed together for the first time at a benefit after Dupond had become the Opéra's director. Unfortunately, Nureyev's choice of casting for the new Bayadère, the prerogative of the choreographer, seemed to bring back those old-time feelings. Dupond was not included in either the first-night cast or any cast thereafter. Nureyev perhaps remembered an Opéra performance of Bayadère's revered white act some years earlier when the then-teenaged Dupond lost control of the long white scarf that wafts through the pas de deux and, by his own admission, very nearly strangled the Opéra's exquisite senior ballerina, Nöella Pontois.

The Bayadère oversight was taken badly, and disaster seemed imminent when Dupond insisted he would not attend the opening night, Legion of Honor or not. A scene was avoided at the very last moment by a hush-hush but loud-and-clear directive from Bergé: be there that night or the ballet has a new director the next morning. Dupond conceded, sort of. Due to an unexpected injury, his entrance at Nureyev's Legion of Honor tribute was made in a wheelchair. Dueling divas are one thing; dueling wheelchairs are something else again.

When Nureyev was a ballet student in Leningrad, the Paris Opéra was the last word in sophistication for his generation of Russian dancers, and was known among Kirov students as "The Grand Opera." Back then, more than one of the shouting matches with his peers that were already a Nureyev signature had ended with his last word on any subject: "You will all see. I will dance at the Grand Opera and you will all still be here." That *La Bayadère* on that very stage should turn out to be his farewell gesture almost seems an act of destiny. Ballet dancers, like sopranos and musical comedy stars, build up a medley of greatest hits over a lengthy career. Like the senior ballerinas he partnered toward his first celebrity—Natalia Dudinskaya, Maria Tallchief, and, most famously, Margot Fonteyn—Nureyev danced a long time, longer than any other dancer of his generation. (The Martha Graham of classic dance, Alicia Alonso remains the recordholder, having spanned generations of *Giselles*.) *La Bayadère* echoes along the full length of Nureyev's life and career. The ballet's tormented hero, Solor, is a perfect match for the Nureyev persona. Nineteenth-century ballet's variant on our rock hero, Solor brings on the best part of the ballet, the fabled Shades scene, by smoking a little opium and then sailing off on a major riff. He is also the ballet hero who upstages his women. The ladies fight over him, rather than the other way around that is standard in classic ballet. Everybody wants a piece of his action. Solor was among Nureyev's most promising roles in his brief career with the Kirov. During that fateful tour to Paris, in the Kirov version of the Shades scene, Solor was the role that introduced Nureyev to the West; it was the last role he danced with the Kirov the night before his defection. Barely two years later, when Nureyev had landed on his feet at London's Royal Ballet, *Bayadère's* famous white act, the opiate "Kingdom of the Shades," became his first effort at staging a ballet. In no time at all, the Shades had become a signature of his instantly fabled partnership with Fonteyn, the nearest rival to their *Giselle* in the headiness of its ether and the picturebook-perfection of its classicism.

Nureyev's fidelity to *Bayadère* was as telling as it was a surprise. Nureyev first took the world by storm as the most vital, virile male dancer in memory. Immaculately classic, the *Bayadère* Shades scene seems a baffling choice for a bad boy danseur. It is, in fact, a clue into the personal contradictions that kept Nureyev a world player years after his dancing had disintegrated.

Particularly in its entirety, *La Bayadère* has its drawbacks. The ballet is more than a warhorse. It's a warehouse of nine-teenth-century excess, a catalogue of the things twentieth-century ballet swept from the dance horizon, saving ballet from the fate that awaited mime. First staged in 1877 by Marius Petipa, the French-born choreographer who became the architect of Imperial Russian ballet classicism, the setting of the ballet is the kind of thing drag queens might think twice about. From start to finish, *Bayadère* plays like one of the overwrought silent-film epics that killed the movie palaces. Golden idols dance. Virgins wield daggers. Temples collapse into rubble. Accidentally Freudian, the heroine, the temple dancer Nikiya, first appears in a shroud and then doesn't even last until the last act, lost to an asp in a basket. Audiences can't get enough of it. Three out of the five major ballet companies in the West—American Ballet Theatre, the Royal in London, and now, thanks to Nureyev, the Paris Opéra —include an all-night *Bayadère* in their repertories. Nureyev's version goes for the kick ass in kitsch. Solor enters astride a life-sized prop elephant on rollers. (The surprise pachyderm also provided Nureyev with his own acerbic in-joke at the ballet's premiere. Fully cognizant that his behavior was being scrutinized for signatures of AIDS, which can include dementia, Nureyev never missed a chance during the first act to roll his head back and repeat, "Have we had the elephant yet? Have we had the elephant yet?")

Asp-kissers and all, *Bayadère* also contains the first great summary of the classic ballet vocabulary. The Shades scene is *Bayadère*'s answer to the shadow act costumed all in white that nineteenth-century audiences expected by the end of an evening at the ballet. (The tradition of the white act began with ballet's Romantic period, circa 1830, with Marie Taglioni in her window, not quite innocently backlit. More cynical quarters hold that its popularity lay with the tendency of gas lighting to give the gauze of the women's costumes that special see-through appeal, what leotards have done for our time. The fact has been widely forgotten, but "balletomane" began as a heterosexual reference.) Overcome by Nikiya's death, Solor brings on the Shades scene by helping himself to those few puffs of the poppy. He is visited by a vision of the other world into which Nikiya has crossed. Filling the stage first, the corps de ballet has one of the most famous entrances in classic dance, an endless, single-file processional of arabesque penchées: deep, bowing steps in which an arm is extended to its maximum forward position while the opposite leg reaches as far and as high to the back as it can. The stage finally is flooded with pools of white and an infinity of lingering limbs. The extended corps adagio, three soloist variations, and pas de deux for Nikiya and Solor that follow are an aberrant blast of purity amidst all the high-color kitsch. The pure dance, abstracted nature of a ballet classicism at once textbook and experimental, prefigures the next three generations of ballet innovators: Lev Ivanov's symphonic flights in the 1895 *Swan Lake*; the symmetry and swirl of Michel Fokine's *Les Sylphides* a decade later; and, finally, the breathless twentieth-century neoclassicism of George Balanchine.

The Shades scene was the only section of *Bayadère* the West got to see Nureyev dance. Over the thirty years of his Western career, Nureyev staged all of the traditional repertory classics, dancing all of the leads himself—with the single exception of the final *Bayadère* for the Opéra. Nureyev was never to perform the complete *Bayadère* outside Leningrad. Western audiences never saw him rip into the camp of the mimed acts—puffed of chest, feathered of turban, a field day for the panther magnetism Nureyev patented during his earliest years in the West. Instead, from that first London premiere, we got what Nureyev wanted us to see of him and presumably remember: the wild thing as unmitigated classicist in the Kingdom of the Shades. It was the sixties, and the world ate it up.

Which is why, at the *Bayadère* premiere, Nureyev's face was such a shock. The gilt of the Legion of Honor medal and its banner of green and white draped about his neck should have helped but they didn't. Their glitter only emphasized what had once been as glittering and was now lost. For a decade Nureyev had responded to the AIDS rumors in exactly the way he'd always countered inquiries about his sexual orientation, by following the lesson Margot Fonteyn had taught him, in the fire, at their famous "pot bust" in San Francisco in 1967: "Just don't say anything." On the evening of the *Bayadère* premiere, all Nureyev's performance signatures were clearly in play—the red-caped theatricality, the all-night drive, the imperial ambition. But Nureyev's face was more familiar to people than his dancing. The gaunt, haunted face above the satin—no other high-profile AIDS case had allowed cameras this close this late—wasn't it. *"La machine,"* Nureyev told a friend not long after, *"est cassée."* [The machine is broken.]

And you saw the break first in what had been his first piece of luck. Mae West said it best in reference to herself: "When I was born with this here face, it was the same as strikin' earl." She could have been describing Nureyev. This was clearly more than a case of those lips, those eyes. Nureyev had the audacity to be physically exotic at a time when the lines of battle were as clear as the Berlin Wall and the March on Selma. This was not a safe face. The eyes traced the subtlest slant upward. The cheekbones were so expansive *Newsweek* called them cruel. The lips were too full to even approximate inexperience, especially with that faint suggestion of a scar tilting off the upper lip and adding the very lightest suggestion of a threat somewhere in the immediate vicinity. (Tellingly, Nureyev got his scar as a child during an altercation with an angry dog he was trying to feed.) From the beginning, photographers lined up. Within a month of his defection, Nureyev already was posing for Richard Avedon. Nureyev became the most photographed figure in his profession and one of the most photographed men in the world. He was, as Maria Tallchief once sighed, "an extremely, *extremely* attractive young man."

At the *Bayadère* premiere, for the only time in his career, Nureyev had to be helped onto a stage. For the first time in his public life, he was seen to weep. "Can you imagine," he told a friend that night, looking out into the gilded vastness of the Garnier. "I am going to have to say good-bye to all this."

Two days later, he set off for his beachfront bungalow at St. Barth's.

Asked in the airport about reading material for the flight, Nureyev's answer was direct.

"I want ass magazines."

ONE

Rudik

One

Born on a Train

"Let them hate, so long as they fear."

—JOSEF STALIN, borrowed from Caligula,
Alex de Jonge, Stalin

Standing on the tired platform of a provincial Russian train station, Farida Nureyeva probably didn't realize that she was about to take the first steps in an epic story.

She probably wouldn't have cared much anyway.

Farida's was not a discretionary trip. The slight, steely woman with the shock of black hair was once considered pretty. Toughened by her lot at twenty-three, now she was simply another shadow in the vast, faceless Russian peasantry. Besides, on that icy morning in March 1938, Farida had more pressing problems. She was aiming at the other side of the world—the Pacific port city of Vladivostok, the farthest post of the sprawling Soviet empire, where her husband Hamnet worked for the new government's burgeoning military machine. The physical distance between Farida and Hamnet was becoming a pressure on their marriage; times were hard enough without having a husband who was always somewhere else, no matter how much the young couple believed in the worthiness of the struggling Soviet nation. Matters were serious enough that Farida had decided to forget the blustery last stand of Russian winter. She chose instead to head

23

east just as the first thaws began their annual attempt to turn Asian Russia into one huge spillway.

But Farida couldn't think about even that, not for the moment anyway. One glance across the platform told her why. The train, when and if it finally pulled into the station, would provide only limited relief. Long years of military conflict had turned the famous railway into Siberia into one long military skirmish, open game for whichever side of the latest conflict got to the trains first. Just getting a ticket for the trip had been nightmare enough. The coming fortnight trundling across the continent would be jammed with refugees from every strata of the unsettled Soviet order. Farida had seen them all before. Long files of soldiers; row after broken row of political prisoners bound for Stalin's latest answer to opposition, the gulag. Scariest of all were the ice-eyed brigands, out to serve whichever side of the struggle offered the best price. Even if Farida was lucky enough to find a place to sit and/or to sleep, she was unlikely to get a moment's real rest until the train reached Vladivostok. She didn't dare take her eyes off the three small figures huddled next to her against the cold.

Farida pulled her daughters closer. Soldiers, she knew, could get ugly; her own husband liked his liquor and it didn't always bring out the best in him. The three children pressing up against their mother's body brought back her greatest anxiety. The girls were careful of their mother's swollen belly. They knew there was a new life in there. Well into her eighth month of pregnancy, Farida knew that were the child to arrive en route, its chances of surviving the cold, the rattle of the train, and the infamously unsanitary conditions of the Siberian railway were virtually nil.

No one could have known that, at the juncture of the central Asian steppes with the mountains of Mongolia, the horizon dotted by Lake Baikal, the highest and largest inland sea in the world, Farida would realize her husband's fondest dream. On March 17, 1938, their baby boy finally arrived, delivered into the arms of his ten-year-old sister Rosa (and ironically, considering where the boy would die half a century later, he was born as the train was speeding past the city of Irkutsk, known locally for its many theaters and grand opera house as "the Paris of Siberia"). His father's absence would prove prophetic. No one could have imagined that his only son would grow up to become the bitterest disappointment of Hamnet's life.

Years later, after Rudolf was the most famous dancer in the world, he recounted the story of his birth with relish and, whenever possible, described it as the most romantic event of his life. He also polished its details to a burnished gloss, eventually reporting that the rumble of the train had brought on his mother's labor pains three weeks prematurely and forced an early entrance. Not a chance. Just as he would year after year in the world's great theaters, Rudolf Hametovitch Nureyev made his entrance right on schedule. From the beginning, the Nureyevs' baby boy knew the value of a big entrance.

Fact and fiction share a special bond through Rudolf Nureyev's fifty-four years. It's no particular surprise for a life begun during the most dangerous days of the Stalinist era, when the border between what's real and what's protective coloring is a matter of life and death. Because he lived in the West for so long, Nureyev's audiences eventually forgot that the man and his character were forged someplace else, somewhere very far away, by realities few Europeans and fewer Americans could ever understand. When Nureyev was a child in the city of Ufa, deep in the Ural province of Bashkir, reinventing yourself was the only way to keep ahead of the hair-trigger local commissars.

Distant or not, the Ufa of Nureyev's childhood was already a valued Soviet industrial center. A decade of slave labor by Stalin's political prisoners had begun forging the network of roadways, train routes, and heavy industries that Stalin needed to connect and control European Russia and his far-flung Asian provinces.[1] Guarded by the Urals but accessible to their mineral wealth, with the added advantage of Siberian coal near enough to keep the foundries busy, Ufa was a vital connecting point of the new system. It was also one of the shadow cities that tended to disappear from maps of the Soviet Union. On official Soviet maps, it is, in fact, still possible to find Ufa located on the wrong side of the Urals.[2] Even today native Russians discuss the city quietly, with a tremble of cautious awe. "The whole area," according to one descendant of Ufa expatriates, "is . . . well, kind of wild."

When the British filmmaker Patricia Foy arrived in Ufa in 1990 to prepare a documentary on Nureyev's life, she and her crew were unable to learn "what was manufactured there. [The locals] were very evasive, but only two months before the area had been forbidden to visitors."[3] The lack of facts hasn't stopped the rumors. The entire Ural region is widely believed to have been one of the centers of the Soviet arms industry. The thirties were the decade when the Soviet government began to build and flex some real military muscle, and the Nazi threat already on the march when Nureyev was born[4] prompted Soviet leader Josef Stalin to invest extra effort in an experiment he'd begun during his first Five Year Plan ten years earlier: evacuating critical industries to the protective cover of the mountains that keep Europe out of Asia. When the war ended, the factories stayed. By 1945, when Nureyev's family finally was reunited in Ufa, the Urals housed fully half of the Soviet metals industry.[5] The adjacent Volga basin already had begun producing the MiG fighter planes that would, for the next three decades, keep the Urals clear of prying enemy aircraft, a warning to the world to be wary of the Soviet bear.

Keeping your mouth shut was a lesson any sharp, determined little boy would have learned but quick, Farida's little lad in particular. Despite Nureyev's fabled gift for expletives in rehearsals, in class, and even in performance, it was a lesson even thirty years of exorbitant celebrity in the West couldn't undo. (After his move to the West, Nureyev never once bad-mouthed the Soviet government to the press.) The first fact of survival in the Soviet Union, Nureyev's capacity to rewrite the past and the present would be a source of contention to the end of his life. But the contradictions of his saga are too outrageous not to have some basis in truth. Raised in a shanty, trained as a toddler to bury his few rations of raw potatoes against the bite of Russian winter and the hungry hands of others, Nureyev died master of an enormous fortune so carefully scattered around the world no one knows exactly where it all is or just how much money is actually involved. (Estimates vary from $50 to $80 million.) The man who taught the world even men in ballet could be butch was also among the most famously promiscuous homosexuals of a randy epoch. The danseur who reinvented the term "Russian ballet" for a nascent global village didn't have a drop of Russian blood in him. Nureyev's lines had none of European Russia's Westernized sensibilities or the "slave mentality" so famously ascribed to the Russian national character.[6] On both sides, his family history traced back instead to the race that had terrorized the Russians for a millennium, the demon Tatars.

What Nureyev also had from the very beginning of his life, firsthand, was a sense of the wide world, and not the unpracticed one Western schoolchildren get out of their geography books. By his fifth year, Farida's baby boy, nicknamed Rudik, had crossed the Asian land mass twice, and then ended up going halfway back east when Farida and her brood resettled in the Urals to wait out World War II. Instantly precocious, a scamp with wide, thoughtful eyes and a crown of flaxen hair—a neighbor from Ufa's first memories of the child Nureyev are of a "lively little rogue who was always naughty, impulsive, and easily angered" —Rudik was the apple of his mother's eagle eye (a responsibility the Soviets would later use to masterful effect in trying to get Nureyev back into the fold). The horizons of his childhood were without limits and among the most dramatic the world has to offer—the Caucasus, the Urals, the forests of fir and birch that blanket central Russia before the brush-cut rigors of the taiga take over. Nureyev's later friends and colleagues marveled at the travel demanded by his grueling performance schedule, as he crossed and recrossed the globe the way most other people cross the street. Helping to invent the international jet set is no mean feat for a man deathly afraid of air travel his entire life. (The great dramatic ballerina Lynn Seymour remembers early flights with Nureyev curled up under his seat, vodka in hand, during take off.) Motion was a habit Nureyev had acquired by five and never lost. Like the father who was always away, young Rudik's real home was always someplace else. Just by looking out the train window from Mamushka's lap, you could see how far away it was.

When Farida set off on her long journey to Vladivostok, she also could not have known that she was a woman who had bumped into history or that the impact would ricochet through her son's life straight through to his deathbed. On that long ago winter morning, Russia was witnessing the arrival of more than just Farida's baby boy, yet another little soldier ready to march in service to the Soviet state. By March 1938 a new set of daily priorities had been wedged into place for the new Russia, a second revolution concluded without the fanfare or good intentions of the first. In place of the euphoria of the 1917 revolution, the operative rules this time were silence and subservience, a numbed assent to the kind of fear that never goes away. Even the tsar hadn't been as good at fear as Stalin, whose adapted name is Russian for "man of steel."[7] When Nureyev was born, after more than a decade of terror, Stalin was in the last stages of achieving his own Russian Revolution by sealing up a stress fracture that had been straining the cause since Kerensky: keep the masses out of it. Don't tell them what you don't want them to know. The unknown is where real power hides. If everyone is busy guessing who will be next to vanish, no one will ever feel safe enough to be a threat. They'll turn on each other instead.

His methodology was the type to scar a nation and its people for life.[8] Things always had been tough for the endless Russian masses. Now, under Stalin, they were worse. By the time the Nureyevs finally had their son, no Soviet citizen of whatever rank could know where and when the fatal blow might come. There were just too many possibilities—a surprise bullet, a show trial, "relocation" to the dreaded collectives, specialist local tortures such as force-feeding prisoners salted fish and then refusing water. A surefire career route for the ambitious, arrests were based on quotas. If the quotas weren't met, the local government officials themselves were arrested and either deported or executed. Not even Stalin's henchmen were safe. His highest ranking officials were required to train two successors to their jobs, just in case,[9] and "those members of the Communist Party who held responsible posts were the most suspect of all. . . . People who had important jobs generally kept two suitcases packed, one at work and one at home, so that they might always have their things ready whether they were arrested by day or night."[10] Stalin's fearsome purges of the party during the 1930s began middecade, after the murder, presumably with Stalin's approval, of his most popular ally, ex-fireman Sergey Kirov. In a surge of national mourning, Kirov's name was given to the Leningrad ballet company where Nureyev first became famous a quarter century later. Nureyev was born the same month as the last of the Moscow show trials that began with Kirov's assassination and concluded in one more round of mass executions.

Predictably, for a boy who would become a man as private as Nureyev, informing was the order of the day, the only sanctioned form of private enterprise.[11] There's a reason the Russian language has no idiom analogous to the Western expression "live and let live." Betrayal—supplying information about friends, family, anybody—was reinvented as an act of patriotism.[12] A backroom politico of the oldest school, Stalin knew that informing on your own was one of the oldest Russian traditions,[13] and the knowledge gave him a mastery of faceless, constant fear that outdid even the Nazis. Stalin had the bigger job all around and even Hitler knew it—more land to watch over, more extremes to control, and, always, more subjects to keep underfoot. "If I had the vast spaces of Siberia," Hitler once remarked to his staff, "I wouldn't need concentration camps."[14]

Ma Joad had an easier time than the Russians. By 1938, the political anxiety pervading Soviet society had made nervous breakdowns and heart attacks a mass phenomenon.[15] When Nureyev made his dramatic entrance, the population of the gulag was approaching 10 percent of the adult citizenry.[16] Stalin already had executed close to five million of his subjects. The estimated rate of dispatch was five hundred victims a day, Sundays and holidays included.[17] Children twelve or older could be tried as adults and then executed.

This was the world Nureyev knew through his adolescence, when all those crucial attitudes toward life, love, and sex were being solidified. And the horrors of a brutal political regime were multiplied each and every day by the first and oldest enemies of the Russian people, twin villains Nureyev knew from infancy: the rigors of the native landscape; and, even worse, a constant cold so bitter it burns each breath into ice. (Soldiers lost in guarding the highest Siberian latitudes during World War II were discovered with their spinal fluid frozen through.) Seeping around every corner of his life, the chill of those early days would pursue the child Rudik right through to the end and the Paris apartment the adult Nureyev always kept overheated, still afraid of the cold. "Those people never get over how they grew up," says a colleague of Nureyev who's made a study of Russian dancers. "It never leaves them. Look at Misha. The melancholy will always be with him. With Rudolf it was the same story."[18]

In retrospect, it's hard to imagine a nomad like Nureyev as expressive of any specifically national character traits. Despite his final decade in Paris, Nureyev died a citizen of Austria, where the income tax structure was more accommodating.[19] His real estate holdings included a ranch in rural Virginia and a beachfront bungalow on St. Barthélemy in the Caribbean. In 1991 Nureyev acquired the final status—the rocky Mediterranean island near Capri, Li Galli, that once belonged to Léonide Massine. (The neighboring resort islands are owned by the likes of Gore Vidal.) Nureyev invested small fortunes in museum-quality furnishings for his Paris apartment on the Quai Voltaire and his seven-room spread in the Dakota apartment building in New York City. Not six months before his death, Nureyev was ordering new pipes for extensive repairs to the outmoded plumbing system in his Tyrrhenian retreat. For all the time, energy, and expense expended on his well-appointed homes, Nureyev rarely was resident in any of them for more than a few short days at a time. Life was on the road. "All I need," Nureyev once observed, "is a room, then a bath, a bed—and a door to get out and start dancing again." [20]

Rolling stones, even stylish ones, may gather no moss, but they can't help leaving behind a trail, the kind of path into the past where the deepest tracks only become more entrenched with time. The exact statistics of Nureyev's background, of course, its names, dates, and places, disappeared long ago into what Pasternak called the "nameless numbers on lists that were later misplaced." Like their son, Nureyev's parents grew up at the eye of a political hurricane. His mother's family were products of the ancient Mongol city of Kazan, the holy capital of the Volga Tatars. Farida was born less than a year after World War I forced millions of unprepared Russians to take on the invading Germans who'd been in training since Bismarck. When the war finally ended, Kazan was the city where the full fury of the new Red Terror was first felt. Farmers for generations, Hamnet's family worked the land outside a mountain village near Ufa in the Mongol province of Bashkir. Hamnet reached young manhood when the horrors of the counterrevolution had attained unspeakable proportions. In the early 1920s, when civil war was at its peak, Bashkir officials recorded more than two thousand cases of cannibalism. [21]

Family trees were not a high priority for people as hard-pressed as these, especially since they were people for whom illiteracy was the norm and who didn't even have surnames to record until the first decades of this century. The family name Nureyev, in fact, first appeared with Rudik's paternal grandfather, who spent most of his life with only the given name of Nurr, a Bashkir word for sunlight. [22] When Nurr and his brother Fasily were given last names by the government of Nicholas II, the attending clerk took an easy way out of a busy job by simply adding the common Russian suffix "yev" to both names. Nurr became Nureyev and Fasily became Fasiliyev, the reason that Nureyev's few surviving relatives don't even share a common name.

For all the anonymity of Nureyev's origins, the outline is clear, and the clues begin with his father. Hamnet was named Murmuhammed at his birth, but, during the whirlwind of wars and revolutions waiting in the wings, changed it to something a little safer, more Russified. Nureyev's bloodlines trail all the way back to the infamous, and hugely successful, Asian invasions of the late Middle Ages, the era of the Golden Mongol Horde sweeping down onto Russia. Since its earliest recorded history, Russia had been plagued by invaders along every one of its endless borders. Even the most notorious of the would-be conquerors, from Napoleon to the Nazis, inevitably failed—with one exception. Over all those centuries, the Mongol Tatars were the only race to make the Russians a conquered people (until, by Nureyev's birth, Stalin had managed to subjugate the nation from within). Independent with a vengeance, the Tatars were a race of survivors who grabbed at their destiny with both hands, or at least with the hand that wasn't wielding a weapon. Horsemen of enduring legend, they tore across the continent as a matter of course. "The Tatar yoke" had Russians trembling for three centuries. The memory never went away on either side and would affect Nureyev's life from both directions.

Nureyev was always acutely aware of his ancestry. Once he'd finally gotten away from Ufa and reached the dance mecca of Leningrad, his unschooled manners and bumpkin accent were an initial and painful problem, a rare instance of real mortification in a life driven by world-class confidence and self-esteem. The favored ethnic slurs of native Russian argot during Nureyev's youth included a healthy helping of ethnic insults that didn't spare the descendants of the Tatars scattered across the Soviet nation. Characteristically, the teenaged Nureyev's attitude to second-class status in an allegedly classless society was defiant. Instead of being cowed by the limitations of his background, Nureyev looked to his ancestry with a reverence just short of ruthlessness.

The quality was not destined to endear Nureyev to the Soviet authorities. From the earliest days of the new regime, the Tatar tribes were the only ones of their subjects the Soviets genuinely feared. The Baltic states were sitting ducks, the Russians too broken and bitter to resist. The Moslems were liable to strike back. When the Soviet Socialist Republics were being outlined, the Bashkirs got a republic of their own, despite the fact that its population was only one-quarter Bashkir.[23] Ufa became one of only four Spiritual Directories allowed an official religion by the atheist Moscow government.[24]

The Bolshevik fear of Nureyev's ancestors was more than the paranoia of revolutionaries. Historically, it was plain practical sense. (The Chinese built the Great Wall to keep the Mongols out.) Even the most enduring historical myths, of course, can be manufactured, as our century has learned better than any other. Witness the cults of Stalin, Hitler, and Ronald Reagan. Three hundred years of Tatar rule, however, left behind data impressive even against the brutal background of Russian history. The name Tatar, in fact, was introduced by fearful Europeans, who derived the term from the mythological gates of Tartarus, the underworld hell. With good reason. Nureyev's conquering ancestors introduced European torture chambers to the knout—a lash with three razor-sharp rawhide tails designed to produce a deep, lasting wound with each blow—as well as an update on the medieval rack, theirs fashioned to dislocate a victim's limbs one by one. (Boiling water dripped onto freshly shaved heads was also a popular favorite.) The Tatars were also responsible for a more lasting contribution that would one day torment Nureyev himself, an all-knowing form of secret police whose methods would be honed by the Romanovs and perfected by their communist successors.

Nureyev's Tatar ancestors were the last two tribes to hold out against the tsars. The Volga Tatars and the Bashkirs remained their own masters until the sixteenth century, almost two hundred years after the rest of their Mongol brothers had given in. One of Nureyev's early Russian colleagues, the incandescent young ballerina candidate Alla Sizova,[25] still remembers a conversation she once had with her new partner at the end of a rehearsal day. The two dancers were returning to the communal apartment they'd taken together after graduating from the Kirov ballet school into the main-stage ballet company. Sizova remembers their talk that day as exceptional because her new young friend from the provinces, normally a very private young man, was for once talking about his family and its antecedents. Looking up at the rows of delicate palaces that were one of the few legacies of Romanov Petersburg the Soviets had had the sense to hold onto, Nureyev made a telling observation. "We were once the rulers here, you know, and for three centuries, too. My people were in control of yours," Nureyev explained with an emphasis at once sympathetic and savage that still impresses Sizova more than thirty years later. "You did," Nureyev concluded, "what *we* said."

"Just a Little Tatar Boy"

Two

CAPITALIST: "What took you so long?"
SOCIALIST: "I had to buy some meat and there was a long line."
CAPITALIST: "What's a line?"
COMMUNIST: "What's meat?"

ureyev had good reason to look back on his ancestry with satisfaction. As a student, his Mongol past was a history lesson with a contemporary application: conquest was his birthright. As an adult, the view from the top of his profession was the richest landscape the Tatar conqueror had seen in centuries. World celebrity was only part of the picture. Like Pavlova,[1] the only continent Nureyev didn't play was Antarctica. Headline interest in his offstage activities waited in every port of call as well, and, intentionally or not, Nureyev always left behind something for folks to talk about. (Fonteyn and Nureyev, in fact, were the only ballet dancers outside the Soviet Union to be taken into police custody twice, once each on their own and then once together.) Like his fellow icons of popular culture, Nureyev was one of those people other people just like to talk about. Uniquely, Nureyev managed to keep tongues wagging without benefit of a personal press representative. He never needed one.

From early childhood, Nureyev managed to create a self-sustaining private world with himself at its axis, and, as an adult, his tight inner circle of friends protected him (while he was alive

35

and especially since his death) with a tenacity worthy of its subject. Nureyev's finances were among the protected zones, although his business savvy was yet another surprising feature for a man raised in a country where, both traditionally and in historical fact, the rich are the enemy of the people. (It's a quality Nureyev shared with the two other dancers in the Blessed Trinity of Kirov expatriates, Natalia Makarova and Mikhail Baryshnikov[2]). Nureyev died with a financial estate worthy of the great Khans.[3] Beyond a sum as staggering as that *for a ballet dancer,* but no less valuable to him, Nureyev was one of the few artists in the history of any discipline to bodily alter his craft, to introduce a change in the actual shape and direction of an art. Nureyev gave ballet a new male body, literally, and his look and line affected every male dancer who came after him. Without Nureyev, there would have been no Baryshnikov, and Baryshnikov is the first to admit it. Without Nureyev, there would not be anything like the current fleet of ascendant male ballet dancers—Ethan Stiefel at New York City Ballet, Nicolas Le Riche at the Paris Opéra, Lloyd Riggins with London's Royal Ballet—who've followed Nureyev's lead in elevating male ballet dancing to the strata of finish, focus, and finesse that had been the exclusive territory of the ballerina since the first half of the nineteenth century. Until Nureyev, women had always out-jumped men, the aberration of a Nijinsky or Nureyev excepted, because women's more intense training straightened their knees, streamlining them for flight. Nureyev, like everyone else in his generation, never could straighten his knees *en l'air* or in pirouettes. He tried but had begun too late. The reason so many male dancers today can straighten their knees for a clean, sailing jeté is because Nureyev refused to stop trying.

But the signature feature of the Nureyev saga is how far he had to come to reach that pinnacle, Horatio Alger rewritten as one half Dostoyevsky and one half Judith Krantz. Unlike Makarova and Baryshnikov,[4] Nureyev had the harshest facts of Soviet life slammed in his face from that first trek to Vladivostok. His most intense childhood memory, the first fact in a litany of deprivation, was hunger, unending hunger. Until he was seven years old, the second constant was violence. The bloodshed of the purges and internal conflicts ravaging the Soviet Union through the first half of the 1940s was a routine fact of Nureyev's earliest life.

Motion was another. Within a matter of months after arriving in Vladivostok, Farida and her four children found themselves back on the Trans-Siberian Railway, accompanied by Hamnet this time and bound all the way back to Moscow. Travel, the children already knew, was second nature for their father, a trait his son would acquire.[5] A son of the new Russia, Hamnet worked for the all-important Soviet military at a job that kept him on the move. He was one of the new company of *politrouks* instituted by the Soviet government. Among the most single-minded dogmatists in the new Russia,[6] the *politrouks* were soldiers assigned to instruct their comrades in the great history of Mother Russia, the glories of the party, and, in particular, their good fortune in a leader as miraculous as Stalin. Low on the power totem pole but guaranteed access to the good graces of the powers that be, Hamnet's work necessitated constant travel from one battalion to another. He generally traveled without his young family. When he was reassigned to Moscow on the eve of a new war in Europe, Hamnet moved his family with him to the potential security of the capital city, the power center of the Stalinist empire.

By the 1930s, Moscow had replaced Leningrad as the seat of power in the new Russia. Stalin and his cabinet of men's men had little use for the elegance and innovation of Peter the Great's "Window to the West." A native Georgian of the most proletarian stock—the few existing photographs of Stalin's mother explain half his neuroses—Stalin shifted power from the marbled corridors of the Winter and Tauride palaces in St. Petersburg, now Leningrad, to the Kremlin, the ancient Moscow fortress with a history that makes the Tower of London look like Disneyland. Stalin projected Moscow as the super city of the future and a showcase for the great Soviet advances in urban technology, such as the vast new subway system completed in 1935 by an up-and-coming new party honcho, Nikita Khrushchev.

The Nureyevs' arrival in Moscow couldn't have been

timed worse. The barely repressed panic in the wake of the last show trials pervaded the city, and, with Hitler on the move a capital city soon turned out to be anything but a refuge. Hamnet was gone again in less than two years. Operation Barbarossa, Germany's surprise invasion of Russia in the summer of 1941, had him off to the front, his *politrouk* manual replaced by a rifle. The family he left behind again was also back on the move almost immediately, just as soon as one of the first German bombs to hit the city hit their apartment building dead-on. Flight was swift and sudden, and Rudik's first lesson in traveling light. The speediness of their departure forced Farida to leave behind most of their few possessions. Her son's earliest memory was evacuating the city "on a wheelbarrow with a kettle swinging from the back."[7]

Farida's destination this trip was the tiny Bashkir village of Tchichuna[8] on the eastern face of the Urals near the city of Chelyabinsk.[9] The two years she and her children lived in the mountain hamlet left her son with his first conscious series of visual impressions. Interestingly enough considering the ferocity of his adult life, the strongest of Nureyev's earliest memories involve being frightened. Nureyev remembered being stranded in a sailboat in the middle of a lake, "crying and shouting with fear," and, with particular emphasis, "the tremendous snowdrifts on either side of the only road in the village. . . . These snowpiles looked to me like dirty mountains on each side of a narrow, frightening path. So it is, then, that the first images of early childhood for me are of an icy, dark, and, above all, hungry world."[10] A couple of other important firsts were also waiting for him in Tchichuna, and they were destined to influence Nureyev to the very end of his life. First, Rudik learned his first scam. And before the family had relocated yet again two years later, Rudik was given something he had not yet known existed—a present, a gift with no strings attached, something that belonged to him and only him.

The tiny shack, or *isba*, where Farida and her children lived in Tchichuna was straight out of the darkest chapters of a Tolstoy epic, one of the makeshift, one-room shanties in which the poorest of the Russian mountain peasantry had huddled for centuries and where amenities such as a toilet were unimagined. Farida and her children were forced to share the close quarters of the *isba* with other families, although their exact number varies with who is telling the story. At least two other people are definite: an aged, intensely religious husband and wife who lived in a corner of the room smothered with icons and who always kept an oil lamp burning before an image of the Virgin Mary. (The vestal lamp was no small luxury for the period, both politically and in terms of the oil that could have helped heat the hut.)

Already the possessor of a keen eye, Rudik took no time at all to learn that, if he joined the old couple in their early morning prayers, he would find himself with a few extra scraps of food as a reward. That lesson under his belt, a household accident soon brought Rudik another reward, one that took him by surprise and that he never forgot. Already a physical knock-about, always in motion, Rudik managed one evening to knock over the pot boiling that night's rations of potatoes. (Nureyev would later refer to the time as his "potato period.") The family lost its dinner, and the water scalded the child so badly he had to be taken to a hospital in Chelyabinsk. The fuss the attending doctors and nurses lavished upon him was an entirely new experience and then Farida topped even the pleasure of all the attention. She brought him some colored pencils and outline drawings of country cows for him to draw on. They were the closest Rudik had yet come to a real present, his first possessions, and his first intimation that life holds gratuitous pleasures as well. He was four years old. "The memory of that burn," Nureyev wrote later, "was a sweet one."[11]

Farida chose to relocate her family again at the height of the war with Germany. By 1943, when the Nureyev children were uprooted once more, 70 percent of Germany's military might had been relegated to the Russian front. The pressures of life in Tchichuna clearly were becoming more intense for Farida by the day. Her daughters were growing up fast. The eldest, Rosa, was already fifteen, an age when peasant girls became peasant wives. The last thing Farida needed now was to lose a pair of hands in the endless struggle to feed her family, particularly to a village as isolated as Tchichuna. Farida also had had enough of the elderly couple and their icons, and was wary of the effect they might have on her stubborn young son. Like her husband, Farida was a passionate communist, and the religious fervor of Old Russia was anathema, both politically and practically. Barely literate, Farida had never studied Marx on "the opiate of the people," but the circumstances of her life were daily proof that, if there was a divine presence, her family was not one of its interests.[12] She could hardly resent the old couple for the scraps of sweet potato and goat cheese they gave Rudik as a reward for his prayers, but her youngest's strength of will had made an unsettling appearance. No matter how angry Farida became over the prayers, Rudik, fully four years of age, refused to ignore any chance for something extra to eat. Food was so scarce that the little boy generally went to bed without dinner, fast asleep before the evening meal of potatoes had finally finished boiling. He had to be spoon-fed in his sleep and, as a result, woke up each morning hungry again without even the memory of a recent meal as solace. But Farida had reason to resent the old people—for the danger they placed her family in. Stalin hated the religion of Old Russia, too[13]—like the old revolutionaries he dispatched by the thousands, religion bred resistance—and guilt by association was the common fare for a one-way ticket to oblivion. Just as frightening, the few reports from the front that had managed to reach the Urals came with a cutting double-edge. The resistance of Leningrad and Stalingrad to the Nazi sieges was already legend— the power of the people at its most heroic—but the stirring news was accompanied by terrifying rumors, terrified whispers of how dear the victory had been in loss of life.[14] When and if the war finally ended, who knew who would be coming back? Best to be with the only people who had to take them in.

In 1943, the Nureyevs were back trekking across the Urals. The only member of the family excited about the move was Rudik, who understood only that they were moving to a city and there would be lots of people there. Their destination this trip was the Bashkir capital of Ufa that would become the family's permanent home once Hamnet had returned from the war. Hamnet had a brother there, and once again his wife and children found themselves crowded into one room with many other people. [15] Like the ramshackle dwellings that still crowd Ufa's poorest corners, a few brightly painted housefronts the only break from the pervading bleakness, the Nureyevs' new home was less than thirty feet square. There was no floor, only the bare earth, plus the added insult of a lean-to roof creating a wedge of an attic the family could never manage to use because they could never manage to heat it. Once again, there were no niceties, not even of the most practical nature. From the vantage point of his vast success, Nureyev would later joke about the privations of his first real home and the problems they generated, such as just what to do about bodily functions in January. The memory remained indelible.

What Nureyev would later describe as the "nightmarish conditions" [16] in Ufa were intensified, day after day, by biting poverty. As in Tchichuna and everywhere else across the Soviet Union, anything of value had become community property with the 1917 revolutions. No one could own anything of worth, especially the poorest classes who had not yet managed to crack the system. As a result, everyone was poor, but the situation for the Nureyevs was especially serious. As refugees, they had to take whatever they could get, go wherever they were taken in. Farida and her children were forced to scour the city for whatever they could find—old bottles, shreds of firewood, scraps of cloth—that might somehow bring in either food or cash. The desperation held real dangers. Nureyev's every account of his early childhood always emphasized one critical event, an encounter that almost cost him his mother. In the last days of the war, Farida's perpetual quest for food led her to visit a family of Hamnet's, distant relations who lived thirty kilometers from Ufa. She set out at dawn in the dead of winter; the trip had to be made on foot and meant one day to get there and then another to return, but the cousins had promised her food in exchange for the last remnants of Hamnet's civilian clothes. Farida sensed potential trouble because the

trip was the first she'd made without taking along at least her
eldest daughter. Her premonition was almost fatal when she
found herself face-to-face with the dark truth behind a local legend. After the first day of walking, Farida finally stopped to rest
in a thicket of fir trees. She soon realized that she was not alone.
The forests around Ufa had long been rumored to house packs of
scavenger wolves that, like the human population, were starved
for whatever food they could work up. Farida was the dinner of
their dreams and would have become exactly that if she'd been
anything less than a born survivor. Within a matter of moments,
she had set fire to her only blanket and then used the flames to
turn the tables on the wolves. *She* frightened *them*, but Farida
was so badly shaken that she kept the story to herself until years
after Hamnet had rejoined his family as the titular man of the
house. In Patricia Foy's documentary film *Nureyev*, released in
1991, Nureyev accords Farida his highest compliment: "A ballsy
lady, eh?"

Hamnet's return introduced a new problem, one that
would haunt his family for the rest of their lives.[17] The fresh hell
was the friction between father and son. As eagerly as Farida had
awaited her husband's safe return, the two soon found themselves
at odds over their youngest child. Hamnet and Farida had radi-
cally different projections for their only boy. Rudik was already
eight years old when his father finally made his way back to Ufa
a much decorated military hero.[18] Hamnet was horrified to discover that his son was a mamma's boy of the first order. Farida
cherished the creative streak already evident in Rudik. (Of all the
gifts she could have brought him in the Chelyabinsk hospital, the
pencils and coloring book were a telling choice, especially since
they were not the likelier kind of homemade plaything and cost
her resources that could have gone to food.) Nureyev always
remembered his mother as a sad woman, already old at forty, and
he could not remember her laughing out loud even once.[19] For all
that, she still possessed a taste for delicacy, a sensibility that her
impulsive son always managed to touch. During all the hard years
since Moscow, peddling everything she owned to keep her family
alive, the one possession Farida refused to part with was the one

that could have brought the biggest bundle, the family radio. Rudik reveled in its sounds from age two. By the time Hamnet was back in Ufa to stay, Rudik's appetite for movement and music were keeping the boy in constant motion. His favorite game was leaping from one of the family's rickety chairs onto another, without the vaguest idea that he was imperiling himself and the chairs.

His son's flights and flightiness sat less than well with a man as severe and withdrawn as Hamnet,[20] but the trouble instantly brewing between father and son had much deeper roots. Rudik genuinely was frightened of his father. He couldn't even look Hamnet directly in the face until he'd become a teenager. Hamnet was no fonder of what he saw in his son. One of the more unusual features of Nureyev's early poverty stemmed from the fact that he had had to wear his sisters' hand-me-downs from birth. For whatever reason, Farida never turned the girls' clothes into outfits for a little boy. Until he'd started school, young Rudik was often dressed as a girl, an unexpected fact that the Nureyevs' few surviving neighbors from that time still remember with clarity a half-century later. That era ended once Hamnet was back. Retired from the military, he found work in the railway industry, but his first real project was his son. Hamnet began introducing Rudik to a man's pleasures—hunting, fishing, anything rugged he could think of. Rudik couldn't have hated it more. Getting up at dawn to sit for hours in the cold and dark, waiting for animals he had no desire to kill—this was not the boy's idea of a good time. Life was uncomfortable enough without searching out more physical privations. The type of father who views male children as "little men" the instant they've quit the birth canal, Hamnet had no scruples about the means he chose for toughening his son into that little man. On their first hunting trip together into the forests surrounding Ufa, Hamnet left his son alone, huddled in a rucksack for the eternity of a full hour. Rudik was blind with fear until his father's return. Hamnet was wildly amused. Remembering the wolves, Farida never forgot the incident and never forgave her husband for it.

Hamnet had taken up the gauntlet too late. Rudik already

had a mind of his own, and that mind had already been made up on a subject that would change all of their lives. On the first day of January 1945, the year Rudik entered the local grammar school, the year the war seemed it might never end, Farida managed to buy a ticket for a gala evening of ballet at the local opera house. Even in tsarist times, the Grand Opera House in Ufa had maintained a more than respectable reputation, not simply for the unexpected splendor of the building itself, but for the quality of its performers.[21] The succeeding Soviet government had kept the standard high, if by default. Undesirables had been shipped to Ufa from the earliest days of the revolution, including many of the St. Petersburg/Moscow intelligentsia. The new government policy of assigning state-trained artists to the provinces was a cultural windfall for cities such as Ufa. Instead of resenting relocation, performers clamored for the assignments and the relative security of distance from the fighting. The dancers Nureyev saw on his first night at the ballet were all products of the ballet mecca —the fabled Leningrad dance academy that, like the company into which its students graduated, was known under the Romanovs as the Maryinsky and, after Stalin, as the Kirov.[22] The lead ballerina that night had studied in a special department of the Kirov school set up to train dancers for the Bashkir republic and was eventually accorded the Soviet government's highest tribute, the rank of People's Artist.[23]

The ballet that New Year's night was *The Song of the Crane*, the first of the new nationalist ballets the Soviet government was hell-bent on promoting.[24] Based on a local legend reminiscent of *Swan Lake*,[25] it was a classic story of the struggle between good and evil in which the shepherd hero outwits the evil landowner for the hand of a village beauty. For Farida and her brood, just getting into the theater for the performance was a battle of wits and willpower to rival the events onstage. Farida had only one ticket for the five of them, but they'd all gotten in, thanks to the crush of the crowd. In the grand Russian manner, the audience finally broke down the theater doors and rushed the auditorium. The near riot was lost on Rudik the moment he first set eyes on the interior of an opera house. This unanticipated new world—gilded, plush, alive with light—was his first glimpse of opulence. The ballet was even better. Sets and costumes in vivid colors, his first experience of live music, men who flew, and women who moved on the tips of their toes. Rudik's life was changed in a night. He was going to be a ballet dancer.

The state had other plans, and, always a good soldier, so did Hamnet. The Soviets had caught on right away to the utility of educating their children. The foundation of a lasting Soviet utopia was children raised by the party, and the first generations of Soviet children, like Rudik's, were critical. The earliest official textbooks taught the youngest Soviet students to write by copying out simple phrases: "The State is good. The State is great. The State will protect me." The effect was more than Pavlovian. It became "a balm of safe certainty and assuredness that the system would find [everyone] a place, watch over him."[26] The Russian Revolution was unique as a political upheaval that moved power from a ruling royalty directly to the lowest strata of society, not to a bourgeois middle class. The chance for an education was among the key selling points in drafting the proletariat. Under the tsars, Hamnet and his peers had not been allowed to go to school. By the time Rudik began school, a system of state organized and supervised schooling was in place. The state provided seven years of mandatory study, beginning at age seven and based on a five-point grading scale. Higher education remained a matter of access, guaranteeing priority for the advantaged and the connected. Children in Rudik's position could at best look forward to vocational training that would provide the foot soldiers of an industrial nation, and there was "no liberal arts curriculum in the Soviet system through which a student [could] search at leisure for his own area of aptitude or expertise."[27] Boys were directed toward industrial or agricultural work. For their parents, the new systemized vocational training was ready access to real jobs, and their belief in its potential took on the fervor of a new religion,[28] the only hope for turning "workers and peasants into mechanics and engineers, into the new cadres needed to replace the old scientific intelligentsia."[29]

Enter Rudik, wearing his sister Lida's weathered cape to his first day of school and carried on his mother's back because he had no shoes. The boy's first response to school was enthusiastic. The new information was exciting and he absorbed it easily. The first encounter with a peer group went less well. His unusual attire, just the kind of thing to turn other children nasty, had started trouble from the first day, and Nureyev's first encounter with people his own age began with him as the butt of their collective jokes. His taste for music and movement didn't help matters. His tormenters developed a hateful nickname for a little boy: Ballerina. (Hamnet used the same epithet.) Even worse, Rudik was the type of little boy little bullies live to torment, an easy target, and he was regularly hounded, hunted, and roughed up.

Farida's son didn't take it lying down, or at least not for long. His teacher's final evaluation in fourth grade describes Rudik as a boy who "cries a lot."[30] By the next year things began to change. Grade five: "The boy is very restless, but somehow disciplined. Sometimes he is rude with his comrades, and sometimes can be very insulting." Grade seven: "Nureyev is very nervous, tends to fits of anger, . . . and fights with his comrades." Grade eight: "He is very nervous, explosive shall we say, and he fights a lot with his classmates." Even the Nureyevs' neighbors began to notice that the boisterous little boy had begun to change with his first years in school. Living more and more behind his own private wall, he spent his little free time alone in the foothills just outside Ufa, caught up in the only sounds of the city—the haunting echoes of the trains leaving the local station, taking some lucky person somewhere else.

And there was a distraction, an important one that was causing warfare on the home front as well. After the New Year 1945 epiphany at the Ufa Opera House, Rudik was introduced to a kind of dancing he himself could do right now. The access was ironic. As part of its effort to instill pride in the students' heritage, the school curriculum included brief classes in national folk dances. Vigorous but specific, circling but crisp and precise, the Bashkir folk dances appealed to Rudik. Two of his gifts were apparent immediately: a natural physical facility and an innate sense of how to translate that into a performance.[31] Just as tasty, Rudik also had his first experience of praise, of pride in his own skills. The children's folk-dancing group from his school acquired a local reputation after they'd begun performing for the patients in the Ufa hospitals.[32] Rudik was always singled out. By the time he was ten and had joined the folk-dance troupe of the Young Pioneers, the party-sponsored youth group Soviet children were obliged to enter, the compliments were returning to the same point over and over again. Rudik had heard the magic words. "You should go to Leningrad."

The odds against that happening were high and not just because Rudik was a peasant pauper a thousand miles from Leningrad. The dancing infuriated Hamnet, especially once Rudik's schoolwork began declining in direct proportion to his increasing absorption in dance. By his last year in the Ufa school, Rudik's marks had dropped to average at best. His teachers knew he could do better, but were also aware that "he likes to dance and gets carried away with his dancing. He very accurately, every day, attends the choreographic club at the opera theater. He dreams of becoming a ballet dancer and he performs in dances at the evening programs at the school."[33] The declining grades and the increasing local profile—as the boy who dances—were not happy news at home. Farida and his sister Rosa were Rudik's only allies. Farida calmed Hamnet down, and Rosa, who was studying to become a teacher, had access to books and lectures that kept her brother's interest alive. (Rosa even somehow managed to bring home ballet tutus for her brother to touch and study.)

Hamnet had a different perspective on the subject. A child of his flesh as a professional dancer cut deep, even deeper than the issue of masculinity. His son's ambition clearly was bigger than Bashkir folk dancing. He was after ballet dancing, a tsarist bauble. Rudik was passing up the education Hamnet could never have had himself. Even worse, in abandoning his schoolwork, Rudik also was shirking his most important duty—to become a productive, useful citizen of a nation that needed every pair of hands to carve out the future.[34] Hamnet had been fighting for that future his entire life. And now his own son was turning his back on the struggle, at ten. The dancing had to stop.

Rudik thought otherwise. Despite his fear of Hamnet, Rudik continued to study and perform, on the sly when necessary, under cover of whatever story he could concoct. He kept at it even after Hamnet's objections got physical and beatings became a regular feature of the household. By then, the boy had had his first stroke of luck, and parental protests were meaningless. The point of no return had been passed. At eleven, Rudik was introduced to an elderly woman named Anna Udeltsova who taught children's dance classes in Ufa. Udeltsova had been a member of the Diaghilev corps de ballet and she'd lived in Ufa since the revolution, when she and her husband, an officer in the tsar's military, suddenly found themselves exiled. Rudik performed a few of his folk dances for her as his first audition. A woman of taste and discernment,[35] Udeltsova knew that something unique had crossed her well-traveled path, despite the fact that the child was clearly "an urchin. Just a little Tatar boy."[36] But she could also see that he was unusually serious about his work and that he had a musical sensitivity that cannot be taught. Udeltsova began giving Rudik his first ballet lessons, gratis—the coherent exposure to the basic ballet steps and positions he'd been craving and that are the basis of a dance technique that lasts. She also gave him another gift every bit as important. In Rudik's eyes, Udeltsova was an experienced woman of the world who took his dancing seriously, who spoke to him of a responsibility to his talent. After a year, Udeltsova knew that she had given Rudik as much as he could learn from her. She sent him to a professional teacher, a woman named Vaitovitch who had once been a Kirov soloist,[37] with one last piece of advice: "You should go to Leningrad. You must study at the Kirov."

The die was cast, whatever the odds. The only real question now was how.

Three

The Walking Crisis

"Venice is lace. Petersburg is marble."

—ALEXANDRA DANILOVA,
New Orleans Times-Picayune

T he answer to the question obsessing Rudik—how was he going to get to Leningrad—is the great requited love story in the Nureyev saga. It's a romance fable in three acts of just the type the Soviets could have put to good use in teaching their youth about the power of the proletariat. No wan, Chekovian wishful thinkers here. The hero is a youth of action: this time, those three sad sisters get to see more than Moscow. The characters in the drama are of more vintage stock anyway, the good folk of legend. The passionate young lover, the beauty in the tower, the distance and dark forces that separate them. Act 1 sets the scene. The valiant teenage hero has had only the most fleeting glimpse of his beloved but he knows that this is The One. He is, of course, from the rudest peasant stock and much stands in his way, like a bitter, recalcitrant parent who thwarts his every effort. But our hero is more than determined. He's resourceful, too, never misses a chance to edge closer to his goal, and the act curtain finds him feverish with plans. Act 2 sends him out across vast distances with only his will and his wits to guide him. The series of trials and the requisite last-minute disasters that almost undo him lead to Act 3, at the gates of the palace. They swing wide and his ideal embraces him.

And that's essentially how seventeen-year-old Rudolf Nureyev ended up on August 17, 1955, in the enchanting nineteenth-century cul-de-sac Carlo Rossi created to house the ballet, music, and dramatic academies of the Imperial Theater of St. Petersburg.[1] The trip to Rossi Street had taken Rudik the four years since class with Udeltsova and Vaitovitch. He'd continued performing in Ufa with the Bashkir companies that played to the villages surrounding the city, despite the fact that many of his peers already were beginning to get their first real jobs and make a much needed contribution to the family income. The only compensations from Rudik's dancing were experience and the odd comic relief, the inevitable onstage mishaps that performers love to remember well after the fact. There's one in every theater company, and Rudik was the boy things happened to. Props collapsed around him. His pants dropped to his ankles twice in a single performance. Nothing could stop him, not even bad luck. When he was sixteen, Rudik found out that a troupe of Bashkir dancers had been invited to perform in Moscow. Despite the vehemence of Hamnet's objection to the mention of the word "dance" —disagreements still became physical—Rudik got his father to go to the opera house and enquire about the tour. Hamnet's procrastination won this round. The company was en route already.

The rest of the story is *The Red Shoes* meets *Forty-Second Street*. Missing the tour was a bitter disappointment but only another setback, especially once Rudik had begun getting work as a supernumerary with the Ufa Opera House. This tasted like theater, and, thanks to his natural nerve and resilience, standing on a real stage for the first time was his second piece of good luck. It leavened the tension at home once he'd inflated his status into "an artist of the Ufa Opera," which became the chance to give dance lessons in private homes. Rudik eventually began earning as much as, and sometimes more than, his father, which may or may not have helped the family situation (and might also explain why Hamnet was so opposed to his son striking out on his own).

Even better, the fantasy had a foothold in reality now and Rudik learned the first rule of the theater: Don't go away and they'll have to use you. He became a fixture with the Opera ballet, going onstage at every opportunity as every spear-carrier and townsperson in the book. He took class with the company whenever they'd let him, and, despite a flowering reputation for his temper, finally was offered a contract. Realistic or not, his sights were higher, and Rudik passed up the sure bet. He declined.

And then it happened, the invitation to the ball. In the summer of 1955, there was to be a festival celebrating Bashkir art in Moscow, and the ballet company from the Ufa Opera House was going to go. At the last minute they were short a soloist in *Song of the Crane*, the ballet Rudik had first seen on that New Year's night ten years before. He volunteered himself for the job without knowing a step of the choreography, got the part, and, by the time the troupe reached Moscow, had overrehearsed himself into a wicked foot injury he was told would take months to heal. He was back onstage inside a week. The Bolshoi Ballet, the Kirov's Moscow rival, was there. It wasn't the Kirov but it wasn't Ufa either. Through the Ufa company's rehearsal pianist, an ally since his days with the Pioneers, Rudik went right to the source —class with the Bolshoi's most famous teacher, the great Asaf Messerer himself.[2] Messerer told him to watch the class and they'd talk once it was over. The discussion never took place. Messerer was called away before the class had finished, but an invitation to study at the Bolshoi school came anyway after an audition with another teacher. It also came with a problem. The Kirov boarded its students, but the Bolshoi didn't. The Moscow offer was for classes only, not room and board. Once again, Rudik went for the long shot. He took what little money he could pull together and bought a one-way ticket to Leningrad. He went straight to the Kirov school on Rossi Street and opened the door.

There's more than romance in the Tatar urchin standing before the elegantly colonnaded facade of the Kirov school. Poetic as the picture may be, right down to the tattered overcoat hanging over his too-thin body in the middle of August, it's also a portrait of sheer nerve for the history books. Even Dorothy Gale made it to the Emerald City with a backup trio, and, if ever there was a real-world Oz, it was the city where seventeen-year-old Rudik was now completely on his own for the first time in his life, without so much as a place to spend the night or the security of a train ticket back home.

Leningrad was not just a city of kings. It was a city of emperors, and, for Rudik, the city literally appeared out of a cloud. He'd gotten onto the wrong train out of Moscow, and the trip had taken sixteen hours instead of eight, all of them spent standing in a crowded corridor. Craning for a first glimpse of the fabled Admiralty Spire, all he could see was the great black mass of industrial clouds streaming over the horizon from the factories in the city's most distant suburbs. The train finally pulled into the station, and he was there, in the city that had once reminded Somerset Maugham of Venice and Amsterdam but "only to mark the difference. The colors are pale and soft. They have the quality of a pastel, but there is a tenderness in them that painting can seldom reach; you find the dreamy blues, the dying rose of a sketch by Quentin de la Tour, greens and yellows like those in the heart of a rose."[3] There was also a scale, symmetry, and splendor the boy would never get over. The city's impact was lasting and profound. For the first time since that first awful day at the Ufa grammar school, Rudik was embarrassed by the shabbiness of his attire, humbled by the tired topcoat he'd put on because he'd mistaken the factory smoke for rain clouds. Many years and much mileage later, memories of Leningrad could still generate one of the adult Nureyev's few concessions to a divine presence, calling the city blessed by God.

It certainly was blessed by something, considering that the most renamed city in modern history literally had been wrenched from the stagnant marshes at the mouth of the Neva River.[4] At the point where the Neva "empties Lake Ladoga into the brackish Gulf of Finland, it forks out between a cluster of islands. For centuries they had been the home of Finnish fishermen and farmers."[5] The Neva islands were the point where Peter the Great had forged his new Russian capital in the first decade of the eighteenth century at the geographical latitude of Juneau, Alaska. (Peter's capital is, in fact, slightly farther north. It is so cold at midwinter that, on an 1843 visit, the poet, critic, and balletomane extraordinaire Théophile Gautier discovered that the moist end of his cigar would ice over while the tip kept its fire.) Although Peter's initial interest was in a military post to cover his flank from invading Swedes, the new city became his country's capital in less than a decade.[6]

Peter also began a tradition of importing the Italian and French architects from the Paris of Louis XIV—Trezzini, Leblond, Rastrelli, Quarenghi—who would fashion his city into a rival of the greatest European capitals.[7] Over the next three centuries, the imperial architects would shape St. Petersburg into a city of unrivaled grace and luxury, a latticework of islands and canals but with a sense of symmetry too. The era of empresses that followed Peter's reign elaborated on his masculine pomp by keeping to his scale but adding the gilt and academic classicism of the Age of Reason.[8] Paris is the city where palaces leap out of nowhere. Peter's city is all palaces. The colors of the Petersburg palaces talk back to the pale Arctic light, working the glow for all its worth—now soft, now strong, now vermilion like the Anitchkov Palace on the Nevsky Prospekt where Nicholas II was raised, now ocher like the Yussoupov Palace on the Moika Canal where Rasputin would be murdered.[9] The crown jewel was the baroque fantasy of the Winter Palace, all pale-green stone and size, that was built for the Empress Elizabeth at midcentury by Rastrelli—1,000 rooms, 2,000 windows, 200 staircases, and fronted by a square so vast it can accommodate a half million people.

Despite the Romanov appetite for grandeur, the visual high C of their capital was a short backstreet. Rossi Street was St. Petersburg's architectural answer to the Fabergé Easter eggs of the last Romanovs. Carlo Rossi, another imported Italian architect, had already made his mark on the city when Nicholas I commissioned him to refashion certain key areas. Nicholas was said to have only two real interests—soldiers and ballet—and he knew that Rossi had good reason to favor the performance arts.[10] (Rossi's mother was a ballerina.) In 1836 Nicholas had him rework the short street behind the Alexandrinsky Theater, the home of the Imperial dramatic theater company. Only one block long, the street was a double dead-end given over to a complex of government bureaus on one side and on the other to the schools that trained performers for the various Imperial theaters, including the ballet. The result was a perfectly measured sonnet in a city of singular visual poetry, tiny as the Fabergé eggs but generating the same kind of hushed first response, then and now. The impact of the Fabergé fantasies is in their elaboration, their rainbow variety and ingenuity.[11] Rossi Street, or Theater Street as it has been known to generations of ballet dancers, hits its mark through simplicity. Twin facades front the quick length of the street, each a double row of double columns and arching windows, all of it cast in pale pink stone and precision rhythm.

This was where Rudik found himself on that sticky August morning, overdressed. In the ten years since *Song of the Crane,* the boy who could not be bothered with academic schoolwork had inhaled every scrap of information he could find on ballet and its history. In every story, all roads led to Leningrad and the heavy wooden door he was now facing. Rudik knew that the most significant feet in the business had crossed this particular threshold. He did not realize in those first flushed moments of rapture that the greatest names in the roster of legends he was about to join all reached their greatest celebrity once they'd gotten far away from the Kirov school and company—Nijinsky and Karsavina with Diaghilev in Paris, Pavlova on every stage in the world big enough to handle a dying swan, Ulanova with the Bolshoi in Moscow (at Stalin's invitation).[12] He had also not yet caught on to the fact that even the loftiest ambitions require planning as well as passion. It was a lesson he'd master in less than two weeks, to the lasting consternation of the school administration that was about to be so generous to him.

The most immediate problems on that first summer morning were practical, such as missing the proverbial boat once again. Despite the amount of traveling he would eventually do and the eagle eye he'd acquire for the minutiae of contract and financial

negotiations, the footwork of itineraries was never to be a Nureyev specialty; that was the dreary stuff he would learn to have
other people take care of. ("If Rudolf could flip out big time
over some detail going wrong onstage," a veteran ballerina once
summarized after years of touring with Nureyev on the rugged,
rural kind of package tours where the company got the milk
trucks and Nureyev the limousine, "how the hell would he ever
have been able to deal with airline officials?"[13]) His first solo
venture was prophetic: first, the train mix-up in Moscow and
then he discovered that the school was still on summer vacation
and not due to begin classes for another two weeks. Rudik's first
view of the hallowed Kirov corridors was less than glittering: no
sylphs, no swans, only workmen and washerwomen busy scrub-
bing down the building for the new term. Still undeterred, Rudik
tracked down the first person he could find anywhere near his
own age and, going right for the top once again, asked for the
office of Chelkov, the school's director. The answer came from a
middle-aged gentleman passing the two boys. "I am Chelkov.
Who are you?" Rudik's reply was equally direct. "I am Rudolf
Nureyev, artist of the Ufa Opera. I would like to study here."[14]
The boy's nerve struck a chord in the director. Chelkov told him
to return in a week for an audition. It was the last civil exchange
the two would ever have.

Nureyev's successful entry into the Kirov school exactly
one week later is another of the critical events in his career that's
picked up an extra coat or two of polish over the years. It was
not, for example, the one-in-a-million exception enshrined by his
subsequent chroniclers. The odds against Nureyev entering the
Kirov school were formidable indeed, but for once, his negative
social status was not a drawback. The Imperial academies had
been drafting its students from the poorest of the poor since the
day its doors opened. The school's very first students were "sons
and daughters of court valets and choir singers,"[15] and even Pavlova the hallowed was, in Richard Buckle's immortal phrase, "the
illegitimate daughter of a Jewish laundress."[16] Even more surprising, Nureyev's age when he entered the Kirov school was excep-

tional only in terms of the heights he would reach, not where and when he actually began serious study. The Imperial Ballet School began training its dancers as children, as early as six and seven years of age. For the purely practical reason of body count, the Soviets had slackened that particular rein by the 1920s and, by the 1930s, the average age for first-time male students was the early teens. Messerer started studying in his early teens, and the famous Vakhtang Chaboukiani himself began his Leningrad training at the same age as the initiate Nureyev.[17]

The audition itself was less than a smash. Nureyev was auditioned twice. The first was a closed examination with a group of Latvian teenagers headed for training in the national dances so dear to the Soviet cultural scheme. The second, on the stage of the school's studio theater, was a solo variation from the classic repertory performed before a handful of teachers and the few advanced students who had already returned for the new term. The round with the Letts suggests that the Kirov was not expecting a shining new danseur but fodder for the more useful folk companies, the ones designed to indoctrinate the masses in their national glories. The repertory solo came close to confirming that prospect. Having previously danced exactly one classic variation before a live audience, and that experience exactly one month behind him at the Bashkir festival in Moscow, Nureyev chose to perform the bravura male variation from the Diana and Actaeon pas de deux, an extract from the old Imperial standard *Esmeralda* that had been reworked by Chabukiani in the 1930s for some serious acrobatic effects. His performance, according to one audience member, "was not very good. No line. No feet. Nothing, how you say, come together. He was all over the place." At the end of his performance, the veteran Kirov instructor Vera Kostravitskaya walked over to the panting young dancer and said, "Young man, you will become either a brilliant dancer or a total failure, and most likely you'll be a failure."

Rudik understood immediately that her observation was a challenge, not a slam, and, to the end of his life, he would remember Kostravitskaya as "the best woman teacher in Russia."[18]

He was in.

■

Nureyev's life until September 1, 1955, the day he became a boarding student at the Kirov school, had prepared him in many important ways for the climb to come. He had learned already the barreling value of single-mindedness. He knew how to fend for himself and could smell an enemy as surely as Ingrid Bergman in *Murder on the Orient Express* "could hear snakes breathe."[19] But independence of mind has never been a welcome feature in the rigidly hierarchical world of ballet, surely one of the reasons even the most sublime ballerinas have been as celebrated for their tantrums as their talents. After the years of home-front warfare with his father, Nureyev at seventeen already was accustomed to making his own decisions and fighting for them, too, whatever the potential consequences. And he had another, even more noisome trait for a student. For as basic a reason as self-preservation, he'd had to learn how to read people for exactly what they are, and on the spot. In the process, he'd also learned whom *not* to listen to. To date he had encountered only three authority figures he accepted, all of them women—first his mother, and then Udeltsova and Vaitovitch.

This combination of qualities meant high winds on Rossi Street. After Tchichuna and Ufa, Rudik was experienced at communal living; it was the only kind of arrangement he'd ever known. Unfortunately, however, though life in the company of people his own age for the first time would have been rugged enough, the nineteen other people in his dormitory room were even worse than his peers. The Kirov curriculum was based on a nine-year course of training, at which point the eighteen- and nineteen-year-old graduates began professional careers. Chelkov had decided that, because Rudik needed so much training in the working fundamentals of ballet, he would begin with the sixth-grade class, which Chelkov himself taught. As a result, the new Bashkir boy was assigned to what was known among the students as the "Mongolia dormitory," the one housing boarders who were fifteen or younger. Rudik was not only the oldest boy in the room but the tallest, and his precious anonymity in crowds was gone for good. The situation was an explosion waiting to happen, and it did—often. "Rudolf," a Kirov graduate of the era remembers, "terrorized those poor children." The lessons of the Ural *isbas* still with him, Rudik instantly staked out a remote corner of the room as his private preserve, and woe befell any trespassers. A fellow student still remembers a characteristic incident on a day when she discovered an unexpected crowd of the smaller children huddled outside their dormitory door, clearly anxious to get back into their room but clearly even more terrified to try the door again. In the brief glimpse she had through the door, two images remain clear almost forty years after the event. One is the boot that was hurtling in her direction, accompanied by a barked command to "get out!" The other was Rudik cross-legged on his bed, listening to a Bach concerto.

Once again, scheduling was a problem. The regimen of the Imperial Ballet school is part of its legend,[20] and the Soviets were the last people to abandon the chance to order anyone around. The Kirov students put in an eleven-hour day: up at seven for breakfast, alternating classes in academic subjects and dance technique until an hour break for lunch at midafternoon, and then three to four more hours of class. The daily routine was fixed, thorough, and closely guarded. Disruption tempted more than professional consequences; in the decade following World War II, a pattern of strict political repression had become a primary feature of the Soviet school system. Following the rules was more than an academic issue, it was the measure of a student's political correctness. Bad students were bad communists.

Unfortunately, Rudik had lived the majority of his seventeen years on his own schedule. The rigidity of the school system only intensified his impatience. There was never a problem with getting to the two hours of ballet class at midday or the class in character dancing that came later in the afternoon. For Rudik, the irritants were elsewhere, such as not only having to live with children but to eat with them. His first rebellions were as small as sleeping late to avoid the breakfast canteen of tired tea and gruel. They'd soon spilled over into more serious areas, such as the academic subjects stressed nationwide by the Soviets. Ballet students of the Imperial era had received the fundamentals of an elementary education; the academic emphasis of their training was essentially over by age twelve. The Soviets had rewritten that scenario by the time Rudik reached Rossi Street; students graduated with a thorough secondary-level education. But Rudik was not a student whose attention could be forced. To the end of his life, Nureyev could abandon himself to the subjects that absorbed his attention—ballet and music, painting, sculpture, philosophy.[21] Unfortunately, his passions were not high on the Soviet agenda. "Mathematics!" he once shouted at a frustrated instructor. "What do I need to learn that for? Counting money? That's no problem." Time spent in pursuit of any subject other than dancing was precious time wasted.

Matters came to a head in less than a week. In strict defiance of every regulation for the sixth-grade students—whatever their actual age—Rudik left the school premises one evening to attend a performance in a nearby state theater without so much as a request for permission. He returned to find his bedding removed and his meal vouchers gone. Scarlett O'Hara couldn't have handled the dilemma better. Rudik reached his ballet class the next day after a night on the floor and no breakfast and fainted dead away, leading to the first in a series of explosive visits to Chelkov's office.

Nureyev's first head-on combat with Chelkov that day initiated important precedents, setting the stage for a series of dangerous scenes that would continue until the very moment the school handed the Tatar troublemaker his diploma; in fact, the most flattering early review of Nureyev's gifts was that the Kirov school kept him on at all. A fellow student and Soviet expatriate, the late Alexander Minz, remembered that "everything, *everything* Rudolf did rubbed Chelkov the wrong way. Rudolf might simply say, 'Hello' and Chelkov would yell and scream at him that he had said it the wrong way."[22] The problem was deeper than an issue of discipline, a student who overslept or was careless in his studies and choice of clothes. When ballet was involved, Nureyev's discipline would astonish friends and colleagues straight through to the end of his life; however late the night before, Nureyev was always in class the next day. The real difficulty was the nature of his rebellions, the cord that connected them. This boy clearly was not destined to become a cooperative member of the Soviet state. There was method in his manner, an independence of attitude and approach that was deeply unsettling in a system where obedience without question was the first commandment. "He was born wild," a fellow Kirov graduate remembers. "If you have a wild animal in your house, you think it won't bite you?"

Throughout his three years in the Kirov academy, Nureyev terrorized the school authorities by flouting the most cherished standards of the era. In no time at all, he'd become, in the words of another student, "the walking crisis." Nureyev's personal manners were less than conciliatory. Just as in the Romanov era, students were required to wear a uniform. Boys at the Imperial school wore handsome "tunics . . . embroidered on either side of the military collar with silver lyres framed in palms and surmounted by a crown."[23] The people's students, Kirov boys of the Nureyev era wore more proletarian uniforms, baggy trousers and high-collared peasant shirts of a heavy, all-purpose (and itchy) gray material. Even after he'd outgrown most of his clothes, Rudik preferred the ragged edges of his own wardrobe to the enforced uniformity, such as the thick leather belt he always wore pulled very tight because, as a classmate remembers, he was very thin "and wanted to have a waist." He not only refused to dress like his peers but also grew his hair well past the mandatory brush cut. A fellow student still remembers her first sight of Nureyev in class: "I thought, 'Oh, my God, Genghis Khan!' Long hair, wild eyes, don't trust anybody, a little wild animal with huge energy."

Rudik lived up to the look, and then some. "When Rudolf first arrived," Minz remembered,

he was already so closed in on himself, with his own life and character defined, that most people simply couldn't understand him and so didn't like him. And then, when the directors, practically from the first day, began to apply pressure on him to conform, that made him even more withdrawn. Every day there was news of some new "outrage" Rudolf had committed—some way he had dressed, something he had said, something he liked. He seemed like some kind of fanatic to everyone. No one knew what to make of him. And so they stayed away from him.[24]

Sergiu Stefanschi,[25] a Romanian boarder with the bunk across from Nureyev, barely got a single full-night's sleep throughout their three years at the school:

> Every night, as soon as the lights were out and the door closed behind us, Rudi would jump out of bed and say, "Get up. Get up." And then we would dance until one or two o'clock in the morning. We danced everything—boy variations, girl variations, all of the pas de deux. We'd take turns partnering one another. We were such fanatics. At the end of our first year, we were moved from the third-floor dormitory to the one on the street level. After that, we would just open the window after light's out, climb out into the street, and wander the city. I still have a special image of Rudi from that time—a white night and Rudolf doing a *grand manège* of *jetés coupés*[26] around the obelisk in the square of the Winter Palace.

Rudik broke more rules than curfew. He dared the unwritten law that boys had best be boys and behave like them at all times. Standards of male decorum were not brushed aside lightly in an era when even a whiff of sexually suspect behavior could open a new file chez KGB.[27] The student Nureyev was too busy to be bothered with such nonsense. He had too much to learn too fast. According to a later Kirov graduate, Mikhail Baryshnikov, "before class, when everyone was standing around, warming up, [Rudolf] would do things like perform Kitri's variation—the woman's variation from the first act of *Don Quixote*—the whole thing, full out, with lots of panache. People just stood there amazed."[28] During Nureyev's student days, men were not expected to have legs with high-reaching extensions; that was ballerina territory. Aware of a critical lack of stretch in his muscles after such a late start, Rudik eventually would engage in extension competitions with the female students just before daily class (and won his fair share). It was exactly the kind of public behavior to arch administrative eyebrows. The androgynous promise of Nureyev's dancing set many a bureaucrat on edge. According to Minz:

> At that time, it was almost impossible for audiences and even critics to cope with any expression of [sex] onstage. Most people simply put it out of their minds. The rest had no adequate vocabulary to discuss what they saw. Sexuality on the stage was something you did not write about or talk about. Any sign of it was taken as some sort of pathology and denounced as a form of anarchism. That was probably Chelkov's attitude on the subject. When Rudi was still in school, for example, Chelkov used to love to call him into his office for long talks about sex. He took a kind of sadistic pleasure in doing that.[29]

Worst of all, Rudik paid the cornerstone of Soviet society —the party—the ultimate insult: complete lack of interest and not the remotest indication of gratitude for the gift of his education. During the postfainting scene with Chelkov, Nureyev was totally unrepentant, and trumped Chelkov's reference to his peasant ignorance by pointing out that he would have received better treatment under Alexander I,[30] the tsar who'd first added rigid intellectual repression to the curricula of Russia's university system. The interview ended with a stunning indictment by Nureyev: "I know what you are trying to do in class, Comrade Chelkov. You are trying to make everyone look like you. Who wants to do that?" The last straw was his refusal to join the Komsomol, the secondary school equivalent of the Young Pioneers every young adult was obliged to join. "The functionaries of the theater tried as hard as they could to turn him into one of their cadets," another colleague recalls. "But it was impossible. The more they brushed him, the spikier he became. It was just not in Rudi to think like a serf."[31]

It took him exactly one more week to crack the system. Within a matter of days, Rudik knew that class with Chelkov was not going to take him where he needed to go. Chelkov had chosen exactly the wrong approach for dealing with a student as intelligent, insightful, and self-motivated as Nureyev. He had opted for intimidation. The choice hadn't worked for Hamnet, and it was doomed to failure this time, too. Chelkov began badgering his new student from the first day of class, and the assault was relentless, a barrage of offensive references to Nureyev's peasant origins,[32] repeated emphasis on his backwardness and country-come-to-town unease, and the type of demeaning insults an unscrupulous taskmaster can work out of a daily routine. Nureyev later remembered that the first section of his tights that began to show wear and tear was their backside, because Chelkov so consistently placed his Mongol nightmare against the back wall of the studio for classroom exercises. Apocryphal or not, the story makes a telling point. Then and now, ballet classes are notoriously hierarchical about the arrangement of students across the studio, and among the ballet students themselves in particular. The last place an ambitious ballet student wants to be is the back row, day in and day out.[33]

Something had to be done and done fast. Even more troubling than the atmosphere in Chelkov's class—again, any chance of anonymity had been given the kiss-off by Chelkov's attention-focusing stream of invective—Nureyev was able to gauge Chelkov's classroom skills with the cold eye of youth. They came up short. Rudik knew right off that, as a teacher, Chelkov did not have the level of facility he needed, and he had found out just as quickly that another teacher in the school did. The means the seventeen-year-old country boy employed to get from one teacher to the other was a masterstroke of ingenuity. A week after the fainting incident, Rudik was back in Chelkov's office, this time of his own volition. He was troubled by a thought he'd recently had and wanted Chelkov's advice. If Nureyev followed the prescribed course of study over the next three years, by the time of his graduation he would have reached the age for military induction. His career would be over before it had begun, and all the time and money the school had invested in him would have been for naught. Chelkov bought Rudik's reasoning, although, ironically, the three-year bargaining point was exactly the amount of time Nureyev would remain at the school, by choice. Starting with the next week of classes, Rudik was moved to the eighth-grade level taught by the teacher he had hoped for, senior male instructor Alexander Pushkin. Rudik came to the man who would change his life with a letter of reference from Chelkov: "I am sending you an obstinate little idiot—a weak-minded evil boy who knows nothing about ballet. He has poor elevation and can't sustain his positions correctly. I leave you to judge for yourself and if he continues in this way we shall have no alternative but to throw him out of the school."[34]

There's an apt irony in the two Pushkins who guard either end of the hall of mirrors that was the life of Rudolf Nureyev. He had not yet encountered the works of Alexander Pushkin, Russia's national poet since the first quarter of the nineteenth century, when Nureyev began working with the Kirov teacher Alexander Pushkin, the hero of male ballet dancing in twentieth-century Russia. The only literature that could keep Rudik's over-worked eyes open during his endless classes in the Russian classics was the great storm clouds of Dostoyevsky. A head-on with Push-kin's literary legacy seems inevitable for a young man drawn to Dostoyevsky for his "generosity and violence,"[35] and Nureyev's taste for Pushkin only grew with the years.[36] The first words spoken at Nureyev's funeral service in Paris were an extract from Pushkin's *Eugene Onegin*. Dead at thirty-eight in a duel, the man behind Pushkin's verse was clearly every bit as absorbing to a born rebel such as Nureyev.[37] The fire of Pushkin's personality is an almost eerie projection of what was to come for Nureyev. Pushkin's outspoken objection to the political repression of his era made him the bane of the Romanov authorities and, as a result, a social exile. By his own count, the woman Pushkin married, and whose infidelities led to the fatal duel, was his one hundred and thirteenth paramour.

In contrast, the Alexander Pushkin whose classes would set fire to Nureyev's dancing was a man famous for never raising his voice. Every discussion of Pushkin by his students and col-

leagues inevitably uses the word "gentle." Dapper, reserved, a
gentleman in the purest sense of the term, Pushkin had begun
teaching at the Kirov school in 1925, the same year he was named
a principal dancer with the main Kirov company.[38] By the time
Nureyev reached his class, Pushkin was his country's most re-
spected teacher of male dancing; even after graduating into the
Kirov, the company's leading men continued regular work with
Pushkin in a special company class. Pushkin's approach was the
antithesis of Chelkov's and had exactly the opposite effect on
Nureyev. Like Balanchine, Pushkin taught by inference rather
than correction, which, in the process of developing a dance technique, develops a performance intelligence based on initiative and
self-reliance. Unlike the "Do it this way! This way!" manner
of Chelkov, Pushkin's suggestions eased his students into the
classroom exercises, and he was one of the rare breed of dance
teachers able to get students "on their legs" by the internal logic
and instinctive musicality of his enchaînements. "If you do his
combinations every day," a graduate remembers, "you start to
dance." The reserve of Pushkin's personal demeanor and the
seeming effortlessness of his classroom method belied the fervor
he was able to invoke. "He inspired his pupils," according to one
of his two best known students, Baryshnikov, "like an infection."[39] The other, Nureyev, felt a comparable intensity: "He
would inject you with excitement about dance."[40]

Pushkin was also smart enough to leave the "evil boy"
Nureyev to himself for their first year of classes. Pushkin, Nureyev wrote later, "didn't even look in my direction for the first
few weeks. . . . I think that everyone believed at that time that I
would study for two years, struggle through the eighth and ninth
grades, and then forget about ballet forever."[41] Instead of discour-
aging Rudik, the relative inattention was exactly the tonic he'd
been waiting for. For the first time, Rudik was allowed to think
for himself, to develop his own method from the inside out. The
choice worked even better than a professional of Pushkin's vast
experience could have anticipated. At the end of the school term,
students were given a classic variation to perform on the stage of
the school; the examination performances were among the most

eagerly anticipated events of the student year. After a single year of work together, Pushkin had decided that Nureyev wasn't ready for a live audience and left him out of the student performance in the spring of 1956. He was in for a surprise. Nureyev took his teacher into a studio one day, locked the door behind them, and performed the male variation from Diana and Actaeon, the very solo through which he had stumbled barely a year before at his audition for the school. Pushkin added Nureyev's name to the list for the student performance, and the pattern of give and take that would characterize Nureyev's most successful performances had been established.[42]

At the end of the next year, after Pushkin had worked more closely with him, it was Nureyev's turn to compromise, and he did, for the first time in his life. The ninth level of study should have been his last year in the school. At Pushkin's suggestion, Nureyev stayed on in the school another year. The extra work with Pushkin in the great male variations of the classic repertory not only consolidated his technique but became the basis of Nureyev's formidable ballet scholarship. (John Gielgud's memory is reputed to include every word Shakespeare wrote; the same is said of Nureyev's familiarity with the classic ballet repertory, including all the additions made to variations, pas de deux, and corps dances over the decades—and by whom and when.) When the majority of the main Kirov company left on tour to Eastern Europe during his second ninth-grade year, Nureyev got the unprecedented chance to dance the male leads in nine repertory standards on the sacred stage of the Kirov itself, from the title role in Le Corsaire to, holiest of holies, Prince Siegfried in Swan Lake.

Nureyev's last two performances as a student—at a national competition in Moscow in the summer of 1958 and then at his graduation performance at the Kirov school theater two weeks later—were the beginning of his professional legend. For the Moscow event, Nureyev returned to Diana and Actaeon, and at both performances he and Alla Sizova danced the work that would become a Nureyev signature, the Corsaire pas de deux. His Cor-

saire variation in Moscow was added to a state-sponsored motion picture being made about Russian ballet, the only dance by a Kirov student to be included in the film.[43] The ovation he and Sizova received after their graduation performance of *Corsaire*, according to one veteran audience member, "shook the walls. Remember—this was only a student performance. I have never heard such an ovation in that theater."

Class with Pushkin and then the first rush of real applause may have determined the future course of Nureyev's professional life, but they did not do a lot to displace the chip on his shoulder that was getting heavier by the day. The arrival of a particularly promising new student causes a ripple through a ballet school, particularly an academy for advanced study such as the one Rudik had entered. The fellow students notice the competition, the instructors notice someone who could bring a significant measure of glory to the art and to their school, and the whispers of "a new one" begin. Nureyev had been in Pushkin's class for more than a year before word began to go out that this Tatar terror might actually have something special. He continued to give the school's administration the opportunity for huddled conferences about his other qualities as well, and there was soon talk of "a taste for scandal." The early rebellions had consolidated into a dependable pattern of behavior. The scenes with Chelkov became daily and uglier as Nureyev's contempt for Chelkov grew more bold and more bald. "I don't have the time for all that," Nureyev shouted at the school's director during one particularly bitter encounter over his academic performance. "Why can't you understand that, you stupid, stupid man!" Interaction with his peers could prove every bit as volatile, particularly once he'd graduated into pas de deux class and begun learning for the first time to accommodate his dancing to the presence of another dancer. More than one aspiring ballerina who found herself in the wrong place at the wrong time also found herself shoved out of his way. Just as in that first encounter in Chelkov's office, Nureyev could be remarkably unrepentant about the mishaps. "Not my fault," he tossed off after sending a partner crashing to the studio floor from a lift neither one of them was experienced enough to negotiate yet. "She should have helped me more."[44]

The offstage tension continued until his very last day at the Kirov school. Nureyev received his diploma with one final threat from Chelkov. The school director drew the line over Nureyev's attire for the graduation exercises. Chelkov told him point-blank that he was to appear for the ceremonies properly dressed: white shirt, tie, suit, his hair cut short and neat. Another graduate that day still recalls the outfit Nureyev chose instead: no tie, no jacket, black velvet pants worn shiny at the knees, and his hair "doing whatever it wanted to do. I said to him, 'You must be crazy. Chelkov will never stand for this. You will not graduate.' All he said was 'We shall see.' " The two dancers took seats next to one another for the presentation, and, by the time the event had reached the actual awarding of the diplomas, even Nureyev was so apprehensive that the two found themselves gripping one another's hands.

Chelkov called Nureyev's name.

Nureyev stepped forward to receive the certificate, returned to his seat, and looked his nervous friend straight in the face.

"You see," he told her. "You must never show them you are afraid. If you do, you will be lost."

Four

Center Stage

"He was like a tank—you couldn't stop him."

—*Mikhail Baryshnikov,*
Vogue, *March 1993*

After the Moscow competition and then his graduation performance, Nureyev was the only dancer in Russia anyone wanted to talk about. Sweetest of all, they were putting their money where their mouths were. By summer's end, the Kirov and both of Moscow's lead companies, the Bolshoi and the Stanislavsky, had offered him soloist contracts. All of them waived the requisite first years in the corps de ballet for the first time in memory. (In his thirty-three years on the professional ballet stage, Nureyev never once danced a corps role.) Flashy as they might have been, the offers were never really a contest, not after a brief conversation Nureyev had at the reception following the graduation performance in Leningrad. A comparable discussion had taken place only once before in the three-hundred-year history of ballet in Russia, and Nureyev knew enough of that history to know it. In April 1907, after Vaslav Nijinsky's graduation performance, Mathilde Kschessinskaya, the *prima ballerina assoluta* of the Imperial Theater and the most powerful woman in Russian ballet, walked directly over to the student Nijinsky and said, in effect, "Young man, you have just become my partner." Fifty-one summers later, history repeated itself, with consequences as far-reaching. The great Dudinskaya herself,[1] the Kirov's revered *prima* and the wife of the company's director, Konstantin Sergeyev, made, in effect, the same proposition to Nureyev. For one of the few times in their careers, both Nijinsky and Nureyev did as they were bid.

Nijinsky, of course, was fired from the Imperial Theater. His career in Russia lasted barely four years; like Balanchine, Nureyev lasted less than three. Nijinsky left Russia for a better offer. Balanchine left because he wanted to. Nureyev left because he had to, and not for the reasons that have become the standard version of his "leap to freedom." The threat facing Nureyev the day of his defection was more than professional, deeper than the absence of artistic freedom. His life was in danger. Nureyev's homosexuality provided the opposition a trump card. Though irritating, provocative, defiant—not joining the Komosol, not dressing like anyone else—these were not a crime. Homosexuality was, something for which one could go to a labor camp or worse.

By Paris 1961 Nureyev's KGB file was a hefty one. When Nureyev put the picture together that final day at Le Bourget, his fear was sharper than never dancing again. Only one other person there that morning knew that the pocket of Nureyev's jacket contained a pair of sharpened scissors that had not found their way there by accident. "If you don't get me off that plane," Nureyev threatened to French dancer and choreographer Pierre Lacotte, "I will kill myself right here." That is not the action of a man whose will to live would later keep AIDS at bay for a decade.

Dudinskaya's invitation after the graduation performance may have cinched his future, but the powers that be were determined to make Nureyev strain just a little bit more for the brass ring. After the Moscow and Leningrad double tour de force, Nureyev decided even he had earned some R & R and took the first holiday of his life. He spent the Kirov's annual August vacation time on a Crimean beach (although still giving himself a two-hour ballet barre every day). When he returned to Leningrad to begin his first year with the Kirov, an ugly, astute surprise was waiting for him: since the Bashkir regional government had paid half his tuition, his career would begin there as a form of return on the loan. His destination was not the Kirov stage after all, but the corps de ballet at the Ufa Opera House. The first threat of exile turned out to be a carefully staged warning, but it frightened Nureyev and he flew into a panic. He took the first flight to Moscow to plead his case, and the official he met at the Ministry of Culture (who was no longer at her job the very next day) told him that there was no room for any bargaining over the Kirov versus Ufa, although a second invitation from the Bolshoi might be considered. Nureyev accepted the Moscow position and returned to Leningrad for his belongings. Nureyev's later account of what happened next, abbreviated events: "When the Kirov director heard I was [back] in town he called me to his office and said in a calm, matter-of-fact way, 'There was never any question of throwing you out of the Kirov. Unpack your things and stay here with us. Your salary is waiting to be collected.' "[2] Others remember a more complex sequence of events. For Sizova, Nureyev's partner from the graduation performance, the incident brought out a side of Nureyev no one had yet seen: "A different aspect of his character manifested itself. I remember that he had conversations with Pushkin at that time and with all the teachers. He begged everyone to let him stay with the Kirov. I remember him crying, saying, 'I don't want to go back! I want to stay here.' " After much pulling of many a string, particularly by Pushkin, the authorities relented, but the scare was sharp and considered.

Nureyev gave his first official performance as a member of the Kirov in November 1958.[3] He graduated straight into the principal male role in a company standard, *Laurencia*,[4] and, as promised, opposite Dudinskaya. The performance was an electric success on all fronts. "The *Laurencia!*" Alexander Minz remembered years later. "It was like an eruption of Vesuvius!"[5] The student star became a professional nova—overnight. The press was ecstatic, the audience was mad for him, and Dudinskaya paid him the finest compliments of veteran professional to heir appar-

ent: she treated Nureyev like a peer and covered for his inexperience. Despite their differences in age and professional stature—
Dudinskaya was already forty-six when she and Nureyev first
performed together—she didn't dance down to her nervous new
partner. Instead, Dudinskaya danced her signature role with a
renewed vitality and abandon, feeding off the energy and challenge of her young partner—literally. That first evening, Nureyev's lack of experience at the practical facts of partnering
occasionally left Dudinskaya in the lurch, never a pretty sight in
ballet. ("If boy not there," a longtime Kirov follower explained,
"girl fall down.") She covered Nureyev's first-night gaffes with
the generosity of a seasoned professional having the time of her
life. At one particularly tricky point in a pas de deux adagio
Nureyev's timing was a hairsbreadth off and he missed the point
where he should have gotten Dudinskaya "on her leg" for a
lengthy balance; digging deep into her fabled technical strength,
Dudinskaya got herself in place on her own, on pointe. When all
was under control, she flashed her shaken cavalier her famous
megawatt smile—over the shoulder—and moved on.

The moment was a forecast of the Fonteyn phenomenon
and more. It was a first glimpse at an area of Nureyev's cumula-
tive impact largely overshadowed by his effect on male ballet
dancing in our time—his impact on his partners—who all return
to one point. "You had to be your best with Rudolf," Antoinette
Sibley explains. "He simply would not allow slippery standards."
"Rudolf was never indifferent on the stage," a Kirov habitué
remembers, "and did not allow anyone else to be indifferent on
the stage either. For example, Kolpakova[6] at first considered him
just another partner. However, her performance with him was
something extraordinary. When they were on the stage together
in *Giselle*, he danced the tender lover Albrecht and he warmed
her dance with his feelings. One had an impression that she
melted in his hands. There were people that have accused her of
being cold as a dancer. When they danced together, you could not
accuse her of it anymore."

Indifference was not a feature on the other side of the
footlights either—or in the wings. A Nureyev cult was already

in bloom before his first *Laurencia*. His student performances had generated a group of followers already approaching the manic. Russian balletomania had been a world standard since the nineteenth century, when the packs of students following Virginia Zucchi, the fabled Italian ballerina who was a regular guest at the Imperial Theater, would unhitch the horses of her carriage and tow Zucchi through the streets themselves.[7] However frozen the Russian night, Dudinskaya's fans, according to one of them, "would always wait for her to come out after her performance. She usually took at least one hour to get ready, so, if we waited for her, we were unable to get to the other side of the Neva River, since the bridges were raised every night. The pleasure of seeing Dudinskaya leave the theater was more important, so we usually stayed." Like Chabukiani before him, Dudinskaya's husband, Konstantin Sergeyev, the Kirov's director and ranking danseur during the 1950s,[8] was attended by a largely male and particularly rabid company of followers who would jam the Kirov theater for his performances and court their hero's offstage attention. Nureyev's following was the only one to begin before he had even turned professional and included, according to a colleague, "a group of young girls who would never miss a single performance of his. . . . If he was leaving the city for some reason, they would come to say good-bye to him at the train station and to wish him luck wherever he was going and then they would always go somewhere to discuss such events among themselves at great length. The only word for them was fanatics." By the time Nureyev joined the Kirov the behavior of his fans, like their hero's, was pushing the envelope. "It was absolutely forbidden to throw flowers to the stage at that time," another Leningrad friend recalls. "Those girls did not care. They would go up to the fourth gallery, the highest one in the theater, with the flowers stuffed up inside their skirts—large flowers, too. Peonies. When the performance was over, they would shower the stage with flowers for Rudi. Unheard of. And for a man. Not a ballerina. Simply unheard of."

Prophetically, the adulation did not always bring out the best in Nureyev:

He could also permit himself unacceptable behavior toward his admirers. It was absolutely unacceptable for an artist to give to another person a bouquet of flowers given by the admirers who waited after the performances. I remember clearly Nureyev leaving the theater one afternoon after a matinee performance of *Don Quichotte*. His fans were there, their arms filled with flowers for him. It was the time when *My Fair Lady* was on tour in the USSR. Later, right in front of all these young girls, his admirers, he gave a huge bunch of flowers that had just been presented to him by the girls to the girl who was playing Eliza Doolittle. Normally after such a gesture the admirers would turn away from such a person, find another person to admire. But everything was always different with Rudik. His followers forgave him and remained at his side, despite the fact that this gesture was ugly and utterly tactless.

The Kirov administration gave the Nureyev fans a lot to see. Although he had to fight for his ground—Kirov director Sergeyev was not a fan—in his three years with the Kirov, Nureyev accumulated a repertory of ballets that the majority of Soviet danseurs had to work a lifetime to achieve. In addition to the requisite "coming of age" roles for the ascendant danseur—the male pas de quatre in *Raymonda*, the pas de trois from the first act of *Swan Lake*, the Bluebird pas de deux from *The Sleeping Beauty*—Nureyev danced in experimental ballets such as Yacobson's *Valse Volonté*. He danced ballets from the full range of the nationalist works perpetually in political vogue, including Vainonen's torchlit *Gayané* suite and the revolutionary fireworks of the *Flames of Paris* pas de deux. He also assumed the male leads in virtually all of the traditional repertory classics—*Giselle, Don Quixote, La Bayadère, Swan Lake, Nutcracker,* and *The Sleeping Beauty.* Almost immediately, he began altering the choreography to suit his tastes and talents and, almost as quickly, Nureyev's emendations became standard. He partnered no less than half the company's considerable roster of ballerinas,[9] most of them more than once and at their requests. The statistics of Nureyev's quick Kirov career become more striking in light of the fact that the

Kirov at the time was a strictly hierarchical company with twenty principal dancers in competition for fewer than fifteen performances a month. Nureyev was the only dancer anyone could remember who didn't have to wait his turn. Even more astonishing, by his second *Laurencia*, Nureyev had eliminated the role's greased-down black wig,[10] redesigned the tunic of the costume, and begun rewriting more than a bit of the choreography. Nureyev was allowed to do virtually as he pleased. No other Kirov dancer had been granted such leverage.

But for every professional step forward, Nureyev took two steps back into dangerous political straits. The latitude he was allowed was without precedent, offstage and on—his own friends, his own steps, his own costumes. Nureyev, in effect, did whatever he wanted to and the Soviets let him get away with it. In the context of the era, Nureyev's innovations were not entirely an exception. The thaw of the early Khrushchev years had had an impact on the Kirov. By the time Nureyev reached the company, according to Irina Kolpakova, his first Giselle, "it was a new era. A lot of people were doing new things, things in a new way." In 1956, Sergeyev was removed from the company directorship and replaced by Feodor Lopukhov, a graduate of the Imperial academy who was both a practiced authority on the Petipa classics and, as a choreographer,[11] one of the two great innovators in the Russian ballet of the early Soviet era. The emphasis of the company repertory shifted from the traditional standards that had been dominated for a decade by Dudinskaya and Sergeyev to an era of invention. The Kirov had a promising young house choreographer in Grigorovich, and Boris Fenster, an established choreographer with an eye for change, was moved from his small experimental company to working with the main-stage Kirov troupe.

The fresh air of Nureyev's dancing was the right gust at the right time, and his energy was infectious. "He wanted to do performances his own way," Kolpakova remembers.

He didn't want to go what Russians call "along the well-traveled road." There were no big scandals at first, but not everyone was happy with what Rudi was doing. Innovation in the theater is not always a welcome thing or a good thing. Change needs a reason or the past will be lost. But, if a person comes out and performs in a vibrant, intelligent way, like Rudi did, the change can be good for everyone. For example, with our *Giselle*,[12] Rudi made changes in the choreography of the coda. I don't remember anyone ever doing that before. And he danced the new steps so expressively, so dynamically, with such éclat, such soul and emotion, that his steps were soon being danced by everyone.[13]

The troubling, and suspicious, difference in the response of the Kirov administration to Nureyev was the degree of freedom they allowed their number one troublemaker. The dominant features of Nureyev's Kirov career—speed, innovation, and intrigue —were not incidentally related. Nureyev had a plan for his future, but so did the authorities. The two blueprints were less than complementary. Nureyev, for example, knew exactly what he wanted to look like onstage. The antique Kirov costuming didn't fit the picture. In addition to altering his *Laurencia* costume, Nureyev reworked everything he wore onstage. He added an ice-white *faux bijou* to Solor's turban with his first *Bayadère* and refused point-blank to wear the bloomer shorts that had been part of the costume for Albrecht, the hero in *Giselle,* since the turn of the century.[14] And he refused more than to wear the *Laurencia* wig. He refused to wear any wigs at all. Until Nureyev, Kirov men always wore obvious hairpieces straight out of a daguerreotype. Like Albrecht's crotch-covering bloomer shorts, the flat, shiny wigs flattered no one, and Nureyev became the first dancer in Kirov history to appear onstage with a contemporary hairstyle. Nureyev's ragged, rebel mop of hair was his era's answer to the ducktail and about as popular with the powers that be.

Of course, Nureyev had to fight to keep his course, but his peers were having a hard time of their own in his wake. They were forced to sit back and watch Nureyev earn liberties they would never be allowed. "You cannot imagine how much they hated him," a colleague from the time recalls. "How much the dancers—the men in particular—resented him for the things he could get away with." Just as at the school, his list of enemies grew by the day, particularly after Sergeyev was reinstated as director in 1960. Fast approaching his fiftieth birthday, Sergeyev had a specific, entrenched concept of the classical danseur, summarized by a Kirov associate as "a romanticized version of a blue-eyed, enchanted bird. It wasn't Nureyev, and that is why Rudolf had to fight so hard to get and return to the great ballets." Insult was added to injury when Sergeyev saw the spotlight he'd cultivated for two decades shift onto the upstart Bashkir crow. The consequences of his enmity were far-reaching, and there are eerie echoes in Sergeyev's reemergence as Kirov director just as plans were beginning for the fateful tour to Paris. The ascendant male dancers also being overshadowed by Nureyev saw a chance to curry a little directorial favor, and in the time-honored Soviet manner. A Nureyev file at the KGB offices began to bulge.

Nureyev's offstage behavior was no help. He rarely smiled and was too intense for social comfort. His intensity easily read as arrogance, an impression Nureyev did little to correct. "I don't think the innovations were the reason for his problems," Kolpakova maintains. "It was his manner. As I said, other people were making changes, too, but slowly, gradually. With Rudi, it was much sharper, much stronger. He had no tact and that upset many people." Nureyev's classroom attitude was particularly abrasive. He swore his way through classes with a string of expletives unlike any ever heard before in the hushed Kirov studios. He balked at the most revered Kirov traditions. The daily obligations of the younger dancers during Nureyev's ascendancy included drawing water from a tap and dampening the antique floors of the studio to make them more malleable and manageable for classroom exercises. Once again, Nureyev called a halt. "He just said, 'I won't do it,' " Sizova recalls. "We were the junior dancers, just starting out, and there were big stars in the company class— all the stars of the company. The newest dancers watered the floor for the stars. Not Rudi. Can you imagine?"[15] (Nureyev eventually conceded the point, to a degree. He took to watering only the spot where he himself would stand.)

His actions had practical ramifications. When Grigorovich began preparing a new full-length work during Nureyev's first year with the Kirov, he cast the new star as the ballet's male lead. The collaboration barely made it to the first dress rehearsal. Nureyev was more interested in rehearsing *Laurencia* and *Bayadère* with Dudinskaya than in working on a ballet that would take a year to reach the stage, despite the fact that he was getting every Russian dancer's dream—an original leading role in a full-length ballet for which all the Kirov's vast resources had been marshaled. "Rudik would be late for rehearsals with Grigorovich," a cast member of the new ballet remembers, "or he wouldn't show up at all or he would come in wearing sneakers. Grigorovich finally said, 'Go. Good-bye. Don't come back.' "

A more serious problem was brewing also, one that would not be resolved until that last Paris morning at Le Bourget. Unlike Nijinsky, who got all the way through the Imperial School without making a friend, Nureyev had made a handful of lifelong friends during his years as a student. That began to change when he joined the Kirov company. Nureyev made a single new friend during his years onstage with the Kirov, a fellow dancer named Nina Alifimova, who was said to be a daughter of the other great Soviet choreographic innovator of the 1920s, Kasian Goleizovsky.[16] Otherwise, his circle of friends was drawn from outside the ballet circle, yet another example of Nureyev's taste for doing exactly the wrong thing. The authorities objected even more strongly to Nureyev's personal independence[17] and taste for privacy than they did to his brash behavior in class and onstage. (During Nureyev's first fight with Chelkov back during his first week at the Kirov academy, the first thing Chelkov demanded was that he turn over his address book. Nureyev refused.) Nureyev could at least be monitored within the confines of Rossi Street. The private time and friends Nureyev kept to himself was another story, and it set the government machine in motion.

The result was the hawkeye treatment, Soviet style. Nureyev was kept where he could be seen and well clear of any contact with foreigners. He was sent out on tour when foreign troupes came to Leningrad and denied the soi-disant privilege of dancing when important government officials were in attendance.[18] For all the freedom the Kirov authorities allowed, technically the tethers were kept tight. In three years with the Kirov, Nureyev danced outside Leningrad no more than three times. The first was a star-cross'd trip to Vienna in 1959 as part of the Kirov contingent at an international dance festival. Things got off to a bad start when, in Moscow for rehearsals with the Bolshoi participants, Nureyev exploded over the conditions of the Moscow rehearsal studios. He treated the horrified company to an extended—and loud—lecture on the priority of individual opinion over collective subservence. After that, Nureyev was kept off company tours, with only two exceptions: a trip to Berlin by bus with a circus troupe, and, a year later, a stint in the polar outpost of Ioshkar Ola—in December, with the same company of circus performers.

When plans for a tour to Paris were announced for the summer of 1961, Nureyev was certain he would not be included —and he wasn't. The plans for the tour changed at the last moment, when the Paris organizers decided that they were interested in dancers younger than Dudinskaya and Sergeyev. Nureyev was the last person to find out that his name had been added to the roster for the tour. "A woman I knew at the time," a colleague recalls, "happened to find out one day that Nureyev was about to go abroad with the company. When she saw him in the theater that night, she told him, 'You are going abroad.' He could not believe it, could not believe that he was being taken along. She told me that her news made a very deep impression on him. It was from her that he first heard this news." Nureyev was ecstatic and apprehensive at the administrative change of position. "It couldn't have been an easy choice [for Sergeyev] to have to make," Nureyev wrote in his autobiography.[19] "He, the most powerful conformist leader of the company and me, its most rebellious nonconformist member." The choice, however, was easier than Nureyev imagined. A trap was in place, and, wild to see the outside world, Nureyev stepped right into it.

Nureyev should have taken a cue from an encounter his first long-standing male lover had had on a state-sponsored visit to Paris the year before. "Alexei,"[20] a mutual friend remembers, resembled Jean Marais very much. So there in Paris during some kind of reception, Alexei and Jean Marais met. It was impossible for Jean Marais not to notice Alexei, because Alexei was extraordinarily beautiful. He was so beautiful that back in Leningrad it was impossible to walk down the Nevsky Prospekt with him, because everyone's head would turn. So Jean Marais invited Alexei to his place. Alexei, who was twenty years old then, did not know what to do. He accepted his invitation. He could not have done otherwise, of course, but what to do next? Should he go or not? Alexei could not think of anything better than to discuss the situation with the KGB official who accompanied him abroad. So, this official told him, "You must go, but I will come with you." Alexei wanted so very much to go by himself, but the official told him, "No, I will come with you."

Back in Leningrad, Alexei described the scene to us. Together with this official, they approached the beautiful house of Jean Marais, who personally met them at the door, wearing a luxurious robe. There was a table for two set in the dining room, of course. The place set for the third person appeared immediately.

Amusing as the story may have been to Nureyev's friends in the Leningrad gay underground, it foreshadowed the danger awaiting him in the City of Light. Paris can be a heady experience. Nureyev drank too much of the City of Light, and for the first time slipped out of discretionary mode. He made sexual advances to someone the KGB had set up as a plant.

Five

The Leap,
or Enough Rope

"What a story! Everything but the bloodhounds snappin' at her rear end."

—MISS BIRDIE COONAN *

he scene is a tea table in a quiet St. Petersburg apartment. The lace curtains are drawn tight. The tired walls are dotted with snapshots of days gone by. The two guests dare to peruse them only with quick, sidelong glances. Their host, a gentleman in his late fifties whose voice is most comfortable in a hush, seems too nervous for any undue curiosity. He is also given to quick, sidelong glances that are, in his case, clearly the habit of a lifetime. The only thing that prevents him from being a Eudora Welty character is the Russian accent.

There were a lot of rumors then that it did not happen the way he described. Sergeyev, who was director of the theater again, was painting a very different picture, but I believed only Rudolf. It was forced upon him. He was provoked. Forced by circumstances. Someone scared him. You cannot even start to understand what it meant to be sent home like that. Before the end of the tour. This is the end! It is not simply that you will never go abroad again. It can mean Siberia or . . . anything else. This is why he ran away.

* *In the film* All About Eve.

It is not by accident that he calls that chapter in his book "Paris Situation." Two or three years after he left, he sent me his book. Actually he sent two copies, one for Alexei[1] and one for me. This book talked about his life and was written in English. He put a bookmark at the beginning of the Paris chapter and he included a little note that said, "Everything that did happen happened the way I describe it here. Believe only that!"

The scene is a Paris restaurant out of a Piaf fantasy. Red-checkered tablecloths, not a demitasse without a cracked lip, waitresses who were never young in black uniforms that were never new. The speaker has enjoyed his meal and is enjoying his souvenirs of an exciting time. Gallic to the bone, he has somehow managed to turn the unforgiving contours of the Naugahyde banquette into a couch.

Of course, everyone was mad to meet the Kirov dancers. First time for us to see such a thing. After the first performance—it was *The Sleeping Beauty* but Rudolf didn't dance. No, he was on second night—*Bayadère*, but actually he did not dance the *Bayadère* variation. He did solo from *Corsaire*. But we already knew about him. So. After *Sleeping Beauty* there was a little reception in the *foyer de la danse* and, the people I was with, they ask Rudolf to join us for dinner. So Rudolf say, "Oh, yes, I would like that but I think that someone else must come along with us." He could not go out alone. Must have someone else from the company with him. So Soloviev joined us.

The scene is an upscale New York eatery, the kind where the choicest table is not in a corner but dead center in the big, big picture window. Our table is conspicuous thanks to a cloud of cigarette smoke. The speaker, a Russian, is too busy lighting up another to notice the glares.

You see, Rudolf was in love with Soloviev. He was an angel. Oh, no . . . not Rudolf. Rudolf was many things, but an angel? No, no. Soloviev. He looked like an angel, he danced like an angel, and the man . . . It's the only word.

Angel. They were in same hotel room that month in Paris. So Rudolf tried, and Soloviev was completely terrified and he told management.

Another brunch, a great American ballerina is days past a tribute to Nureyev. She is still shaken.

"Yes, I think I will have another one of those, please. Ask them to make this one . . . well, more spices and . . . you know."

I do as I am told.

"I'm sorry, but I don't think I can continue with this. We'll talk again another time. I promise."

She stares at her drink until I switch off the tape recorder. Her face hardens for the first time.

"You know the defection was completely fucked up."

"Beg pardon?"

"Totally. It wasn't supposed to happen that way at all. He had no choice. He was betrayed at the last minute by someone who later shot himself."

My face freezes for the first time.

"But that can only be one person. It has to be Soloviev."[2]

"I never said that. But I will say one thing. If you ever associate that statement with my name, I will simply say you are lying. Oh, yes, this drink is much better."

Three decades later, the Kirov tour that led to Nureyev's break with his homeland appears to have been more than a welcome exchange of artists in a politically tense era. Double meanings and ulterior motives ricochet like handballs. Everyone was up to something. Even the timing of the tour is odd. Considering how hot the Cold War was getting, the Kirov could not have picked a more volatile moment to make its debut in Western Europe. The company left for Paris exactly one month after the fiasco at the Bay of Pigs; by the end of its July season in London, the Berlin Wall was under construction.

The Kirov tour was an integral part of a star-cross'd attempt by the Khrushchev regime to put on a happier face for its Western adversaries. Stalin had opposed contact with the West, so what little interaction there had been had taken place under the strictest supervision. A Kirov visit to Stockholm in 1947 was timed for the single week of the year when all of the local ballet dancers would be out of town. But only a year after Stalin's death, a contingent of no less than forty-four dancers, drawn from both the Kirov and the Bolshoi, was in rehearsal for a three-week Paris engagement. The company roster was heavy with big guns—not only Dudinskaya from Leningrad but both Ulanova[3] and the resplendent Raisa Struchkova[4] from Moscow. But, at the last moment, the French government decided that the week immediately after the fall of Dien Bien Phu might not be the best time for Soviet guests, and their invitation was withdrawn. As a measure of the political significance attached to the Soviet appearance, the international press already assembled in Paris for the Russian season, such as John Martin of the *New York Times*, extended their itineraries to include Leningrad.

The next effort at exchange took two years. The ballet equivalent of a May Day parade, the Bolshoi's London debut in the autumn of 1956 was an historic success. The Soviets had gained a foothold in European ballet. The vigor and virility of the Bolshoi men whipped European audiences into a frenzy. Margot Fonteyn later admitted that her first sight of Ulanova was unsettling, the first challenge to her supremacy in many a year. The success of the tour had the PR advantage of deflecting attention from less sanguine news back home. Pasternak began submitting *Doctor Zhivago* to publishers in the summer of 1956, and the government ban on the manuscript was firmly in place by the time the goodwill ambassadors from the Bolshoi reached London. The engagement began exactly one day before the first armed clashes in Budapest that led to the Soviet invasion of Hungary less than a week later.

The 1961 Kirov tour was an even more massive undertaking than the Bolshoi invasion. This time the plan was more than a one-stop visit. The company was scheduled to open May 22 for two weeks at the Garnier and then move to the Paris suburbs for another two weeks at the massive Palais des Sports. A month at

Covent Garden would precede the annual August vacation and then the company would reassemble for its American debut at the Metropolitan Opera House in the autumn and a seven-week tour of North America.[5] They did not travel light. In addition to the full-length *Giselle* and two programs of repertory highlights, including the *Bayadère* Shades, the Kirov tour included the largest, most technically complex ballets—*Swan Lake* (four acts, half of them in palaces), *Sleeping Beauty* (prologue and three acts, three set in palaces), and Grigorovich's *Stone Flower* (three acts in eight scenes, including one in the Kingdom of the Copper Mountain). The 120 dancers were barely half the assembled company, which included musicians, technical and administrative staff, and enough security to keep the entire outfit in line. There was not an uncomplicated aspect to the enterprise. Simon Virsaladze's sumptuous, emphatic sets, for example, designed for the chamber-hall proportions of the Kirov Theater, had to be adapted to the grand opera house proportions of the Opéra and Covent Garden by a stage crew that couldn't speak or read either French or English.

An effort on that scale was the last place the Soviets needed a troublemaker like Nureyev, but he was chosen, the first of several odd events. The Kirov was, always had been, and probably always will be the Bolshoi's artistic superior, and the troupe that left Leningrad in May 1961, was the equal of any ballet company in Europe. Backed by senior artists as exceptional as Osipenko and Shelest, the fleet of emergent dancers who were to replace Dudinskaya and Sergeyev included, among the women, Kolpakova and Sizova and, in addition to Nureyev among the men, the vibrant young Yuri Soloviev. (Nureyev was, in fact, not scheduled to dance until the fifth night of the Paris season, although he was given the *répétition générale* that precedes a Paris premiere and is traditionally considered the opening night.[6]) Even more odd than taking Nureyev along and then not using him *tout de suite*, the kind of attention he was likely to attract was exactly the type the Soviets discouraged—intense and highly personal.

Why make Nureyev a star when they didn't need to? Fresh success was liable only to make him bolder, perhaps bold enough to finally overstep his bounds?

Most suspicious of all, why allow him an unprecedented degree of free rein offstage and on—in a foreign country, no less? Although he was tailed at every turn by the unmistakable KGB undercover agents, Nureyev was allowed a stunning level of personal latitude in Paris, even after his extracurricular activities began making him late for rehearsals on a daily basis. From that first reception in the *foyer de la danse* at the Garnier, Nureyev cultivated a company of new friends who were all only too delighted to show him Paris in the way only Parisians can. The rest of the company saw the sights primarily from the windows of the charter bus shuttling them back and forth between the Opéra and the Hotel Modèrne in the Place de la République,[7] not the city's liveliest quarter. Nureyev lunched in the student hotbeds of St.-Michel and St. Germain-des-Près. He saw Notre Dame and the Louvre by day, Montmartre and Pigalle by night. He went to the movies and saw *Ben-Hur*. He rode the *bateaux-mouches* and bought (or was bought, since the ruble was hardly a player at the Bourse) an expensive toy train at the Paris equivalent of New York's F. A. O. Schwartz, Le Nain Bleu on the Rue St.-Honoré. Each evening at eleven, when the rest of the dancers climbed aboard the bus back to the hotel, Nureyev joined his new Paris friends, who were always waiting at the stage door, and drove off with them into the night. Acquiring a taste he would never lose, Nureyev's guides were the local crème de la crème and regularly included, among others, the formidable Opéra ballerina Claire Motte, the promising young danseur and choreographer Pierre Lacotte, and, most often, a twenty-one-year-old Chilean heiress named Clara Saint, who had once been engaged to a son of the French minister of culture and would be a key figure in the events at Le Bourget.

The independence Nureyev relished was not confined to offstage. During a performance at the Palais des Sports late in the season, Nureyev became so irritated with the orchestra's erratic tempos one night that he walked offstage in the middle of a performance, an offense that would have been grounds for immediate sanctions back home and was doubly offensive for a representative of Soviet art performing for the outside world. Nureyev was back onstage at the next performance without a word of official reproach.

Nureyev's option for self-exile was, and remained, many things to many people, from the defining moment of his career to the clarion call of a rebel era. It was also the cultural equivalent of nature's molting phenomenon—not just in Nureyev's unprecedented change of citizenship but, over the years, as an event that resiliently shed its facts. No other incident in Nureyev's oft-altered life was as rewritten as those famous weeks in June 1961. The most consistent editor was Nureyev himself, who hated the term "defection" to his grave. His account of the bolt at Le Bourget became the inverse of his born-on-a-train number. The latter was embellished with the years, the former steadily stripped down and dedramatized. Nureyev loved to recall his birth, which, of course, he couldn't possibly remember. But he avoided describing the steamy Paris morning that changed his life, a curious attitude toward an act fired by the call to freedom of expression. Until Nureyev's last interview,[8] only three aspects of the "Paris situation" were irrefutable. A twenty-three-year-old Soviet dancer got a new address. The course of ballet history changed in a day. The fuse was lit for a decade of violence and romance.

Nureyev went straight into a seclusion so tight the French press had better luck tracing the Algerian terrorists currently blitzing the sidewalks of Paris. The doggedness of the newshounds left Nureyev with a distaste for the press he never lost. The tactics smelled too much like home: "I didn't like the way in which I was dished up as a public sensation, and I resented the public curiosity about everything concerning my person."[9] Nureyev would not so much as speak to journalists during the week required for the paperwork on his request for political asylum to be signed and sealed. When he did, he "forgot" most of the English he knew,[10] but he could still manage the classroom correctness of tense in the concluding observation of his first interview: "I shall never return to my country, but I shall never be happy in yours." The Soviet authorities were left to confirm the facts, leading to much misinformation. In London, the Kirov company manager refused to admit that anyone had left the company. (He was removed from his job that very day.) The *Sunday Times* of London identified the central figure in these events as Yuri Nureyev. The first photographs made available were all of Soloviev, including those appearing in the *New York Times*, the *New York Herald Tribune*, and *Time* magazine a full week later. The Kirov dancers themselves had no idea whether Nureyev had remained in Paris or gone back to Russia. And while Nureyev himself dated his defection as Saturday, June 17—and yet another example of seventeen as his lucky number—the dateline on all of the initial reports on the Le Bourget incident is Friday, June 16.

As always, there was method at work—both from Nureyev and from the authorities. Seen from the distance of thirty years, Nureyev looks like a man with a plan. He made friends easily in Paris because he was the single Kirov dancer who spoke a second language, English. Although his enchantment at the privileged view of Paris was clearly genuine, he also ladled on the "innocent abroad" routine with a trowel. It worked every time. (Although they eventually were estranged, Saint still delights in remembering Nureyev's wonder at the Left Bank's bookshops. He was overwhelmed by the idea that they were not libraries, that their bounty was available to anyone—despite the fact that Nureyev had been haunting the Leningrad booksellers since his arrival on the Neva.) Most striking of all, and an intimation that the Kirov authorities were not the only ones with a plan, Nureyev's most consistent purchase on his shopping expeditions was theatrical wigs. He scoured Paris for them. The wigs are an unlikely choice for a dancer who'd spent three years refusing to wear them. The prospects of a budding personal wardrobe for a new soloist career, however, seems all the likelier in light of a choice Nureyev made just before leaving Leningrad for Europe. After six years as the Kirov's resident shaggy dog, Nureyev had his hair cut short and neat, making him look not only presentable but decidedly unrebellious.

Once again Nureyev and the authorities were at cross-purposes, and the difference had become acute by the time the company was scheduled to leave Paris for London. Nureyev would later insist that he was unaware of an impending problem until the company boarded the airport bus that last morning and an official began distributing individual tickets to London. The Kirov traveled as a community, and dancers never handled their own tickets. The Nureyev sonar then, he said, went on alert. Something was up, and whatever it was, it got uglier when the company reached Le Bourget and the tickets were recollected. Soviet bureaucrats were not the kind to do extra work without a reason.

Nureyev was, in fact, already well aware that trouble was in the offing. His relations with the company administrators had been deteriorating steadily since the company became an established hit and began raking in money at the Palais des Sports. Nureyev kept taking more and more liberties and the KGB began trailing him more and more closely. For all the tension, he had no intention of remaining in Paris. Clara Saint has clear memories of Nureyev's last evening as a Kirov dancer:

> The last night, after *Bayadère*, we went out with Claire Motte. He did not want to sleep that night. He wanted to see Paris all over again. I can't remember where we ate, but I remember walking a lot on the bridges over the Seine. Claire eventually went home and I stayed alone with him. I escorted him to his hotel around four in the morning. We said our good-byes, and I reminded him that we would be together soon in London. He said he was looking forward to being there.[11]

Whatever happened next, Nureyev was a different man within a matter of hours. By 7:00 A.M., the nostalgic reverie was history, and Nureyev was on the phone to Pierre Lacotte, a French dancer with whom he had spent a great deal of time during the

Paris season. Nureyev begged Lacotte to come to the hotel so that they could drive to the airport in Lacotte's car. Lacotte calmed Nureyev down and convinced him that a European escort might not be the best tactic. Nureyev left the hotel with the company, but the scissors were waiting in his pocket. Lacotte drove to Le Bourget and joined Nureyev for *café à cinq* with Dudinskaya, Sergeyev, and Claire Motte. "We were all having a coffee together," Lacotte recalls, "when Sergeyev said he needed to talk to Nureyev alone. They stepped away from the table, Sergeyev said something to Rudolf, and then Rudolf went absolutely white. Sergeyev came back to the table and said that Rudolf was not going to London but back to Moscow on the next flight. His mother had been taken gravely ill. Everyone stood up and went over to where Rudolf was still standing. When the others were gone, he said to me, 'That's it. I am finished. Help me or I will kill myself.' "[12] KGB agents were beginning to circle. Nureyev showed Lacotte the scissors and repeated his threat.

By 8:30, Clara Saint was on her way to Le Bourget. She'd been called from the airport by an Opéra dancer named Jean-Pierre Bonnefous, who'd come to the airport with a group of friends to say good-bye to the Kirov dancers. After a relay of notes from Lacotte, Bonnefous had been given a slip of paper with Saint's number and instructions to have her come to Le Bourget immediately. Bonnefous told her, Saint remembers,

> that the Russian group was leaving for London but Rudolf had been stopped from boarding the plane by two representatives of the Russian Embassy.
>
> I took a taxi to the airport and was told he was in the bar. Two enormous men were guarding him. I thought, "This is terrible. If he goes back to Russia, he will never be allowed out again." People said that there was nothing we could do. The other dancers had left for London and Rudolf would be flying to Moscow in an hour or two. I walked toward Rudolf but the two men blocked my way. "What are you doing? What do you want" they said. I said I just wanted to say good-bye to Mr. Nureyev. I went over to kiss him good-bye and, when I did, he whispered, "Do something."

I had no idea what I could do but then I noticed an arrow on the wall with the word POLICE pointing to a stairwell going to the first floor. I went up. I knocked at the door and I found two men in uniform. I explained the predicament Rudolf was in. Once they were sure he was a dancer and not "some scientist," they told me the only way they could help and remain within the law was for Rudolf to come to them. So I went back downstairs and approached Rudolf once again and again the guards blocked me, asked me what I wanted this time. I used the same line as before. I leaned over to kiss Rudolf on both cheeks, and, while this was going on, I explained to him in his ear what he must do so the French police could take him into their custody. As they promised, the French police followed me by five minutes and stood at the bar. The two guards were unaware of them, and, after about five minutes more, once Rudolf felt his guards had relaxed, he ran about seven or eight meters to the two waiting French policemen. The Russian guards followed and there was a fight between the French policemen and the Russian guards. Eventually one of the French policemen pointed out that this was French territory and the Russians had no choice but to stop. The Russian guards gave in, and Rudolf went with the French police. A Russian Embassy attaché came to the airport police office and spoke with Rudolf. They spoke Russian but I suspected he was trying to convince him to change his mind. He left after about twenty minutes.[13]

It was not quite 10:00 A.M. The entire episode had taken barely an hour.

Nureyev was on his own again, this time without so much as a change of clothes and with less than ten dollars in his pocket.

Everyone anywhere near Le Bourget that morning agrees that Nureyev's decision to remain in Paris was spontaneous, an act of the moment. "Osipenko was the last one to board the plane," a Leningrad colleague recalls. "She told me that he was standing there and crying. She could see tears in his eyes. He was

very, very upset." The possibility of a break was an option Nureyev certainly had been entertaining: the English lessons, a new
language he hardly could practice with his Kirov peers but could
turn off and on at will; the horde of new and influential friends,
all of whom were in a position to offer him help in securing a job;
the wigs. There has to have been a reason for Nureyev to invest
time and energy on such extracurricular activities. (There *has* to
have been a major reason for him to spend what little money he
had on acquiring his own costumes, which, were he planning to
go back to Russia, would have been tantamount to dropping his
own cash on something the company would have paid for.) His
Kirov colleagues in particular all agree that separate paths were
an inevitability. Nureyev clearly felt the same way. At twenty-
three, he was still fighting the backlog of wasted time in his late
start as a dancer and was not one to squander his energies. Like
the authorities, Nureyev did things for a reason.

It was an aspect of his character that the Kirov authorities
came to appreciate because it made him impatient and, ultimately,
indiscreet. The directors finally had managed to turn Nureyev's
impetuosity to their advantage with the company's month in
Paris. Nureyev had been a thorn in their sides for six years but,
as far as anyone outside the Kirov administration knew, he had
never done anything that was actually illegal, made any breach
that qualified as grounds for exile. That perception changed in
Paris, when the sudden decision to return Nureyev to Russia
changed him from a troublemaker into an enemy of the state.
The most ardent communists among the dancers did not believe
for a second that Nureyev's mother was ill. Nureyev was headed
back to Russia for exile—at best. Something had happened in
Paris that was an indisputable ground for serious charges. Nureyev, after all, was the biggest news of the Paris season, and London was awaiting the arrival of the prodigy with bated breath.
Barely a year after Pasternak was hounded to an early grave,
the Soviets hardly could risk the international humiliation of an
unwarranted assault upon another of its artists, particularly one
as young and commercially viable as Nureyev. Whatever it was
the authorities knew, even the born fighter in Nureyev knew that

they had him this time. It must have been particularly galling for Nureyev to realize that his enemies had simply given him enough rope.

Kolpakova remembers the KGB agents trailing Nureyev in Paris as "complete idiots and cretins . . . [who] sat every night in the hotel and watched to see when everyone returned."[14] Someone was still smart enough to know that, if Nureyev was ever going to overstep his bounds, Paris was just the intoxicant to make him clumsy. Two approaches conflicted. The first was to let Nureyev do as he pleased and wait for the slip, hence the ever more strict surveillance once Nureyev had had his first two weeks of *la vie parisienne*. But Nureyev was too smart for them at first. He kept his activities strictly aboveboard, in plain sight of the guards he knew were always there. His company was irreproachable; even Saint had recently been engaged to a public figure, nixing the possibility of a love match. He made no effort to contact the press and bad-mouthed no one. Nureyev was out late every night, but every night still ended back in his hotel room.

Plan number one—allow Nureyev whatever he wants and he'll finally go too far—did not succeed. The backup plan worked better. The most unusual aspect of Nureyev's presence on the Paris tour, particularly to students of Soviet gay history, is the fact that it broke an unwritten law of the Kirov system: the only dancers allowed to tour were married couples. Thanks to the information they had accumulated through surveillance and the helpful intimations of his Kirov enemies, the KGB knew why Nureyev was still unmarried at twenty-three. Nureyev was already a discernible figure in Leningrad's shadowy gay underworld. Sex between men had been recriminalized under Stalin[15] and, by the time Nureyev reached Leningrad, homosexuality was a blackmailer's dream come true—not only against the law but a violation of every social and moral code in a heavily homophobic society. Until Paris Nureyev covered his tracks too well for confirmation, despite the fact that the most notorious cruising ground in Leningrad was the public gardens near the Kirov. ("Imagine," a Kirov contemporary of Nureyev still vividly recalls, "I am boy from provinces. I am fourteen years old and go for little stroll first day in Leningrad and this man in that park suddenly opens his raincoat and exposes himself to me. Who knew about such things?'')

Nureyev steered well clear of any chance for a public surprise and, even more shrewd, kept his gay socializing a goodly distance from his colleagues in the ballet. Nureyev guarded his privacy closely and always managed to be one step ahead: he stayed just inside the border of the permissible. Nureyev was too discreet, for example, to work the public gardens that separate Rossi Street from the Nevsky Prospekt. Elena Tchernichova, who graduated from the Kirov with Nureyev, was a friend until his death, and is one savvy woman, remembers having ''absolutely no idea that Nureyev was homosexual back then. The thought never even entered my head.'' His gay friends were drawn instead from local artists and intellectuals who met more often in private apartments than in public. According to survivors of the Nureyev group, he had at least one long-term relationship with another man before his defection, again under the strictest cover. Sizova remembers that, during the time she and Nureyev shared an apartment together, he spent hardly any time at home. All of Nureyev's free time was spent with his friends, and his sister Rosa, who was working in Leningrad as a teacher, used the apartment more than Nureyev did. He was so discreet that even Sizova did not know that his nights were being spent at clandestine gay gatherings or with his ''special friend.''

The KGB officials knew what they were seeing in Nureyev's de facto cohabitation with Alexei and, masterfully playing off personalities, gave Nureyev a backup temptation for the Paris tour, just in case the liberties they allowed in Paris should not lead Nureyev into troubled waters. They gave him Yuri Soloviev as a roommate; Soloviev's wife, the soloist Tatiana Legat, had for some unknown reason been left behind in Russia (although she danced on the second leg of the tour in America later in the year). A man who's been described as a combination of cherub and truck driver, Soloviev was Nureyev's only rival onstage, the only male dancer Nureyev ever spoke well of other than the great Danish dancer Erik Bruhn and a genuinely docile personality. Nureyev took the bait. The last week of the tour he finally made sexual advances to Soloviev, who panicked. When Soloviev cracked under questioning, Nureyev was hooked, and he knew it. The minimum sentence was seven years at hard labor. The only thing to do was bolt.

Although he was a man who knew how to hold a grudge, to the end of his life Nureyev never had a bad word to say about Soloviev. In 1972, when Nureyev coached a young Canadian dancer named Frank Augustyn for his first performance of the Bluebird pas de deux from *The Sleeping Beauty*, a role that had played no small part in Nureyev's early Kirov notoriety, he had a single comment to make after the ballet. Augustyn, who went on to a major career with the National Ballet of Canada and now directs the Ottawa Ballet, still remembers Nureyev's words. "He said," Augustyn recalls, " 'You are now the best Bluebird in the world. With one exception: Soloviev.' "[16]

The Kirov made its London debut, as planned, on June 19, although, due to a last-minute change in programming, the premiere program was switched from *The Sleeping Beauty* to the more Soviet-flavored *Stone Flower*. Four days later, after a week in Paris, Nureyev gave his first performance with a Western company as a principal dancer with the International Ballet of the Marquis de Cuevas, in the Bluebird pas de deux. The performance provoked a riotous response from Soviet sympathizers, who pelted the stage with coins and filled the Théâtre des Champs-Elysées with harsh shouts of "Traitor!"[17] Despite signing a six-month contract with de Cuevas, Nureyev had left the company by the end of the summer and soon relocated in Copenhagen, ostensibly for classes with the expatriate Russian teacher Vera Volkova. Copenhagen was also the home of the great Danish classicist Erik Bruhn; back in Russia, Nureyev had seen a brief film of Bruhn and was determined that they would meet. They did, and the great love affair of both of their lives began, from all accounts, within minutes.

An unexpected telephone call changed Nureyev's professional life as well. Shortly after Nureyev arrived in Copenhagen, Volkova received a call from Margot Fonteyn, who was planning a benefit performance in London.

"Vera," Fonteyn asked, "do you know where I can find this Russian boy?"

"Yes," Volkova answered, opening a major chapter in the history of twentieth-century ballet. "He's right here."

TWO

Rudi

Six

The New Breed

"He was never too proud to learn."

—*NINETTE DE VALOIS, Interview, London*

he dance world sat up and took notice when Nureyev made his London debut at Fonteyn's benefit for the Royal Academy of Dancing on November 2, 1961. The London *Weekend Review* summarized, "It was as if a wild animal had been let loose in a drawing room."[1] Despite his initial request to partner his hostess on the program, Fonteyn chose to sit out the first dance, to wait and see. Instead, Nureyev performed the Black Swan pas de deux from *Swan Lake* with Rosella Hightower, and *Poème tragique,* a solo created especially for him by the Royal Ballet's founding choreographer, Frederick Ashton (to selections from Scriabin that Nureyev chose himself). From all accounts, those who saw the Ashton solo never got over their first sight of a bare-chested Nureyev. "Nureyev rushed forward to the front of the stage," the British critic and Nureyev biographer John Percival wrote, "then hurtled into a short, fast series of fiendishly difficult steps. What left the most abiding impression, however, was not his virtuosity, but his temperament and dramatic quality. There were plenty of people to point out that if Nureyev jumped high, he sometimes landed heavily, and that his tours en l'air were not strictly vertical, but there was no missing the deep fires that burned in his eyes or the strangely relaxed intensity which hinted at more exciting things to come."[2]

Thirty years after the fact, when ballet technique has reached an unprecedented level of facility and audiences have become unshockable, it's hard to understand just what sent critics and spectators into such frenzies over Nureyev's first appearances in the West. Based upon the early films of his dancing, particularly with Fonteyn—*Les Sylphides* and the *Corsaire* pas de deux in *An Evening with the Royal Ballet,* the BBC films of their *Giselle* and Kenneth MacMillan's *Romeo and Juliet*—and the still-breathless memories of his friends and followers, only one element is absolutely clear: there was much more than just dancing going on. Nureyev was certainly capable of some breathtaking technical feats—his famous exploding jeté that hung in the air like holiday fireworks, the dervish ferocity of his turns. His in-your-gut impact, however, was never simply the result of what Nureyev did. The power was in how he did it—the sinuousness that still sizzles in his *Corsaire* solo, the Byronic abandon of his Albrecht in *Giselle,* his aching, ardent Romeo. Nureyev's earliest reviews all return to the kind of charged but highly personal phrasing that suggests out-of-control hormones on both sides of the proscenium. They were terms that had not been used to describe a male dancer since Nijinsky: "alien," "androgynous," "pantherine," "exotic." "Nureyev wasn't just using his body in a square manner," the great French ballerina Violette Verdy remembered. "He was using it poetically—as an instrument of exploration. I had never seen such a vulnerable, exposed quality."[3] Simply by virtue of what the man looked like—and how skillfully he emphasized his physical beauty—Nureyev's appeal inevitably plucked more than heartstrings. "Rudi was always a wild man onstage," his Kirov colleague Elena Tchernichova remembers. "He would do whatever came into his mind. It was easy to see why people were so shocked." Nureyev, in fact, did more than shock his audiences. He unnerved them. "He [came] onto the stage as if it is an arena," Verdy recalls. "Is he going to be eaten by the lions or not? That is the feeling of danger we [got] from seeing him perform. He dances without a net."[4]

No one had ever seen anything like it. Nureyev appeared in the West like one of those snakeskin strangers in late Tennessee Williams—a man with a past, bashful but basking in his own beauty and trailing chaos in his wake. Nureyev's audiences throughout his career came to the theater to see more than steps. They were there to be astonished; thirty years later, it's startling to realize how often terms such as "otherworldly" and "not quite human" occur in Nureyev's early reviews. In addition to his exotic physicality—the cheekbones, the elasticity, the sheen— Nureyev's personal signatures were qualities that wove their way into the fabric of his dancing. They were not qualities traditionally associated with the male dancer. According to an early biographer, David Daniel, Nureyev was the first male dancer since Nijinsky to bring a sense of mystery to his performances, a sense of the ambivalent, of the sexually ambidextrous. "There was always something elusive in the early Nureyev," Daniel remembers. "You never knew what he was going to do next. Even in his curtain calls. He could stand in front of the curtain and slowly, deliberately open his arms over the house. Or he could bow and bolt offstage and not come back, however much applause. It generated a sense of mystery surrounding whatever he did."[5] He projected a sense of a burning intelligence at work, a mind as agile and astute as his dancer's body.

The definitive statement on Nureyev's native intelligence came from Dame Ninette de Valois, the founder of England's Royal Ballet and Nureyev's greatest champion in the West. "How many people have you interviewed for this book?" Madame de Valois asked during a recent conversation about Nureyev. "How many were dancers? How many were smart?"[6] As a result of Nureyev's singularity, the character of male dancing—not just the character in the ballet but the impulse behind his dances— had changed for good.

Nureyev did things that no male dancer had ever done before. He was fearless. He was sexual. He performed in minimum costuming and maximum makeup. (There is a legend that Nureyev arrived at one early rehearsal with his hair in curlers.) Nureyev himself typically was evasive on what he was trying to achieve onstage: "A dancer must give quite different *readings* of ballets," he told the London *Times* shortly after he'd joined the Royal, "as if they were poems." In her own inimitably cryptic fashion, Martha Graham got as close as anyone to scanning Nureyev's special verse in her posthumous autobiography *Blood Memory:* "Many people have asked me why I did *Lucifer* with Rudolf Nureyev. Lucifer is the bringer of light. When he fell from grace he mocked God. He became half god, half man. As half man, he knew men's fears, anguish, and challenges. He became the god of light. Any artist is the bringer of light. That's why I did it with Nureyev."[7]

However poetic his ambitions, Nureyev also introduced another new feature to dancing—more than a little of that old showbiz razzle-dazzle. He was as shrewd as a vaudeville veteran. Maria Tallchief remembers a rehearsal for Nureyev's American debut, when he danced the *Flower Festival at Genzano* pas de deux with her on a *Bell Telephone Hour* broadcast in January 1962. Tallchief was not particularly impressed with Nureyev during rehearsals. "He had no elevation, no jump, and I thought, 'Well, what's all this about?' I found out during the actual performance, when he was flying across the stage. The studio had a concrete floor, you see, and he was saving himself. Rudolf was very smart in that way, shrewd."[8] He knew how to work up an audience from the very beginning, and pound-for-pound technical prowess was only part of his first burst into celebrity. Nureyev was indeed the rebel poet Western dance had been waiting for, but he was also a showman of the first magnitude, a man who knew in his blood how to get maximum mileage out of a cape. The combination of idealism and ham bone was irresistible. "Rudolf knew exactly when to browbeat his audiences," John Wilson, a former manager for Hurok Concerts, remembers, "and he knew exactly when to smile at them. He could get them to do whatever he wanted them to do."[9] A longtime Nureyev follower is even more specific: "Every woman in that theater knew in her soul that he was dancing for her and her alone. It was like seeing Frank Sinatra for the first time. Every hair on your body stood on end. At least half the men there felt the same way." The world had certainly seen stronger, cleaner dancers—André Eglevsky, Igor Youskevitch, and Royes Fernandez in the United States; Erik Bruhn and whole generations of Danes—but there had never been anyone even remotely like this slender, savage Pan who, in effect, deflowered the serving-man ballet prince in public and made him into a star in the process, as bright—and important— as any ballerina.

Understandably, after his defection, Nureyev became the one dancer everyone in the know had to see. He also became the man everyone wanted to know offstage as well, and in the biblical sense if possible. However much Nureyev reveled in the applause of his new Western audience, he took less well to their offstage intrusions. The tradition of the Nureyev "court," the tight inner circle of devoted friends Nureyev learned to keep close by, began within the first six months of his defection as a means of warding off the uninvited personal interest. The inner court remained a feature of Nureyev's personal environment for the rest of his life, only adding to the sense of distance and mystery that surrounded him. The faces in the circle shifted over the years, as Nureyev moved more and more freely through the new worlds of show business, international society, and haute gaydom. During his earliest days in the West, however, there might as well have been a sign over Nureyev's head, the same sign that hangs somewhere backstage in every opera house in the world: DANCERS ONLY. NO VISITORS PLEASE.

Even when the inner circle was drawn only from the class-room and the rehearsal studio, Nureyev remained an enigma to virtually everyone around him. He saw to it himself. Among the people who first knew Nureyev in the West, no two describe the same wunderkind. The personal aloofness created by Nureyev's inbred mistrust of strangers—not to mention his conveniently fluctuating grasp on the English language—left his new friends to fill in the blanks on their own. Their memories run the gamut.

Many were enchanted by what they saw, just as many were appalled. Some saw only the charm, others could not get past the cunning. Some, mostly women, saw a lonely, courageous young Adonis, alone in a strange new world. Others, mostly men, saw a crude, rude, abrasive arriviste, already too good at playing prima donna. And then there were those, Fonteyn among them, who saw both sides and didn't care about the contradictions—or about the potential violence in Nureyev's hair-trigger tantrums. "Yes, I know it can be awful," Fonteyn was fond of saying, "but isn't it worth it?" A fact that has been largely overwhelmed by Nureyev's subsequent celebrity, at least at the beginning of his Western career, there were many who answered Fonteyn's starry estimation with a resounding "No." The ranking British critic, Richard Buckle, thought Soloviev the far better dancer and described Nureyev as "the dancer with the most publicity." Chief among those who took exception to Nureyev was the chief dance critic of the *New York Times*, John Martin, the single most powerful critic of the day. "As a Tartar," Martin wrote in a famous review of Nureyev's first American tour with the Royal, "Nureyev has inherited the predacity of that somewhat older and until now better known member of his race, Genghis Khan. In other words he moves in and takes over." For Martin, Nureyev was "erratic, undependable, and moody, and condescends to dance well only when the wind is in the right direction." Even Fonteyn couldn't escape the taint: "She has gone, as it were, to the grand ball with a gigolo."[10]

Because Nureyev gave the world so many extracurricular reasons to notice him—the defection, his haunted manner and fits of temper, the sexual glamour that registered from five hundred paces—the facts of his dance technique largely have taken a backseat to the impact of Nureyev's personal magnetism. His fame certainly wasn't based on the purity of his classical technique, despite his immediate beatification as the new Nijinsky by critics who'd never seen Nijinsky dance. A woman who would know, the great Tamara Karsavina, Diaghilev's prima ballerina and Nijinsky's partner, felt that Nureyev was indeed a better dancer than her fabled colleague—less for his purely technical skills, however, than for his variety and his gifts as a partner. Nureyev's first *Laurencia* may have been shaky in the partnering department, but he soon developed into a reliable and resourceful partner. "You are very lucky to have such wonderful partner," Karsavina told Fonteyn when she came to coach her and Nureyev in *Giselle*, adding, with a sad, downward shake of her head, "I . . . had Nijinsky."

No one knew better than Nureyev himself that there was much major work still to be done if he were to become what he most wanted to be, a *danseur noble* in the classic tradition rather than the *demi-caractère* also-ran that was his physical birthright. His determination to clean up his technique was the reason Nureyev was in Copenhagen when Fonteyn's fateful telephone call came. Nureyev had made a point of knowing that Erik Bruhn was in Copenhagen for a series of guest performances with the Royal Danish Ballet, and he knew something else too: without ever having seen Bruhn dance, Nureyev considered him "the only dancer who has anything to show me I don't already know."[11] Nureyev had been shipped to East Berlin on his first tour when Bruhn, the great classicist of the era, danced in Leningrad with American Ballet Theatre in 1960. Shortly before his defection, however, Nureyev saw a brief bootleg film of Bruhn dancing Balanchine's *Theme and Variations* on the Ballet Theatre Russian tour. In a flash, he saw in the flesh the image that had been evolving in his mind for the ideal male dancer, the one he'd been working so hard to mold his intractable physique into—not the square, squat, bounding bricklayers of the Soviet man's man but a long, clean sire of the blood royal, elegantly proportioned and articulate. Bruhn was everything Nureyev was hell-bent on becoming as a dance artist.

On his own in the West, with ready cash from the de Cuevas tours hot in his pocket, finding Bruhn was Nureyev's first priority. An introduction was arranged by Maria Tallchief, and Nureyev met his only hero for the first time at Copenhagen's Hotel Angleterre in the autumn of 1961. The encounter changed the course of both men's lives onstage and off. Sonia Arova was a popular ballerina of the day and became part of the small touring troupe soon organized by Bruhn and Nureyev. "Rudi's regard, his respect for Erik's dancing," she recalls, "was the basis of their entire relationship. Rudi sought Erik out so he could learn from him. Whatever came later, it all began with that."[12] Under Bruhn's sponsorship, Nureyev began taking class with the Danish company and with Volkova in particular. Like Nureyev, Volkova was a Russian and an alumna of his alma mater, the Kirov academy, but from back when it was still the Imperial Ballet School. Since emigrating to the West with her British husband, she had become one of the most influential ballet teachers in Europe.[13] The new Russian visitor in Copenhagen made a clear impression on a fifteen-year-old apprentice dancer with the Royal Danish company named Peter Martins: "Rudi was what we called a 'dirty' dancer. Not clean, not finished. Russian. A rough, rough, rough . . . I want to say 'diamond' but that would not be quite right. It took Rudi years of concentrated effort to clean up his technique, to discover that there was more to dancing than what he had been taught in Russia. He worked his whole life to try to become a pure classical dancer like Bruhn. He never did become Mr. Clean."[14]

Onstage or off.

Just as it had in Russia, the aggressiveness of Nureyev's offstage manner, his gift for insolence and merciless bad manners, left a less than glowing impression on those around him. Despite his position in Denmark as Bruhn's guest, Nureyev's behavior toward the Danes in general, Martins also remembers, "was just plain obnoxious. He was . . . what? Twenty-two, twenty-three years old and already acting like a star. I was taking the adult classes when he first came to Copenhagen, and my first impression of him was that he was rude, enormously rude to everybody —to the other dancers, to the pianists, to every single one of the teachers with the exception of Volkova. And Erik let him get away with it, or tried to make it all into just a joke."[15] Not everyone was amused, and Nureyev's brittle, biting personal style became a genuine liability once he'd left Copenhagen and set off in search of a job. Although from the distance of three decades Nureyev seems to have had no trouble finding work, the facts of his first year in the West suggest things might have been otherwise. Despite the success of his London debut at Fonteyn's RAD gala and the sensation created by his first *Giselles* with Fonteyn in February and March 1962, for almost a year after both performances Ninette de Valois remained uncertain about whether to take Nureyev into the Royal on a regular basis. In the meantime he was looking elsewhere as well—and with no luck. The biggest problem was his smart mouth. At Bruhn's suggestion, and in spite of unofficial pressure from the Soviets to keep Nureyev from finding a home in America, Lucia Chase, the founding director of American Ballet Theatre, took Nureyev into her company in the winter of 1962. He lasted a week, until he had insulted Chase to her face one time too many. Nureyev's manners didn't improve even after de Valois offered him a position as "permanent guest artist" in London. He even managed to alienate the company's founding choreographer, the great Frederick Ashton.

"Like all Russians," Nureyev told Anna Kisselgoff, the chief dance critic of the *New York Times*, "I thought I knew better than anyone else about the classics."[16] Nureyev finally so infuriated Ashton that, however ecstatic the response to Ashton's *Marguerite and Armand* for Fonteyn and Nureyev in 1963, a full five years were to pass before Ashton created another original role on Nureyev.

Nureyev's technical imprecision and lack of civility didn't matter for a minute in performance. He was more than the paradigm for a new breed of male dancer. He was a whole new species, and men in dance learned a completely new vocabulary. "Rudolf was a revolution in male dancing," Tchernichova explains. "Everybody else looked like truck drivers next to him."[17]

Until Nureyev's arrival in the West, the danseur was the lord of only one domain—the Kingdom of Second Billing. Balanchine's fabled assertion "Ballet is woman" was more than just an opinion. It was a job description for the male dancer: tote that swan, lift that sylph. With the death in 1929 of Diaghilev, who had reserved the star spot in his Ballets Russes for his string of boy prodigies—first Nijinsky, then Léonide Massine and Anton

Dolin, and, finally, Serge Lifar—ballet choreographers largely lost interest in men, unless, like Lifar at the Paris Opéra, Robert Helpmann at the Sadler's Wells in London, or Chabukiani in the Soviet Union, they were making ballets for themselves. Everywhere else, the ballerina was at the top of the heap. Ashton found his muse in Margot Fonteyn and in the United States Balanchine, ballet's Ziegfeld, built a repertory and a company glorifying the long limbs and limitless energy of the all-American girl. The male dancer was back out in the cold, the reason why even the great and important danseurs of the twentieth century were always associated with a single reigning ballerina—Dolin with Markova, Frederic Franklin with Danilova, Youskevitch with Alicia Alonso, Eglevsky with Maria Tallchief. Yes, Nureyev had Fonteyn, but his list of partners is a who's who in tutus: Lucette Aldous, Sonia Arova, Yvette Chauviré, Eva Evdokimova, Carla Fracci, Cynthia Gregory, Sylvie Guillem, Marcia Haydée, Rosella Hightower, Patricia McBride, Natalia Makarova, Yoko Morishita, Merle Park, Nöella Pontois, Lynn Seymour, Antoinette Sibley, Maria Tallchief, Ghislaine Thesmar, Martine van Hamel. Like Nijinsky, however, he would still have made it as a solo act.

Nureyev put an end to the male dancer's second-class status. Under his tutelage, men in ballet learned three things: to let go, to step forward, and to fight back. His innovations were the result of his quest for the grail, the public viewing of a lifelong personal struggle, Nureyev's battle to reshape and redefine his recalcitrant body. A ballet dancer, the saying goes, has to be born with two assets: the right body and the right parents. Nureyev lost on both counts. A major contribution his parents had made to Nureyev's success was by default. A mother desperate to give her favorite child a taste of a finer life and a father determined to dictate the future of his only son can generate enough friction to get a real fire burning, and the combination helped to forge the blind determination that characterized Nureyev's life from beginning to end.

Fate was not much kinder in the body department. Nureyev was not tall and broad-shouldered like Bruhn; he barely scraped five feet nine inches. His body was slight, between 148

pounds and 160, and without any of the physical specialties ballet
dancers need for success. Nureyev's struggle to correct his body
never ended, not even during the painful last decade of his career,
when he danced the majority of his performances bound and
bandaged from injury after injury. (Nureyev eventually came to
feel that he danced his best when he was most tired, and more
than one of his later partners agrees.) With the single exception
of a generous turnout, the all-important capacity for a dancer's
body to fan away from its center, the inborn gifts that can determine a ballet dancer's career—proper proportions, natural align-
ments, steely insteps—simply were not there. According to an
early colleague at the Royal, Georgina Parkinson, "ballet was
never easy for Rudolf. He had to work terribly hard for what he
had. And he was willing to sweat blood for it."[18] Verdy, who
knew Nureyev from his earliest days with de Cuevas, agrees:
"Rudi's body was not an easy one to work with. He is self-created
in that sense. He made his body—made an instrument of it at
the same time as his soul and his talent were revealing themselves. He was the battleground on which all this took place, from
the beginning."[19]

Even Nureyev's famous exploding jeté was a gift Nureyev
gave to himself. "Rudolf did not have a real jump, a natural
jump," Tchernichova explains. "He was not like Misha, who was
born with absolutely astounding coordination. You throw him
out a window, he'll land on his feet. Rudolf was not like that. He
taught himself how to jump." The goals were fixed in Nureyev's
mind and so was the opposition. " 'Those idiots!' " the student
Nureyev complained to Tchernichova when he'd been hit with
another classroom correction for performing pirouettes from an
elongated position high up on his feet rather than closer to the
earth with the real men. " 'They are so stupid! Don't they understand that I have bad proportions. I have short legs and a long
body. I have to be on a high demi-pointe or I will look ridiculous.'
It is a big part of why the company hated him—I mean, hated
him. He was not purely classical. He was a wild man onstage. He
danced on a high demi-pointe. He had high extensions. These
were against all the principles of Kirov training. But he knew

what looked right on him."[20] Sonia Arova is of the same opinion: "Everything Rudolf had technically he worked for. He really worked for that jump, really worked on his head and *épaulement* thoroughly and carefully. And he wanted to do it his way. Rudolf was going to do what Rudolf wanted to do."[21]

Setting another pattern that would continue until the last months of his life, Nureyev set his sights high and refused to settle for anything less, even after he easily could have descended into the sum of his specialty acts. His resistance to the easy way out was evident as early as the film of Nureyev's *Corsaire* solo at the Moscow Competition in 1958. At the top of the variation— which is basically one pyrotechnic punch after another from start to finish—the dancer must perform a series of three air turns on a diagonal. They're not your standard up, down, and twice around "double tours." These are Soviet *tours en l'air*, barrel turns with pointed feet. To ensure as many obstacles as possible, the dancer travels backward on his diagonal, face to the audience, from just under the proscenium to the farthest upstage corner of the stage. He spins in on his body in the air, rather than outward as with the easier "outside turns." At the same time he brings both legs tight up underneath himself, his arms looped to his shoulders. In the Moscow performance, Nureyev comes out of the first pass like Karen Black at the controls of a 747 in *Airplane 1975:* "I can't fly this plane! I can't fly this plane!" Nureyev's back foot deserts him completely in a landing planned as a deep, reaching lunge and he comes within millimeters of biting the dirt. Instead of easing up for the next turn, Nureyev slams the accelerator to the floor. The second turn is higher, faster, and cleaner and the lunging return to earth is virtually a full split, solid as a rock.

Nureyev never lost that appetite for risk. In the West, instead of sticking to what he could do, Nureyev set relentless technical challenges for himself straight through to the end of his career. Nureyev, Verdy remembers, "was merciless on himself. The solos he has written for himself in *The Sleeping Beauty* are things other people would hesitate to try in a classroom."[22] They were also proof that Nureyev's career, however lucrative, was much more than a commercial enterprise. Nureyev took chances

he didn't have to take. Past master of the Russian school of nuclear male dancing, his first targets in the West were the fiendishly filigreed ballets of the nineteenth-century Danish
choreographer August Bournonville. The Bournonville danseur,
of which Bruhn was the high priest, is everything the Russian
dancer is not—buoyant rather than bounding, precise rather than
pushy, articulate rather than loud. All Nureyev really had to do
to lay them in the aisles was put on a pair of harem pants, but
Nureyev was determined to master the intricacies of Bournonville
technique. When he was finally invited to perform again at the
Kirov theater in 1989, Nureyev's choice of ballets to show his
former comrades what he had learned in the West was evidence of
how deep his steadfastness still ran: Bournonville's *La Sylphide*.
Nureyev's will to dance better—and better and better—reinvented the possibilities of the male dancer. "Whatever else anyone might say about Rudolf," Peter Martins summarizes, "and
I've heard all the stories. That he could be a real bastard, all that
stuff. In the final analysis, if Rudolf had had to choose between
the glamorous life, the money, the attention, and all that and
dancing, he would have chosen dance. Absolutely."[23]

"Male classical dancers in those days," Arlene Croce wrote
in *The New Yorker* shortly after Nureyev's death, "were not
nearly as turned out as they are now, and it was Nureyev who
made the difference, but when he first appeared with his feet
placed at nine-fifteen he seemed altogether absurd. And he was
absolutely adamant about it. The truly remarkable feature of that
signature step of his—the 'double assemblé'—was the tight fifth
he held from takeoff to landing. It was the double revolution in
the air that caught the eye, and at first everyone who tried the
step stumbled coming down, as Nureyev himself sometimes did.
Then his imitators caught on, and the step today is a common-
place, along with full turnout. Nureyev would go into his perfect
fifth even when he had nothing to do but support his partner. He
would draw himself up, his feet locked, his head high, and only
then would he offer his hand to his ballerina, as much as to say,
'Let's make this one legit.' "

Nureyev's determination to fine-tune his technique

changed the course of male dancing. Just as he first burst into celebrity, Nureyev's battle of the hour was his concentrated effort to adapt Bruhn's elegance and exactness of execution. "Rudolf was the last in the line of dancers," New York City Ballet principal dancer Heather Watts explains, "who wouldn't always land in fifth position but would fix his fifth after he'd landed. He could afford to be academic on stage when he wanted to be because he had all this other stuff going on as well."[24] As the most famous dancer in the world, he gave the Bruhn paradigm a platform for worldwide exposure and acclaim. Nureyev never fully embodied his ideal, but he set his peers moving in that direction.

He also left behind an unexpected self-portrait—his ballets.

Trying to pinpoint autobiography in the work of any artist is like trying to give the Medusa a perm wave. Nureyev's work as a choreographer embraced both original ballets and his versions of the traditional classics. Neither met with universal acclaim. Nureyev's own ballets tended to be overwhelmed by other issues, by his interest in poetic or thematic concerns rather than the finer points of choreography. His stagings of the Petipa repertory were as personalized and given to a numbing taste for perpetual movement: every note gets a step. As a producer and choreographer, Nureyev spent a lot of time tripping on a Freudian slip; there's something going on with a choreographer who can turn Prokofiev's *Cinderella* into an icy essay on cynicism and greed.

Nureyev's ballets are as close as Nureyev came to explaining himself to his public. His first original work, *Tancredi*, staged for the Vienna State Opera in 1966, set the tone. Nureyev was not only the central character but, in concept, the only character in the ballet. The other dancers were either projections of himself or demons in pursuit. "In particular he is torn between Sacred and Profane Love," Alexander Bland[25] wrote of the ballet's premiere. "After a succession of hallucinatory experiences, his personality splits finally and fatally in two, and, after a last struggle, he sinks back into the primordial chaos from which we saw him born."[26] The picture was little cheerier when Nureyev made his Byron ballet, *Manfred*, for the Paris Opéra Ballet fifteen years later. Once again, Nureyev was the ballet's centerpiece, and everyone around him had the predatory possibilities of the dancers in *Tancredi*. Endlessly pursued by masked figures, Nureyev's Byron figure is a hero always at a distance, a lone, hounded exile: he is finally swallowed whole by a sea of deep blue silk.

For all his sacred commitment to the preservation of purebred Petipa, the imagery Nureyev added to the traditional classics, at least according to Alexander Bland, was for "the Jung of heart."[27] Two productions are especially telling. Ninette de Valois considered Nureyev's staging of *Nutcracker* "the best I've ever seen,"[28] and, in the quarter century since its first performance at the Royal Opera house in Stockholm, it has been performed by more companies and in more theaters than any other version of the ballet. Nureyev even extended *Nutcracker* into the sociological. The guests arriving for the traditional Christmas party reach the festivities braving street toughs and the occasional mugging. The unexpected becomes the norm for a *Nutcracker—Nutcracker!*—in which the Arabian dance is set in a den of iniquity, the party guests double as vampires, and the young heroine is presented with an immodestly oversized nutcracker. Nureyev's controversial staging of *Swan Lake* for the Paris Opéra Ballet in 1984 makes the same point sotto voce. The entire ballet is set in a room from which there is no escape. Nureyev may have spent his life on the road but, against the background of his creative output, the very restlessness of his schedule sounds like the cry of a man who sees himself as hounded, as trapped.

Seven

The Last
Imperial Ballerina

*"And all that's best of dark and bright
Meet in her aspect and her eyes"*

—GEORGE GORDON, LORD BYRON,
"She Walks in Beauty"

Anyone attempting a biography of Rudolf Nureyev is, of course, volunteering for a stroll through a minefield. Half of the story centers on subjects you're not supposed to talk about in mixed company—sex, money, violence, passions that would make a Brontë blush. The first half of Nureyev's life was spent in a place where secrecy was the norm, the second in a profession that lives to talk, but hushes "don't quote me."

The biggest problem is not the web of privacy Nureyev's perpetual motion spun about his private life. It's the alabaster and ebony goddess née Peggy Hookham who, as Dame Margot Fonteyn, was Nureyev's guiding light, determining his professional life and outlook.[1] Fonteyn's life and career were every bit as dramatic as Nureyev's. Nureyev leaped over the Iron Curtain. Fonteyn was deported from Panama for gunrunning. The endless rhapsodies on the love-in between the ivory *assoluta* of the Royal Ballet and the Mongol tiger misses the most important point of the story, the reason they were what they were together: different as night and day, Fonteyn and Nureyev were, in fact, variations on the same theme. The most difficult job in assessing their impact in performance when the Fonteyn/Nureyev event was in full sail is remembering to watch Nureyev. It's not that he is at any less than his most exhilarating in their *Corsaire* or *Romeo and Juliet* or *Giselle* or even in something as flaccid as Ashton's *Marguerite and Armand.* It's simply the difference between heat and light. Fonteyn is ballet as pure light. Try taking your eyes off her. Nureyev won't let you, because he can't either.

Fonteyn's telephone call to Vera Volkova in the autumn of 1961 was an apt beginning to a lasting and complex relationship between two very shrewd professionals. Despite the "do you know where this Russian boy is" routine with Volkova, Fonteyn knew exactly where Nureyev was at the time of her call. The ballet world is small and close-knit. Word travels fast. Fonteyn was the most powerful woman in European ballet after her boss, de Valois, and she was a diplomat's wife to boot. Her husband, Roberto de Arias, was the scion of an important political Panamanian family. For a time, he was Panama's ambassador to the Court of St. James. Though aware of the cash and cachet Nureyev's presence would bring to the benefit matinee she sponsored annually for the Royal Academy of Dance, Fonteyn was not on the lookout for a new partner when she offered Nureyev the chance to make the London debut that had been postponed by his defection. Her career plans were looking in an entirely different direction. After the Royal's tour to Russia in July 1961, Michael Somes, Fonteyn's principal partner for the previous fifteen years, had announced his retirement. At forty-two Fonteyn was doing more than considering the same option: just before Nureyev's arrival for the RAD gala she had given her "farewell performance" in one of her many signature ballets, *Swan Lake.*

The idea of a new partner was so far removed from Fonteyn's mind that when Nureyev, asking for the moon as always, requested her as his partner for the benefit, she chose instead to perform the relatively undemanding role of the somnambulant heroine in Fokine's *Spectre de la rose* with the great English danseur John Gilpin. Nureyev's insistence on partnering Fonteyn at his debut—Volkova told Fonteyn that he was "adamant" on the subject—did not produce a favorable impression. "The more I hear of him," Fonteyn told a friend, "the worse he sounds. I don't mean as a dancer, but why should he decide to dance with me when he's twenty-three and I've never even met him? He sounds rather tiresome to me."[2] Nureyev bowed to Fonteyn's objections and, assuming a pseudonym to throw off the press, flew to London for rehearsals. The future partners met over tea in Fonteyn's home on Nureyev's first afternoon in London. Conversation was initially quiet, polite, and wary, until, as Fonteyn wrote in her autobiography, "I said something light and silly. Suddenly he laughed and his whole face changed. He lost the 'on guard' look, and his smile was generous and captivating. 'Oh, thank goodness,' I said. 'I didn't know Russians laughed.' "[3]

Despite her improved opinion, Fonteyn was still hesitant about dancing with Nureyev when de Valois invited him to London for guest performances of *Giselle* with the Royal in early 1962. (De Valois said later that she got the idea to invite Nureyev to guest with the Royal during his curtain call at the RAD matinee. "It was quite a spontaneous gesture he made, extending his arm out over the audience," de Valois recalled, "and all I could see was him in *Giselle*."[4]) A savvy professional woman to the bone, Fonteyn asked for time to consider de Valois's offer to work with the boy wonder: "I immediately thought, 'He's twenty-three. I'm forty-two. That's going to be like mutton dancing with lamb.' So I said, 'Well I would like to think about it.' And I did think about it and I suddenly thought, 'Well, he's going to be the big sensation all this season. If I don't dance with him I will be an absolutely back number, a nothing, because everyone will rush to the Nureyev performances, and somebody else will be dancing with him. So I took my courage in both hands, and I said, 'Yes, I'll do *Giselle* with Nureyev.' "[5]

The partnership began with the first Fonteyn/Nureyev *Giselles* at Covent Garden on February 21 and March 1 and 6, 1962. They took everyone completely by surprise (de Valois excepted). The performances themselves were a surprise to several members of the Royal Ballet. A guest appearance by Bruhn in March, partnering Nadia Nerina in *Swan Lake*, had been announced with some fanfare, as Bruhn would have been the first guest danseur to appear at Covent Garden as the partner of a Royal ballerina. Ten days before Bruhn's scheduled debut with the company, the Fonteyn/Nureyev *Giselles* were added to the regular schedule, according to one close source, at Fonteyn's insistence. Despite the curiosity generated by the prospect of a Fonteyn/Nureyev *Giselle*, the odds against anything more than a fleeting PR event were considerable. The twenty-year difference in age and professional experience was the least of it. There could not have been two more different dancers—in style, in temperament and approach, in authority. Fonteyn was the classic ballerina at her most crystal-line—refined, reserved, immaculate. (Right down to her finger-nails. According to a corps dancer with the Royal during the 1950s, her impeccably manicured hands set a tacit standard for all of the company's lead women: "No one could ever have dirty nails because Margot didn't.") Nureyev was Bacchus in tights. Fonteyn was famous for never complaining about anything. The Nureyev temper was already a fixed part of his legend. After many years at the top of her profession—"the Royal didn't so much believe in *Beauty*," the American critic Arlene Croce once wrote about Fonteyn in her great signature role, the Princess Aurora in *The Sleeping Beauty*, "as [much as] it believed in Margot"[6]—Fonteyn was not a woman accustomed to being ques-tioned. Nureyev questioned everyone and everything. The first rehearsals for *Giselle* were nervous and unsteady until, as Nure-yev said later, "Margot began to trust me."[7] The rest, of course, is history. Fonteyn dropped all mention of retirement.

Both dancers were changed irrevocably. "To make a good partnership," de Valois explains, "each side must do something unconscious to the other. That's what they did for each other. He brought out a flamboyant quality in certain of her performances that hadn't been there before. She definitely inflamed the poetic side of his work—not just in terms of his technique but his natural flamboyance."[8] The English critic Clement Crisp got even more specific: "It was an artistic love affair conducted in public."[9] The romance of it all, half Barbara Cartland, half Joyce Carol Oates in her *Bloodsmoor* mode, is in the characters involved.

Older woman, younger man. Society doyenne, backwoods boy. Emily Post and Brando's *Wild One*. Fonteyn had been Europe's ranking ballerina for almost two decades when she and Nureyev met. In one of ballet's favorite legends, de Valois first saw the fourteen-year-old Peggy Hookham in a class at the Vic-Wells School. De Valois turned to the teacher of the class, so the story goes, and asked, "Who is the little Chinese girl in the corner?" Fonteyn's shiny black pageboy had confused de Valois about her origins, but the talent was instantly clear. Fonteyn made her professional debut at age fifteen as a Snowflake in *Nutcracker* with the Vic-Wells Ballet (the precursor of the Sadler's Wells Ballet that became the Royal in 1956) and danced her first Odette/ Odile in the full-length *Swan Lake* the year Nureyev was born. When the company's prima ballerina, Alicia Markova, left the Vic-Wells to start her own troupe de Valois moved Fonteyn to center stage and kept her there for the next thirty years.

By the time Fonteyn met Nureyev, she was not just a luminous international star in the grand manner. She was an institution, Mount Margot, the summit of dance artistry[10] in Europe. "No dancer today can match Margot Fonteyn in the simple gift of line and movement," the English critic Alexander Bland wrote in 1956 about Fonteyn's Princess Aurora in *The Sleeping Beauty*, a role she had already been dancing for seventeen years. "To this she now triumphantly added theatrical *excitement*, a glow of dancing for the love of it, an inner *bravura* which stung the audience into enthusiasm."[11] (The list of ticket prices at the Covent Garden box office included matinee, evening, weekend, and Fonteyn performances.) Miraculously, once Fonteyn began dancing with Nureyev, her performances actually improved, the ballet equivalent of a Caballé or an Aretha Franklin suddenly discovering yet another octave at the top of her range. Ballets that had eluded Fonteyn, like *Giselle*, suddenly were added to her great signature roles, and even her technique became stronger. "Margot really didn't have a jump for the majority of her career," a colleague from the Nureyev years remembers. "Rudolf arrives and suddenly she has a big, beautiful jump." The personal qualities of her dancing took on new colors. "Margot's partnership with Rudi revived her," Royal Ballet ballerina Nadia Nerina explains, "and for the first time she danced with womanly abandon, her movements flowing with a genuine quality of sensuality. She also 'gave' as a woman. She was, of course, in love with him, and she fused her movements with a warmth and a softness that had not been apparent in her dancing before."[12] Nureyev himself once summarized Fonteyn's impact on him: "The first thing she taught me was great professionalism. The way she worked. Her work [was] very thorough. Get out. Do it. Do it well and have a good time. Don't linger. Get on with it."[13]

They became, according to *Time*, "the hottest little team in show biz,"[14] abandoned to one another's gifts, egging one another on to higher and higher strata. "Public became enthralled." Nureyev explained later, "I think public was enthralled because we were enthralled with each other, with what we did with the roles."[15] The mutual challenge, the first either had known in quite a while, was suffused by the sheer pleasure they took in one another's company: Fonteyn and Nureyev were famous for making upstage faces at one another, screwed up lips as if to say "Oh, my. Aren't we on tonight?" or rolling eyes that said "What step was *that?*" They became a personal and artistic phenomenon that kicked ballet into a realm of popular appeal it had never known before. Audiences were mad for them. "I'd seen hysteria before," says John Wilson, a key member of the Hurok Concerts staff during the Royal's American tours in the 1960s. "I'd never seen anything like this. People camping out three days in front of the Met to get any ticket they could. Well-connected people who had never before had difficulty getting a seat for anything calling and begging, 'I will do anything.' In a funny way, Margot and Rudolf sort of spoiled the box office. We could always sell the Royal before but then all we could sell was the two of them. I remember during one New York tour there was a matinee of *Giselle* that wasn't selling at all. I mentioned this to Mr. Hurok, who said, 'Take out an ad that says, '*Giselle*, Fonteyn Nureyev.' It was sold out in a matter of hours."[16]

The obvious question, of course, is why two such different but powerful personalities fit so beautifully. The first clue is in Nureyev's behavior with Fonteyn from the very beginning. Nureyev had been past master of the "instant read" on the people around him since the Ufa schoolyard. According to the great Dutch ballerina Martine van Hamel, "He was a very perceptive man and able to read people's motives instantly. He judged people well too and very cleverly, especially when someone was trying to use him."[17] Sonia Arova agrees: "Rudi had a cunning kind of mind and kept his distance until he knew when someone was coming to him as a friend or coming to get something out of him."[18] He was also among the world's foremost authorities on pushing the envelope and, as early as his first weeks in Copenhagen with Bruhn, Peter Martins still remembers, "he was always seeing what he could get away with, how far he could go."[19] Twenty years later, the attitude was still in place. Laura Young, a ballerina with the Boston Ballet who spent three years of rugged touring with Nureyev, remembers him as a man "who was always testing the waters. You could never show fear or intimidation. If he saw he was getting to you, he went for the jugular."[20]

Never with Fonteyn. He knew on sight that this was the big leagues. Nureyev's acquiescence to Fonteyn's refusal to dance with him at the RAD gala was completely uncharacteristic, the first time since his defection that he had not gotten exactly what he wanted, right now. His obvious willingness to work *with* Fonteyn in the *Giselle* rehearsals—to suggest rather than demand, to prove his trustworthiness—indicates that Nureyev caught on quickly that he wasn't going to get away with anything untoward with Fonteyn. "They got on as well as they did," the French ballerina Ghislaine Thesmar explains, "because for the first time in his life Rudolf got as good as he gave."[21] One imagines that at their first meeting Fonteyn thought: "Oh, young man, have I got your number," while Nureyev thought: "Oh my God, she can read me like a book." Fonteyn all but says as much in an interview for Patricia Foy's 1991 documentary portrait of Nureyev: "The first thing I thought was that he looked pale and pinched. Somehow I wasn't expecting that. I would say that we were sort of eyeing each other a little bit, perhaps trying to size each other up. Very soon afterwards there was a press conference for his performance and he was doing a television interview. I thought, 'Well, I'd better go and look and see if he needs any help.' Well, he answered one or two questions and I thought to myself, 'That boy doesn't need any help at all. He knows exactly what he wants to say.' He always managed to hit the nail right on the head and make his points."[22] Nureyev himself once summarized Fonteyn's chastening savvy. Shortly after their first *Giselle*, Fonteyn invited Nureyev back to London for one of her performances of *Swan Lake*, suggesting that he consider dancing the ballet with her. Nureyev went to Fonteyn's dressing room, duly impressed but also convinced that he would only disrupt the sublime completeness of Fonteyn's performance. "There is no place for me in that," he told her. "I would destroy everything." Fonteyn looked him dead in the eye. "Just you try."[23]

More than one-upmanship was at work. Fonteyn recognized the method in Nureyev's manner because, in her own quiet way, she'd been doing the same thing since before Nureyev was born. Surprisingly, their early stories align much more than they diverge. Fonteyn was not a hell-raiser in the Nureyev tradition —no tantrums, no swearing, no broken furniture—but she was also never the submissive, dewy-eyed dancerette of cliché either. When Fonteyn's mother took her six-year-old daughter to see Pavlova dance her *Fairy Doll*, the little girl left the theater less than impressed. She had, after all, been taking dance classes herself for almost two years by then and thought "that I could do pretty well too, especially in my favorite dance, the Irish Washerwoman's Jig. I really didn't like ballet dancing very much because it was stiff and rigid and, frankly boring. And I liked something where I was banging a tambourine and stamping about in heeled shoes. Rhythm and movement. That sort of thing."[24] As the daughter of a prominent international businessman, Fonteyn knew a childhood of security and privilege worlds away from the Ural poverty of Nureyev's youth, but her early years were every bit as peripatetic. She first saw the fabled Shanghai Bund at the ripe old age of eight, when her father was transferred to Asia.

Until she settled in London with the Vic-Wells in her midteens, Fonteyn's girlhood was spent shuttling back and forth between London and China, as her mother tried to determine whether or not her dark-eyed little girl had a real shot at a dance career.

In an almost eerie echo of the early Nureyev saga, once Fonteyn was the Vic-Wells's clearest ballerina candidate, she did not go passively along the anointed path. In discussing the ascendant Fonteyn, both de Valois and Ashton consistently return to the adjectives "stubborn" and "willful." Fonteyn was in complete agreement with their assessment. "I was considered stubborn and a 'little devil,' " she wrote in her autobiography. "After I had been at the school a little time, however, I noticed that new arrivals fell into one of two categories as far as Miss de Valois was concerned. 'She's a nice child,' or, 'She's an absolute devil, but very talented.' It was the latter group that always seemed to get on. I tried to be a nice child, although I realized it was a compliment to be shouted at all day long."[25]

Ashton later told a somewhat grisly story about the means he had to use to rein in the new star who became his muse: "I didn't sort of get on with her. I found her inadequate in what she was doing and she also seemed to me to have a sort of superior attitude which didn't appeal to me. And also I sensed a streak of stubbornness. [In a rehearsal for *Le baiser de la fée*, Ashton's first original ballet for Fonteyn], I bullied and bullied and bullied her. She got more and more into a state and then finally she burst into tears, rushed up and put her arms around me and said, 'I'm sorry. I'm doing the best I can. I can't do anymore.' So then I realized that she'd really conceded to me and from then on we'd be able to work together."[26]

Irish by birth, de Valois reveled in Fonteyn's willpower, as she would later with Nureyev: "I have never known a great artist who hadn't in some part of their make-up moments of a stubborn quality. Otherwise, I don't think that they'd be a great artist. Because a great artist must have some idea of how they want—*they* want—to do a role. Whether it's right or wrong, it's an idea. It's creative. I'm all for arguing artists out of a wrong idea rather than finding myself working with an artist who hasn't any ideas at all. Fonteyn had a lot of South American blood in her, you know. She had Irish blood, too. She wasn't one hundred percent English by any means."[27]

Fonteyn shared more with Nureyev than his talent for taking a stand. There was, for example, a world-class sense of humor: the tights Barbra Streisand wears in the *Swan Lake* spoof near the end of *Funny Girl* ("Vhataya gonna do—shoot the svans?") were a gift from Fonteyn. Despite the ivory sheen of her stage image, not all of the common ground with her new partner was admired universally. "Look at the history of the Royal Ballet," a seasoned international dancer explains, "from the time Fonteyn replaced Markova until—well, for the next thirty-five years. Name another ballerina with that company who danced as much as Margot, who became such a public figure. You think that was an accident? The woman was no fool." De Valois, of course, was a key figure in the equation. Just before the Royal, then still the Sadler's Wells, made its fabled New York debut in October 1949, the impresario sponsoring the tour, Sol Hurok, asked de Valois who he was to emphasize and advertise as the company's prima ballerina. Despite the fact that Moira Shearer was the more established star in the United States as a result of her box office success in the film *The Red Shoes* the year before, de Valois told him to feature Fonteyn. (In Chicago, people who wanted to see that red-headed woman from *The Red Shoes* exchanged their Fonteyn tickets for the Shearer performances.) Hurok got Fonteyn on the cover of *Time*; *Newsweek* picked up the story and ran her picture on its cover the same week, and Fonteyn's de facto reign over the Royal was institutionalized. Fonteyn's opening night performance in *The Sleeping Beauty* got thirty-five curtain calls.

The spotlight took to Fonteyn and she took to the spotlight. Her appetite for center stage rivaled Nureyev's; before their partnership was barely two years old, they had already danced almost two hundred performances together.[28] By that time, Fonteyn had been guarding her position carefully for almost two decades, and with the shrewdness of a no-nonsense professional:

when Karsavina first came to coach Fonteyn in Fokine's *Firebird*, a role Karsavina had originated, the studio rehearsals were closed to the rest of the company, at Fonteyn's insistence. Like Nureyev, Fonteyn knew how to work a house, even in rehearsal. An American critic remembers a visit to a Royal Ballet rehearsal in which, when Fonteyn learned the press was afoot, she redirected her classroom work in the critic's direction. "Obviously, [Fonteyn] was much helped by the influence of the company in which she developed," the critic Clive Barnes said at a tribute to Fonteyn shortly after her death. "She was much influenced by being the chosen muse of the great choreographer Frederick Ashton. But very much she pushed herself with an almost steely, I suspect, ambition. . . . Certainly she always appeared very modest off-stage, at least in her public way. But I suspect that she wasn't that modest in other respects, and I think that she had an absolutely overpowering ambition."[29]

Like Nureyev's debilitating impact on the company's senior male dancers when he joined the Royal, the number one spot Fonteyn held onto with such tenacity eventually had a dispiriting effect on the company's second-ranked ballerinas, who often had no more than a single performance every six weeks. In 1953, when the Royal ballerina Beryl Grey scored a major personal success at Sweden's Royal Opera House, the general administrator of the Royal Opera House, Covent Garden, David Webster, felt compelled to write a letter of complaint to the editor of the Swedish publication *News Chronicle:* "In an article in your paper headed 'VIOLETTA [ELVIN] TO GET A BREAK IN US' (*News Chronicle*, 22 April) it is suggested that during the forthcoming American tour of the Sadler's Wells Ballet the role of prima ballerina will be shared by Margot Fonteyn and Violetta Elvin. This is not true. Miss Fonteyn is ballerina assoluta of the company and shares a position with no one. The company enjoys the services of three ballerinas. We place them in alphabetical order—Violetta Elvin, Beryl Grey, and Nadia Nerina."[30] By the mid-1950s, Shearer, Elvin, and Grey—all three of them barely thirty years of age— had left the Royal for greener pastures. "Nobody doubted that [Fonteyn] deserved her position of eminence as prima ballerina assoluta," Grey's biographer David Gillard wrote, "but it was the degree to which she dominated the British ballet scene that was so hard [for the Royal's other ballerinas] to come to terms with. Every ballerina, from the infant days of the Vic-Wells, had grown up in the shadow of Fonteyn. And that shadow was to loom ever larger as the years progressed. Even the next generation of British dancers [after Grey and company], headed by Antoinette Sibley, were to find themselves sometimes stifled and often intimidated by the magnitude of Fonteyn's legend."[31] In her book *Ballet Master*, which ranges over the whole field of twentieth-century dance from Nijinsky to Lincoln Kirstein, Moira Shearer never once mentions Fonteyn.

The all-important difference between how Fonteyn managed her hold on the Royal and Nureyev managed his—first with the Royal, then with the National Ballet of Canada, and finally with the Paris Opéra Ballet—was the manner of approach. Haughtiness—comments on the order of Nureyev's numbing assertion that Bruhn was the only man alive who knew more about dancing than he did, at twenty-three—was never a feature of Fonteyn's style. During her first years as the Sadler's Wells ballerina, Fonteyn shared digs with two other women from the company, hardly the attitude of an *assoluta*. Later, particularly after her marriage to Roberto de Arias, Panama's delegate to the Court of St. James, made her an ambassador's wife, Fonteyn was no longer "one of the girls" but the new distance was practical rather then exclusionary. She was a regular guest at all-company social events—picnics, outings, and the like—and, when Fonteyn received social invitations as a representative of the Royal Ballet, she declined those that did not include the rest of the company's dancers as well. "Margot had a rule," Hugh Pickett, a longtime friend and colleague, explained, "the whole company or nobody."[32] She was also setting a tone. "If the prima ballerina of the company didn't put on airs," Pickett adds, "how could the rest of the company?"[33] Although Fonteyn knew when to put her foot down onstage and off, she also learned early on a lesson Nureyev would never comprehend, or have the time for. Fonteyn was as genial as Nureyev was disruptive, and she was experienced enough to know that squeaky wheels can get very annoying. Blessed with patience, she let others see to the problems and, in the process, made no enemies (although there is the legend of a photographer who lost a considerable chunk of his camera for clicking away just a tad too close to Fonteyn while she was sewing the ribbons onto her pointe shoes before a big rehearsal). The dancer Joy Brown, one of Fonteyn's friends for more than thirty years, remembers visiting Fonteyn during a particularly trying rehearsal: "It was a long and tedious rehearsal, and, while we were chit-chatting, [Margot] said something to the effect of, 'At times like this I never complain about anything at first—costumes, lights, whatever is bothering me—because somebody else almost always notices it as well and it's corrected. At the end, if something still isn't right, I will mention it then and at that point I'll be complaining about only one thing and not a half-dozen.' "[34]

Fonteyn first met her husband—Tito to his many friends—during the 1930s, on tour with the Sadler's Wells. Their divergent career paths kept them in different worlds for the next two decades. Reunited in the mid-1950s, they were married in Paris in February 1955 at the center of a media blitz, another of the international love stories among people in high places that were so cherished by the press and public of the Grace Kelly/Prince Rainier era. (The only available footage of an antagonized Fonteyn is in films of her wedding ceremony, where the crunch of reporters is clearly not her choice.)

About two years later, Fonteyn, the mistress of calm and clarity, found herself at the center of a political cyclone. During her "break from the ballet," she joined her husband in Central America for a few days of beaches and boating, just as Arias and his political colleagues were in the process of initiating a revolution to unseat the current Panamanian government. The dinghies for Fonteyn's seaside vacation were being used to smuggle arms into Panama. If there is any proof of Fonteyn's absolute fearlessness, it's the home movies she made at sea, in boats she knew had false bottoms stuffed with guns and ammunition. The plan was discovered and the authorities moved in. With surveillance planes circling above them, Fonteyn and Arias set sail in different boats in opposite directions, Fonteyn's serving as a decoy for Arias's escape. She was promptly placed in jail for the night and then deported to Miami.

Fonteyn left behind a film legacy of many extraordinary performances, and perhaps her most unsung gift was her instinct as a great actress. (In Ashton's *Marguerite and Armand* she is Garbo's only rival as Camille.) Nothing that survives matches her performance on her return to New York after getting the boot from Panama. That chin never drooped and her smile never faded, not even when a local woman reporter shoved a microphone in Fonteyn's face with an adenoidal request to know "Miss Fontanne [*sic*], what does it feel like to be a ballerina behind bars?" Gliding through a situation that could have crippled the career of a less steely artist, Fonteyn told the press absolutely nothing. "What are you trying to get me to say exactly," Fonteyn asked one persistent reporter, with a giggle. "Why don't you tell me what it is you're trying to get me to say and I'll tell you if I'll say it or not. Because you're fishing around for something and I can't quite get the gist of it."[35]

Arias's political misadventures eventually led to a genuine disaster, both for himself and for Fonteyn. In June 1964, as Fonteyn was completing rehearsals for Nureyev's staging of *Raymonda* at the Spoleto Festival, Arias was critically wounded in what was described as a "political assassination." Despite the persistent rumors that Fonteyn was planning to divorce Arias over his blatant womanizing, she went straight to his bedside where, in effect, she was to remain for the next twenty-five years. According to Fonteyn, Arias survived a fever that topped 108 degrees, but the injuries he'd sustained from the gunshot blast left him completely paralyzed from the neck down. The astronomical cost of his lifelong medical care was as important a factor in the length of Fonteyn's career—forty-five years—as was the arrival of Nureyev. Her devotion to Arias was unswerving. In the 1989 documentary film *Margot Fonteyn*, Ida Bromley, a therapist at the Stoke-Mandeville clinic in England where Arias was taken for treatment and whatever rehabilitation was possible, explains how well Fonteyn tended her husband: "When such a patient with great disabilities returns home, the family has to make many adjustments. For example, someone has to get up every night and turn the patient, once at least and maybe two and three times. But concentration has to gradually turn from disability to ability, and the fact that Tito, after nearly twenty-five years, is so fit, able to manage his farm, and to travel all over the world, is largely due, I'm sure, to his own indomitable spirit and to Margot's constant care." When she was not on the road earning their keep, Fonteyn was the person who turned Arias's body over in the middle of the night. She did it in spite of a fact that has been kept a closely guarded secret by a tight circle of friends: Arias was, in fact, not crippled in an assassination attempt. Arias's assailant was not a political dissident but a jealous husband who had discovered that his wife and Arias were having an affair. The identity of the gunman remains unknown, and no one was ever prosecuted for the crime. One school of thought holds that Arias was shot by his own chauffeur, because of an affair with the housemaid, the chauffeur's wife.[36] The second school, epitomized by Peter Watson in his *Nureyev: A Biography,* credits a political colleague incensed over his wife's relationship with Arias. Fonteyn, according to Watson, only further confused the picture with her first response to the news. Informed by a friend of long standing that the assassin was an old political rival, her reply was reported to be: "No! You've got it wrong. No! No!"

According to Nureyev biographer David Daniel, Fonteyn was "a combination of the warm and the glacial." "She was the most genteel person I ever met," New York City Ballet ballerina Heather Watts recalls. "I met her in her house in London and I was also introduced to her husband. I was about seventeen at the time, young enough to put my hand out to shake his, and she simply took his hand and put it in mine. She covered for me. Imagine this stupid kid putting her hand out to someone who was a complete quadriplegic. So she simply held his hand in mine."[37]

Were Nureyev and Fonteyn lovers? There are those who say they were and those who say they weren't and those—close friends, too—who swear that Fonteyn miscarried Nureyev's child: the miscarriage, according to Peter Watson, "was, in its way, fortunate. She was forty-five and intended to have an abortion. As it was, she did not have to suffer the indignity of consulting doctors and persuading them to operate. She did not tell [Nureyev] that he had made her pregnant until it was too late. For a budding homosexual, Nureyev already had a considerable list of heterosexual conquests."[38] In Russia, Nureyev was sexually involved with Pushkin's wife, and Maria Tallchief all but admitted to at least a dalliance during Nureyev's first months in Paris.[39] Fonteyn was clearly possessive to a major degree when Nureyev was concerned. "Margot virtually never let Rudi out of her sight," a colleague from the Royal recalls. She also did things for Nureyev that she would never have done for anyone else, such as clean his dressing room. One evening after a performance in Vancouver, Hugh Pickett passed the open door of Nureyev's dressing room and "there was Margot—picking up his tights, his shoes, his leg-warmers, packing his bag."[40]

Another incident is even more telling. In the midsixties, after Nureyev had begun working with Sol Hurok, Fonteyn found herself enmeshed in a raging difference of opinion between Nureyev and Hurok. While tempers were at their most tense, she received an invitation to a gala dinner that, at Nureyev's request, did not include Hurok. Fonteyn was clearly a woman of fierce loyalties, and she was under serious professional obligation to Hurok. Not only had he made her an international star with the Royal's New York debut, but Fonteyn was also one of the artists who got the lavish Hurok treatment on a regular basis.[41] At each of her New York debuts in a major classic role, Hurok gave Fonteyn a special opening night gift: a ring, one with a coral rose for *The Sleeping Beauty*, a pearl with a giant crown for *Swan Lake*, a diamond dewdrop for *Bayadère*. When forced by a Nureyev/Hurok row to make a choice, she chose Nureyev. Fonteyn accepted the dinner invitation, despite the snub to Hurok. For his part, Nureyev kept the picture out of focus. "In rehearsals with Fonteyn," a dancer with the Royal Ballet recalls, "Rudi often played the fool. He frequently treated her with disdain, was rude, and often showed that he was the dominant sexual partner in a relationship, to the embarrassment of members of the company, who would turn away pretending not to have noticed how she was being humiliated by him." Nadia Nerina remembers Nureyev's penchant for skating on thin ice:

> An amusing incident happened some years later in Paris, at a Sunday lunch at the Mediterranée. The company was appearing at the Champs Elysées Theater. The lunch was Margot's idea. It included my husband Charles Gordon and I, Yves St. Laurent and his chief "vendeuse," Margot and Tito, Rudi and Claire Motte [the French ballerina]. In the middle of the meal the maître d' came to call Rudi to the phone. After several minutes he returned and announced: "I am not Mr. Fonteyn yet," and turning to Tito, he said, "Tito, it's for you." The atmosphere froze, Yves half disappeared under the table. Tito, making no comment, went to the phone. Rudi sat down in silence. He realized that he had gone over the top. But, as always he was not going to admit to any fault. Seeing Margot looking at Charles for support, he said, "Charlik, you think I am lousy dancer." "Not lousy, Rudi, but very lousy," replied Charles without hesitation. Rudi burst into gales of laughter, and Margot relaxed. Yves reappeared from under the table. Tito returned smiling— after all he had been a successful diplomat—and the luncheon proceeded with some gaiety.[42]

There is a moment near the end of the adagio in the Fonteyn/Nureyev *Corsaire* on *An Evening with the Royal Ballet*. It's a small moment, a relatively unimportant upstage transition step. For all the symmetry of their dancing, they're still an unanticipated couple—Nureyev in his harem pants and golden armbands, Fonteyn in her Dresden teacup tutu. Positioning themselves upstage for the next set of steps, they extend one foot forward and sweep the sky with big circling port de bras. Without the remotest evidence of effort, their arms align right down to the crook of their little fingers. Nureyev lifts Fonteyn skyward and then kneels at her feet, and there you have it, Fonteyn/Nureyev: Priapus unleashed, and what does he worship? The ideal in white.

Eight

Pop Danseur

"I know a lady in Venice would have walked bare-foot to Palestine for a touch of his nether lip."

—*Emilia, in* Othello

he scene is the Adriatic coast of Italy at a summer sunset in 1983, a plain of azure water stretching to a horizon streaked with the last light of day. Under a billowing white canopy, the staff and dancers of the Boston Ballet are celebrating the end of a rugged tour, three weeks of bus and trunk at its most literal. Long picnic tables are laden with the local bounty—mountains of fresh pasta, antipasto by the kilo, glass after glass of the ripe local chianti. High spirits are flowing as freely as the vino.

Suddenly, a noise, a loud noise, flat and sharp. Like a clap of thunder.

Or a slap.

And then silence, as the entire company turns in the direction of the last sound anyone expected at a closing night party.

The source is obvious, a far table where the star of the tour, Rudolf Nureyev, is seated with the company's director, the effervescent French ballerina Violette Verdy, and several of the troupe's principal dancers. Nureyev is seated next to one of the young male leads, whose face, in the resounding silence, is undergoing an unexpected change in color—or at least on one side, where a bright red handprint is in full bloom.

After a few tense minutes, Nureyev is on his feet and headed for the exit, followed by his faithful Italian masseur/bodyguard, Luigi. Every eye in the place follows Nureyev's exit, and he stares right back at them. He's got one arm stretched out, the fingers wiggling in a Bashkir evil eye.

The Boston dancers, of course, wouldn't know one evil eye from another and assume that Nureyev, who was in a fine mood when the evening began, is waving good-bye. They begin to wave back.

"Bye, Rudolf!"

"See you, Rudolf!"

The misperception sends Nureyev over the wall and barking. He launches into an explosion of expletives. Before Nureyev has quite finished, a gentleman of the corps de ballet, his hand gripped more and more tightly around a hefty glass of beer, has had enough insults for one day. He lifts his glass and turns in Nureyev's direction.

The producer of the tour decides he'd like to sit elsewhere and walks directly into the liquid flying toward Nureyev. The producer gets the full stream square in the face, but a few drops rain down on Nureyev, at which point Luigi has had enough.

Before anyone can stop him, he's grabbed the corps dancer by the collar and is holding him down on a picnic table, his fist grazing the young man's face but never actually hitting him, scare tactics rather than the real thing. At a distance the corps dancer looks like he's getting the beating of his life, which sends the rest of the company's male contingent leaping from their seats and headed straight for the melee.

At which point Nureyev picks up the nearest plate of pasta and flings it straight into the crowd. In moments, the hills are alive with marinara.

Three weeks later, Nureyev and the Boston Ballet are back on tour together.

· · ·

The public and private Nureyevs were never separate characters. The two, in fact, fed off each other to such a degree that
Nureyev's onstage manner could sometimes suggest the kick-
your-shoes-off attitude of a man alone in his living room. "Rudolf was so completely at home onstage, he could do some mind-
blowing things," a dancer colleague remembers. "If he'd have a
problem with his tights or something, or his shoes, he'd just pull
and tug until everything was okay, until the lines were all right
—as if he were in a dressing room instead of right out front for
the audience to see. The stage was his home, his habitat. That's
where he lived. It's almost as if he was most completely himself
only when he was onstage." Inevitably, the qualities Nureyev
introduced to male dancing, the vigor and independence, were
also among his signature qualities offstage, and none of them had
a farther-reaching effect than the liability Nureyev fashioned into
an asset—the kind of old-school star temperament that sets audiences stampeding to a theater and theater administrators staring
longingly at window ledges. Less than six months after Nureyev's
first *Giselles* with Fonteyn, one of the Covent Garden administrators told *Time* magazine: "I'd rather deal with ten Callases than
one Nureyev."[1]

Once again, Nureyev presented the male dancer with an
option he hadn't known for quite a while: the choice to throw a
fit. That, of course, was ballerina territory and figured in many a
cherished ballet legend. Every performing art has its quota of
raucous backstage stories: the opera singers who kayo their partners by chewing on a little garlic just before an intimate love
scene; the possibilities for sudden pratfalls in a costume with
train. Callas excepted, no diva ever got more mileage out of tantrums than the leading ladies of the ballet, and the most outland-
ish were inevitably the most rarefied in performance: Pavlova,
Makarova, and, of course, Gelsey Kirkland. In his autobiography,
Far from Denmark, Peter Martins once described what a ballerina
can look like from behind: "Ballerinas come in all shapes and
sizes. Some are nice, some are not so nice. But they all possess in
common those elements necessary to make a ballerina: They are
all tough, merciless, self-centered, narrow-minded, and without

awareness of or interest in her male counterpart. When a ballerina looks in the rehearsal hall mirror she only sees herself; and when her partner looks in the same mirror he sees not himself but only her."[2]

Nureyev changed that for all time by embracing the signatures of the great ballerinas—the dramatic slap, the bruising rejoinder, the threats. As celebrated as his jeté, Nureyev's fits of temper came in all shapes, colors, and sizes: little ones over a misunderstood request, daily ones over the ineptitude of yet another conductor, and, especially in Paris, great big ones at the fumbling administration. The rages appear to have metamorphosed over the years, from the tantrums in the early days of a petulant and pampered male starlet, to those of a seasoned professional who knew when to put his foot down—and on whom. Just as discussion of the early Fonteyn returns to her willfulness, accounts of the early Nureyev are inevitably seasoned with words like "spoiled," "infantile," and "demanding" (all the more astonishing since the people doing the indulging were figures on the order of de Valois, Bruhn, and Fonteyn). They tend to involve a great many shattered objects: wineglasses, dinner plates, and, according to one legend, a collection of fifteenth-century Venetian glass belonging to a famous Italian film director while Nureyev was a guest in said director's home. By the crest of the "Rudi" phenomenon in the midsixties, under Fonteyn's tutelage, Nureyev had learned to conserve his energy for professional rows and the occasional arrest. The brooding young exile caught on to the local ground rules. "I never felt that my hands were tied with Rudolf," remembers Sheila Porter, a publicity director for the Royal Ballet at the height of Rudimania. "He did not say me nay. There were things that he did not like to do, like schedule interviews and the like too far in advance. It made him feel trapped. But I never got the impression that it pleased him to make trouble. When he did, there was always a good reason. I remember once in New York there was a problem over the order of a repertory performance. Rudolf was in more than one ballet and really put his foot down. 'I know what my body can do,' he said. 'This will be the order.' "[3] His taste for projectiles, however, never did diminish and neither did the threat of violence and injury. Nureyev is known to have sent at least two male dancers to hospitals, a corps dancer from the Boston Ballet Nureyev kicked in the crotch and an Italian dancer on the last Nureyev and Friends tour he kicked in the backside, both during the course of a performance.

Two instances of the demon Nureyev illustrate the central tenets of his commitment to his profession—do the job right and get on with it.

Merle Park was Nureyev's partner for the infamous New York premiere of his *Nutcracker* in 1970, the one in which he stormed off the stage of the Metropolitan Opera House during the pas de deux that opens the ballet's second act:

> Rudolf was under an enormous amount of pressure at the time. He was dancing the ballet. He was producing it. He had one day to get it onto the stage. The scenery wasn't working and so he was very uptight and in the second act he walked offstage because he thought the music was too fast. The music was fast, so I was doing it fast and he wouldn't. He didn't expect it to be that fast and then our feet caught, got tangled. He said, 'Stop, girl. We'll start again,' and I said, 'Rudolf, you can't do that. Just go on.' And it must have just got too much and he walked to the front of the stage and put his hand up to Jack Lanchbery [the conductor] to stop, and Jack put his head down and continued. So Rudolf walked off the stage and left me out there alone for about three minutes. I choreographed. I ran to the side of the stage and called, "Rudolf! Come back, Rudolf! Rooo—dolf!" I heard him stomping and screaming about. Finally the ballet mistress had got him to come back onstage. After the performance he came to my dressing room—there must have been a million people there—and he apologized. [4]

A truce with Natalia Makarova took longer, after a famous standoff three years later. A fellow Kirov expatriate, Makarova shared Nureyev's gift for theatrics onstage and off, and their first performance together was that accident just begging to happen. Nureyev and Makarova were scheduled to dance an open-air performance of *Swan Lake* with the Paris Opéra Ballet in the Cour Carrée of the Louvre. Many a version exists of exactly what took place that night. Nureyev slapped Makarova. Nureyev pushed Makarova. Nureyev tripped Makarova. Only two things were absolutely certain. In the middle of the White Swan adagio, Makarova found herself unattractively splayed along the floor. The next morning, at a hastily summoned press conference, she issued a statement: "I will never dance with that man again." Nureyev looked very bad, Makarova looked very hurt. The truth was, in fact, a little more complex, according to a corps dancer who stood about ten feet away from where the incident occurred:

> Rudolf did not hit her or trip her or any of those things. That's not what was going on at all. Rudi taught Natasha a lesson. Natasha was, of course, a very beautiful dancer, but, well—how shall I say this? She heard her own music. It was very beautiful music but not necessarily the music coming from the pit. And I guess she was accustomed to partners who didn't mind the extra work. Rudolf was, of course, a perfectionist and Natasha was driving him mad by not keeping to the music. It was almost as if he was chasing her around the stage. I guess he finally had enough. Natasha took one of her big beautiful balances just a little bit ahead of where she was supposed to be on the stage and basically he just let her fall. And she had to get up onto her hands and knees because Rudolf just stood exactly where he was supposed to be and waited.

Nureyev signed up as a client of Hurok Concerts in 1965. Until joining the Hurok stable, Nureyev could well have remained a ballet specialty act, familiar from his defection but with a public profile largely limited to his own profession. Having seen the Beatles, Hurok didn't need to ask de Valois whom to push when Nureyev made his second American tour with the Royal in 1965, and Hurok's creation of the "Rudi" event is a testament not only to Nureyev's theatrical excitement but to Hurok's eye for whom to promote and when. Nureyev was clearly the PR subject of the hour, Hurok pulled off another *Newsweek/Time* cover story coup, and Nureyev was on his way to an entirely new strata of celebrity. Until the 1965 Royal tour, the American dance critic Arlene Croce wrote, "the hard ticket was Nureyev-Fonteyn. Nureyev by himself didn't sell out the Met until the Hurok office released its publicity barrage in 1965."[5] Nureyev was never a performer who courted the press. "Interviews were not standard with Rudi," a former Hurok staffer remembers. "His self-exposure was limited. He didn't come into town, for example, a week early to do interviews." For the 1965 tour, Nureyev seems to have been more agreeable than usual to meeting with the press, although interviews still got edgy when Nureyev felt he was being manipulated. One remark to a *Los Angeles Times* reporter—"I hate the audience," his fingernails scratching their disdain into a tablecloth—generated a storm of ill will that simply disappeared into the Rudi snowball. "Hurok cultivated an image of grand and exotic artists for his clientele," another Hurok staff member concludes. "And the whole 'Rudi' thing fit right into that." The result was something the ballet world had never seen before, a dancer—*a ballet dancer*—who made the leap to mainstream celebrity.

Ballet went from coterie to cult on the strength of Nureyev's personal flair, as expressed through the Hurok publicity machine. Hurok's timing could not have been better. He initiated the Rudi phenomenon just as two larger cultural phenomena were about to change our perceptions of the world around us. The first was the media explosion that sired the new global village, the age of the "medium is the massage." Mass media discovered that it was as much a part of current events as the events themselves. The media began to cover itself, and the era of the media baby was born. To the manner born, Nureyev was among the first of another new breed, a star who stayed famous for being famous. In the decades since the Hollywood studio system had taught the world just how to sell a product, the American mass media in particular focused on individual faces. The personality approach was one Americans enjoyed; particularly after the television boom of the 1950s, celebrities could come right into your own living room. According to the media scholar Jeremy Tunstall, "The American popular press from its earliest days stressed personality and celebrity. The Associated Press, when it appeared, was the perfect mechanism for imprinting a few prominent names on the minds of all Americans. Press agentry grew up around the promotion of theatrical personalities."[6]

Enter Nureyev, a theatrical personality out of a publicist's fantasy life. Again, however, Nureyev's larger-than-life persona —the drama of his defection, the idealism of his quest, the sharpness of his tongue—might have remained a "dancer's only" phenomenon, respectably well known but not everyone's cup of tea. The key to the Nureyev crossover is when it took place. "When [Nureyev] arrived in the West," Arlene Croce has written, "it was at a moment of upheaval in public morals and popular culture. Nureyev's behavior on and offstage appeared related to a new trend, and he may even have instigated it, in part. It was amazing how many British rock stars suddenly turned up looking like him."[7] (Peter Martins remembers that Nureyev's appearances in classes at the Royal Danish Ballet school were "like having John Lennon in class."[8]) The sixties were a special time, "years of mass protest, for civil rights and black power, for liberated education, for poor people, women's liberation, gay rights, Chicanos, American Indians, and the Vietnam War."[9] Change was everywhere.

Nureyev fit a time of upheaval like a glove. Sol Hurok surely had noticed the winds of change stirring with the Beatles earthquake on *The Ed Sullivan Show* in 1964, and he made a critical connection. Nureyev was a born rebel and, as such, a potential gold mine in a rebel era. The Rudi Event was underway. Nureyev certainly had the wiry, shaggy-haired look the mass audience of the era seemed to love so loudly. Sired in an act of rebellion, he also was exactly the kind of hero the sixties latched onto with both hands. Hurok kept Nureyev where he could be seen, in *Time*, in *Life*, in *Newsweek*, the *New York Times*, and the saturation level worked. Nureyev caught the eye of a whole new audience, the counterculture crowd that was about to start spending some serious money on enjoying itself. Anointed by his defection and his hair, Nureyev, like the best of the beaded, uninhibited counterculture he helped develop, was exactly the mix of contradictions that was scaring the pants off the powers

that were: "bright, innocent, tender, spontaneous, playful, joy-
ful, spiritual, mystical, sensual, and full of reverence, [and] just
as easily . . . dark, dirty, terrifying, mindless, self-indulgent,
lonely, mad, and hurtful."[10] Nureyev also had, in spades, the
rebel sexuality that had been bankrolling major mainstream careers since Elvis first wiggled those hips and James Dean first
pouted those lips; by the end of the decade, Nureyev had done
for the turtleneck what Lana Turner had once done for mohair.
The most popular buttons among the Rudi groupies went right to
the point: "We want Rudi in the nudi." The combination of
rebel, poet, and stallion Nureyev embodied in appearance, in
manner, in the context of his own history was right out of
McLuhan:

> The poet, the artist, the sleuth—whoever sharpens our per-
> ceptions tends to be antisocial; rarely "well-adjusted," he
> cannot go along with currents and trends. A strange bond
> often exists among anti-social types in their power to see
> environments as they really are. This need to interface, to
> confront environments with a certain antisocial power, is
> manifest in the famous story, "The Emperor's New
> Clothes." "Well-adjusted" courtiers, having vested inter-
> ests, saw the Emperor as beautifully appointed. The "antiso-
> cial brat," unaccustomed to the old environment, clearly saw
> that the Emperor "ain't got nothin' on."[11]

Nureyev even managed to get arrested, not once but twice.
His first trip to a station house took place in Toronto in 1963, on
Nureyev's first American tour with the Royal Ballet. After an
opening night reception by the Canadian audience and at least one
opening night party, Nureyev was arrested for dancing through
moving traffic along Yonge Street, the bustling center of Toronto's gay district. According to the version of events Nureyev
himself told a friend, he was approached by a police officer who
announced he was taking Nureyev to the station for dangerous
and disorderly conduct. "You cannot arrest me," Nureyev told
the policeman. "I am Rudolf Nureyev." The officer's response
was as direct: "Yeah? And I'm Fred Astaire. Get in the damned

car." Nureyev was detained at police headquarters for an hour and then released.

The time in the station house was a little longer with the second arrest, the famous "pot bust" with Fonteyn in San Francisco in 1967. Fonteyn and Nureyev in police custody made headlines around the world and made them the unlikeliest heroes of hippiedom. Fonteyn wore white fur through it all. The evening before a Royal Ballet engagement in San Francisco was due to conclude, Nureyev and Fonteyn received an invitation to a party in the city's then-bustling Haight-Ashbury district. They arrived late—about 3:00 A.M.—by which time the party had been in progress for quite some time—and growing steadily louder and louder. When a pair of tom-toms worked their way into the din, the neighbors complained to the local police, who reached the party moments after the Fonteyn/Nureyev entourage. Although the police originally intended only a warning, matters took on a different color when the officers saw a handful of marijuana joints lying on a table, and the partygoers suddenly began to scramble from the scene—some up the stairs, some onto the roof, others straight out into the street. Nureyev and Fonteyn finally were discovered on the rooftops of two adjoining buildings, Nureyev flat on his back, Fonteyn huddled in a dark corner, in a full-length white ermine coat. They were piled into a paddy wagon with the rest of the revelers, taken first to the Park Police Station and then to the city prison at the Hall of Justice, fingerprinted, photographed, and held behind bars for the next four hours. Once again, Fonteyn smiled her way through a sticky situation without telling the press anything other than a single cultural observation: "You know, in England, they don't allow the press in jails."[12] Under strict instruction from Fonteyn, Nureyev also managed to keep his mouth shut and wait for the bail of $330 each to be posted. He almost succeeded. "Would you please call a policeman," he shouted to a curious neighbor as the partyers were piling into the police wagon. "We have another party to go to." At the police station, when a photographer got a little too close, Nureyev exhaled heavily onto the lens of his camera, blacking out the photograph. With a second photographer, Nureyev ran his hands through his hair and then wiped his fingers on the lens of the camera.

On the wings of that kind of coverage, Nureyev went from being a dance phenomenon to an event of much wider scope: he became one of the most famous personalities in the world. "If Rudolf blew his nose," former Hurok manager John Wilson concludes, "it made headlines."[13] When Nureyev danced on the *Hollywood Palace* variety hour, ABC built a complete replica of the Hollywood Palace in order to accommodate Nureyev's frantic schedule; the segment, according to the show's producer, "cost more than the whole rest of the show."[14] Socially, he became the ultimate "A list" party guest. Gay Talese noted in the *New York Times* the string of New York society hostesses "competing for his presence, caring little if he smashed plates against the wall in displeasure over the menu or the service."[15] Everything Nureyev did became news—when he had his tonsils removed, when he was knocked over by a motorbike in London. The Russian Tea Room added a Nureyev cocktail to its menu—vodka and white crème de cacao—and he became the first man allowed into "21" without a tie. However celebrated the company around him, Nureyev invariably drew focus. "Jackie, Ari, Rudi, and Margot popped into P. J. Clarke's," the *New York Times* recorded in 1968, "and guess who monopolized the stares? Rudi with tight pants, boots, cap, and short fur jacket."[16]

Nureyev's visibility didn't hurt ballet any either, and two more traditions of male dancing were headed in new directions. Nureyev brought a completely new audience to the ballet, the vast mainstream that had never really noticed toe dancing until Nureyev forced their attention. According to Barbara Horgan, the head of the Balanchine Trust in New York City and a woman with forty years of experience in ballet administration and management:

In my opinion, Rudolf was one of the most important elements in the popularization of dance in the United States. I truly believe that Rudolf—Rudolf's ability, Rudolf's star

power, Rudolf's personality—was instrumental in making
ballet the popular art that it became in the late sixties and
the beginning of the seventies. There are a lot of people out
there who didn't know ballet. They think it's funny people
in tights and tutus. But they would know what the word
"Nureyev" meant. That meant Star. He was on *Ed Sullivan*.
He did television. He was in the newspapers, of which we
had many more. There were pictures. There were photographs. He was glamour.[17]

Peter Martins agrees: "Rudolf made a huge new audience
aware of ballet. Before Rudolf, you could introduce yourself as a
ballet dancer and people weren't quite sure what that meant.
After Rudolf, you said you were a dancer and people said, 'Oh, a
dancer.' They knew what a ballet dancer was for the first time,
thanks to Rudolf."[18] A decade before Nureyev's arrival in the
West, the United States had barely seventy-five resident dance
companies nationwide; within four years of his arrival, there
were 225 and the ratio of female to male dance students had
shifted from fifty to one to fifteen to one. Nureyev's vitality,
virility, and visibility achieved the unthinkable: he made it acceptable for a man to put on tights. Nureyev's early television
appearances changed the course of at least one life, an eight-year-
old Canadian boy named Frank Augustyn who, under Nureyev's
tutelage, would become his country's first world-class danseur. "I
had never seen anything like the way he moved, a man and an
animal," Augustyn remembers. "It seemed like he just jumped
into our living room. For boys who grew up on sports, it was like
looking at Wayne Gretzky. You thought, 'That's what I want to
do.' "[19]

A famous incident late in Nureyev's career epitomizes the
disparate elements of the temperament that made him a household name—his ease before an audience, as comfortable as someone in his own living room, his zest for the grand gesture, his
don't-tread-on-me professionalism. Nureyev was a guest performer in his *Don Quixote* in an Italian opera house. As part of the
deal, he had agreed for three minutes of his performance to be

filmed for Italian television. In the middle of performing his vigorous Basilio, Nureyev still noted exactly when the little red lights of the television cameras went on. Four minutes later, he knew that someone was trying to pull a fast one. The producers obviously figured that they had Nureyev by the details. What was he going to do—stop in the middle of a performance? He did. After giving the cameramen a few more moments' grace, Nureyev walked downstage, indicating to the conductor to cut the music. The music kept going, so Nureyev pointed to the two cameras for the audience to see that they were filming. The cameras stayed on, so Nureyev finally jumped down into the house, strode over to the metal stairs leading to the cameras, climbed up onto the catwalk, and turned the camera away from the stage.

The performance resumed and concluded without further incident.

Nine

The Great Gay Myth: "I Slept with Nureyev"

*"Ain't nobody started calling me Mam'selle 'til I
was seventeen and getting a little bone structure."*

—*Madeleine Kahn as Trixie Delight
in* Paper Moon

*T*he Trap is the sleaziest, slimiest, most wonderful
gay bar in Paris. A gateway to another era, it's
the kind of hole-in-the-wall dive that doesn't
need a sign over its flat gray door, just a line of iced blue neon
spelling out "Bar." Those who want what *Le Trap* has to offer
have always known where to find it, wherever they are. They
also know to make other plans until midnight, when the Trap
opens. One minute past midnight and the place is swarming with
gay men in their choicest whoredrobes, most of it tight, tighter
in key areas for an assist to the right spot-check (the lighting is
not the brightest), *cuir* at every turn. Once you've knocked on
the door, been snarled at by the doorman, and finally pushed
your way to the bar, you might think you were in any gay cruise
joint anywhere in the world. Pinball machines. A garish jukebox.
Just a touch too much red light.

And that's when you register the stairs. Once upon a time,
back in the early eighties, when sex was still a verb, the stairs
leading to the second floor of the Trap were a little harder to find.
They were flush against the back wall of the bar, and might easily
have been just a service route for the bar staff, were it not for the

constant flow of men up and down. The service upstairs wasn't for the staff (generally). It was for the patrons, by the patrons. The famous Trap staircase was, in fact, a ticket to a world in which only time stood still. Everything else was as mobile as a shower room. By the mid-eighties, the Trap's stairway to paradise had been shifted to the center of the room. The new visibility served only to stiffen the resolve.

It's a hell of a place to see an international superstar off-stage for the first time, late one wintry Paris night in 1985.

"Look over there."

"Where?"

"Down near the end of the bar. The guy with the leather cap."

"Which one?"

"The one who's laughing. Who does that look like to you?"

"Oh, my God."

Nureyev.

On a so-so, middle-of-the-week night, leaning comfortably against the bar, clearly in good humor, making no attempt at all to draw attention to himself, as if he had to. With one last swallow of his drink, Nureyev tips his hat to the jokester he's been enjoying and mounts the stairs. First at a trickle, then en masse the entire room follows. What came next, and more than once too, was a sylvan blond youth grinning from ear to ear, once he could straighten his back again, and among the most fervently attentive audiences of Nureyev's career. A paparazzi crush without the cameras.

For all the ego and self-absorption involved, Nureyev's career was really an almost unbroken string of contributions. Nureyev left behind his fair share of turkeys—*Valentino, Washington Square,* or the notorious Blackglama ad with Graham and Fonteyn (combined ages: 164 years) that Nureyev had withdrawn from public view. But he also left the dance world more than his fair share of gifts.

Like a real-world approach to sex.

Offstage, Nureyev was a legend for doing all night what most people take all night to do, while his sexualization of ballet is the gift he tattooed on the backside of the dance world. His contribution to the sexual vocabulary of dance lies midway between those of his two great predecessors in the field. Balanchine eroticized the interaction of steps and Graham eroticized her projection of herself. ("All my life I have been a devotee of sex," Graham wrote, "in the right sense of the word. Fulfillment, as opposed to procreation, or I would have had children."[1]) If Balanchine and Graham made sex an inevitable fact of their masterworks, Nureyev was its embodiment. He eroticized the air around him. "He has only to wiggle a toe," an early London critic observed, "to set pulses beating like tom-toms."[2]

Until Nureyev came along, the male ballet dancer wore a tailored straitjacket. Sexual projection was a no-no.[3] The neutering was due in large part to the ambivalent attitude of both audiences and dancers at the sight of a man in tights. The issue went the way of the dodo the moment Nureyev first set foot on stage. He didn't have time for ballet's sexual identity crisis. Once again, no man had ever done the things Nureyev did. In the traditional classics, particularly *Giselle*, he didn't have to move to suggest, for the first time, an Albrecht who might really and truly deflower Giselle. The more free-form events, such as the *Corsaire* pas de deux, *Bayadère*, or MacMillan's *Romeo and Juliet*, gave his sensuality more license, and Nureyev took the advantage. No one had ever moved in the blissfully erotic way that Nureyev moved and still managed to look like cock of the walk. In place of the foursquare, speak-when-you're-spoken-to vocabulary that had been forced upon male dancers, Nureyev introduced curves and circles and hips whenever possible and still looked like a classic dancer. The American ballerina Eleanor d'Antuono, a seasoned professional who spent three decades at American Ballet Theatre, has clear memories of her first *Corsaire* with Nureyev, her entrance in particular: "I bourréed onto the stage, just as I was supposed to, over to where Rudi was kneeling. When I reached him and looked down at this incredibly sexual man writhing at my feet, the sight actually took my breath away. For the first and only time in my professional career, I did not know where I was."[4]

Nureyev knew exactly where he was and exactly what he was doing. A key factor in his early career in Russia and in the West was Nureyev's running campaign to undress himself as much as possible in performance—shedding Albrecht's crotch-shrouding bloomers at the Kirov, going bare-chested in *Corsaire* and even *Don Quixote*, wearing white tights over an inner set of more sheer silk tights to suggest bared skin. He also mastered the art of the tease and got his audiences to live for it. In the version of *The Sleeping Beauty* he made for the National Ballet of Canada in 1972, Nureyev, as was his wont, was first seen swathed in a floor-length cape. For the removal of said cape, Nureyev turned his back on his audience and then slowly, but ever so slowly lowered the cape down his back until it finally came to a lingering rest, just below the circle of Nureyev's finest asset. It was a skill at Nureyev's disposal for the remainder of his career. A veteran of many a Nureyev performance, asked if she had ever seen him willfully upstage another dancer, smiles for a tense moment and then smiles for real: "Yes. There was this thing Rudolf used to do, regularly, when he wasn't actually dancing but thought the dancing that was being done was less than interesting. He'd walk upstage, turn his back to the audience, and flex his butt. It worked every time." The French ballerina Violette Verdy sees even the intensity of Nureyev's sexual vitality as yet another swerve in his contradictory nature:

Rudi [was] a dancer of such multiple beauties that you can almost say he *has* no sex. Or you could say that, as a dancer, he has *both* sexes. He goes beyond being a regular, ordinary, square male dancer. And the matter is beyond one of simply having feminine qualities. It's almost as if he creates another type of sex altogether. He's a kind of dancing *creature*. You don't see a male or a female—you see a *dancer*, a great dancer. Something like a faun or a bird, something wild and very beautiful. He has *all* sexual qualities. So that when he dances, having a woman with him is simply a bonus—with him, a ballerina offers what is necessary to complete the communication. But, in himself, Rudolf is complete.[5]

Early in his *Dance: A Short History of Classic Theatrical Dancing*, Lincoln Kirstein, the pit-bull guardian of ballet in our time, makes an unexpected observation. After a lengthy, discursive analysis of the human impulse to movement, which somehow involves the Bacchic maenads, D. H. Lawrence, and African-American spiritual music, Kirstein finds a surprising connection, one only he would have dared make in 1935. Our bodies, Kirstein writes, are "the most delicate and frankest instruments of all our actions, cerebral and physical."[6] When the body is honed to the exorbitant demands of ballet, an extra element is generated: "Competitive dancing is an index of sexual vigor."[7]

Nureyev was a very competitive dancer from first to last, from top to bottom and vice versa. The number of his sexual adventures perhaps has been exaggerated since the theatrical orgasm of his first celebrity, when a huge photograph of Nureyev nude from the waist up hung in the window of the Royal Vauxhall Tavern, a gay bar in South London. "I know his bed was empty many a night," one of Nureyev's companion bar-crawlers in Paris remembers. Especially among gay men now of a certain age, if all the people who claim to have slept with Nureyev did, in fact, have sex with Nureyev, he would not have had time for a career. Whatever the legend, Nureyev's sexual career was not simply one more case of anything goes.

Rumors of a cold heart to the contrary, Nureyev was, for example, capable of deep and lasting love relationships, encounters that changed the lives of his partners forever. However much globe-trotting Nureyev did, he spent most of his life in the West with a significant other somewhere in the not-too-distant background—Bruhn in the sixties, Wallace Potts in the late sixties and early seventies, Robert Tracy through the last decade of his life. Nureyev's relationships with Potts and Tracy demonstrate the contradictory effects he could have on the people closest to him.

Nureyev's relationships with Wall Potts and Tracy could

not have been more different. A Southern gentleman in the handsomest sense of the term, Potts first met Nureyev while the former was a physics major at Georgia Tech with multiple interests (he would go on to produce one of the classic movies of gay pornography, *Le Beau Mec*), and, for Potts, "it was awe at first sight. And then once I got to know him . . . well, he was the only person I've ever been in love with in my life."[8] Nureyev and Potts lived together for almost seven years in Nureyev's rambling Richmond Park estate just outside London. "[The house] backed up to East Sheen Common, which backed up to Richmond Park," Potts remembered after Nureyev's death, "which made it so idyllic. And then we broke up. Why? I don't know. I wanted to have my own life. But we remained friends. Probably became better friends. You don't have the same passions but you don't have the same anger or jealousy either."[9] Potts remained devoted to Nureyev for the rest of his life and was a vital contributor to the support system of friends who saw Nureyev through the final years of his illness.

Nureyev first met Tracy during rehearsals for Balanchine's *Bourgeois Gentilhomme* in 1979. A student at the School of American Ballet, Tracy was one of a dozen apprentice dancers that Balanchine cast in the ballet as a company of lackeys attending the hero, Nureyev. By his own admission, Tracy was Nureyev's lackey for the next thirteen years. The relationship was a stormy one, but it served both men well, up to a point. Nureyev found a steady lover who doubled as a manservant, and Tracy found himself in daily contact with the likes of Judy Peabody, Jessye Norman, and Jacqueline Onassis. Things eventually soured on both sides. "From the first day," Tracy told Bob Colacello in *Vanity Fair*, "Rudolf was testing me, seeing if I would make him tea, bring him a Coke. . . . He wanted friends to be servants, because he was too cheap to pay real ones."[10] A week before Nureyev died, Tracy received eviction notices from Nureyev's lawyer at the New York apartment in the Dakota. Tracy already had hired Marvin Mitchelson as his legal counsel for a threatened palimony suit. (The parties apparently reached a settlement, and Tracy briefly worked for the Nureyev Foundation.)

Nureyev's relationship with Bruhn was of a different order, something large and explosive. Although their union collapsed under the pressure of two considerable careers—and Nureyev's wandering eye—the mutual affection and regard was lifelong. "Their sexual relationship didn't last very long at all," a friend of both men recalls. "Rudi was already into playing around and that was very difficult for Erik." The professional competition proved crippling. "Rudolf completely overpowered Erik in everything," their partner Sonia Arova concludes. "He had existed before Rudolf came along, he'd had success, he'd had a career and then suddenly there was all this attention to Rudolf, Rudolf, Rudolf. I think he felt that deeply and he was left feeling very hurt."[11] A second friend agrees:

> Just as Erik was hitting his stride, along comes this animal magnetism, this glamour. Europeans were stars but a Russian out of Russia was like some wild animal back then. My impression is that Erik felt overwhelmed by the money and the stardom and the glamour. Erik was a bitter man by the time I met him in the early seventies. He felt cheated. He was a great, great dancer, but a dancer's dancer. He had a very public career, but nothing like Rudolf's, none of the money, none of the fame.

There are those who feel that Nureyev was a less-than-innocent contributor to events. "Rudi's effect on Erik was devastating," a colleague from the Royal remembers about Bruhn's aborted guest engagement with the Royal in 1962, mere weeks after the smash sensation of the Nureyev/Fonteyn *Giselles*. "Erik did not finish the season. Rudi demoralized him to such an effect that he had to leave to go into a nursing home in Denmark to recover. He never did recover completely. One can date the beginning of the sad decline of this superb dancer from the beginning of his relationship with Nureyev." The constant spotlight on both men did not help matters any. "The press saw us together," Bruhn remembered later, "and they watched us like hawks, and it was as if they had placed bets on which of us was going to survive."[12] Nureyev told his friend the actress and singer Monique van Vooren that

"Erik finally sent Rudolf away. He sacrificed their relationship for Rudolf's career, so that Rudolf could go on to do all the things he needed to do."[13]

On some level, a cord remained unbroken.

Bruhn was diagnosed with cancer in the mid-1980s. His condition quickly deteriorated and he died on April 1, 1986. Nureyev was among his last visitors.

However celebrated the numbers, Nureyev's driven, compartmentalized attitude toward his sexuality was too complex for labeling. "What no one ever talks about," a Nureyev protégé remembers about her offstage time in his company, "is that there was a very prudish side to Rudolf. He could be very protective— like, make sure that our escorts were not liable to overstep their bounds, sexually speaking. There were certain things he would not allow. I remember once he kept me from getting a ride home with Mick Jagger from a club because he thought Jagger might try something." (Nureyev had reason to be wary of Jagger's motives. The most recent Jagger biography, Christopher Andersen's *Jagger Unauthorized*, records a brief liaison between Jagger and Nureyev in the late 1960s. Can we talk four fabulous lips in one bed?) For a man who always used his own name to sign the register at gay bathhouses across the globe, there were certain forms of public display that were not acceptable behavior. Nureyev never publicly acknowledged his homosexuality. The closest he ever came to speaking his truth was a comment during a Mike Wallace interview in 1979: "I know what it is to make love as a man and a woman." (Variations on the same metaphor cropped up in interviews for the rest of his life.) "Rudolf was pretty much out there as a gay man well before it became mandatory," a New York friend concludes. "He was about as 'out' as you can get for the seventies." When Nureyev couldn't get a ticket to see the original production of *The Boys in the Band*, he attended a performance anyway, sitting on the lap of a male friend.

If the number of conquests is perhaps inflated, it is not, one suspects, by much. The stories of Nureyev visits to the baths and the tearooms, the back rooms in porn bookstores and the

Ramble in Central Park have been part of gay legend since the Stonewall era. During his first years in the West, when the amount of available sex first sent the Tatar tiger prowling, Nureyev saw a wide field for satisfying his already compulsive sexuality, however thin the ice he had to cover. According to a very close source, Fonteyn and Nureyev were on one of their earliest guest tours, performing in Melbourne with the recently founded Australian Ballet. They were performing one of the full-length classics and, during the intermission before the final act, Nureyev threw a bathrobe over his costume, rushed out into the street in full stage makeup (and wearing a wig), and ran about one hundred yards to a public lavatory that was, in fact, the best place in town for a quickie. On bended knee before "a young, tall bloke," Nureyev suddenly found himself with an unanticipated audience —the local vice squad. After a frenzy of telephone calls and a very long intermission, Nureyev returned to the theater and finished the performance. "That was one time," the source adds, "when Margot was furious with him for days."

Despite Nureyev's winking assertion that he was "almost a virgin" when he left Russia, by the time of his defection Nureyev already had mastered the act of darkness. An old and valued Russian friend claims that Nureyev, by his own admission, was involved in a sexual relationship with both Pushkin and his wife. According to legend, neither of the Pushkins knew what was up with the other, but Nureyev learned a great deal about himself, as he explained to his ancien comrade: "He told me that he would have sex with Pushkin's wife in his dressing room at intermission, and quite often. In those days at the Kirov, men were taught that sex should be avoided for many days in advance of a performance because it drained energies and distracted from focus. I asked Rudolf how he could possibly fuck during the interval and then go out and dance. 'Never a problem,' he said. 'Just opposite. It taught me how much energy I had that day.' " Within the close, closed circle of his gay friends in Leningrad, Nureyev developed an early reputation as the Tatar boy with the temper. An early friend from Leningrad still remembers the fireworks and still trembles at the potential aftermath:

I ask you, please, do not mention any names. We have to respect the rights of these people. It happens sometimes, you know. He was one person when he was young, and then suddenly he got married.

The group of people that I am now describing, and to which I belonged, had a very good relationship with Rudik. Despite his explosions. He was very explosive, easily hurt. I defended him often in my conversation with others. Different people had different opinions of him. Some used to think he was a savage.

He had a very difficult relationship with Alexei. . . . Both of them were very sharp, very independent. Alexei was simple, very proud. . . . Rudik was not well-mannered. He was all raw nerve. He did not know the rules of propriety.

One evening, very late, Alexei, Gregori,[14] and Nureyev, all three of them came to my house in the country. . . . I doubt that I can tell you all the details. . . . Anyway . . . One young man used to live in the town where my house was. . . . He was a frequent visitor in my home. . . . Suddenly Rudik, Alexei, and Gregori appeared absolutely unexpectedly. They were not supposed to come. . . . They brought some food and wine. The young man was really upset. Only much later did he tell me that this particular evening he had a special goal, a special idea. Upon their arrival, I only noticed that this young man became tense. . . . Almost immediately, there formed a sort of disagreement between Rudik and the young man. Right in the middle of their argument, Rudik suddenly got up and said to the young man, "Just get out of here." The young man would not leave. He said, "I was here before you came. We were very comfortable. We had an interesting conversation and I will not leave." Rudik told him, "Nobody wants you here. Leave!" Such outbursts were typical of him. I tried to calm them down, saying about my young friend, "He is a very nice young man. He lives near here. In the town." . . . In a word, it was an ugly scene. When it finally ended and the young man left, everybody blamed Rudik for his behavior. He was hot-tempered. He was lacking in tact. He was not "gallant" in that sense.

The impact of Nureyev's years in Russia has been largely overlooked in the recorded history of Rudolf the Eternal Erection. The pressure cooker of his formative years, repression as the norm, and the fear of reprisal—they send you to the gulag—were a critical factor in Nureyev's attitude toward his sexuality, right up to the deathbed refusal to acknowledge his AIDS diagnosis. The Russian language does not even have a word for homosexuality.

Stalin's recriminalization of consensual sex between men in the mid-1930s, according to Kevin Gardner, an American AIDS activist currently at work in Moscow, was more than the average run-of-the-mill fag-bashing still so popular among straight men insecure in their sexuality. "Stalin's action legitimized harassment of gay men," Gardner explains. "The goal wasn't always to put homosexuals away, although people did disappear into the prisons. It was used to blackmail people, to enlist them in the KGB to inform on each other. It was an efficient tool for threatening people with prison. The beauty of the Soviet legal code is that there were plenty of laws that could be used to harass almost anyone. There were two other laws—Article 121 on male sodomy and Article 120 on sex with a minor—that were infamous for being used disproportionately against gay men. The fear level among gay men became very high." The only option by the Nureyev era was "these closed circles of gay networks. In terms of meeting other gays outside your circle, there were really only the parks and the public works. The one club I've been told about from the 1950s was an exception. There was nothing like that anywhere else in the country that anyone knows about. It's really only been in the last year or two that these new, kind of semiunderground gay discos and gay bars even started opening up in Moscow and St. Petersburg."

Even the closed circuit held its very real risks:

The biggest fear in the various circles was that someone would come into the circle who would inform on them and everyone would be sent away. They were always being pressured to name each other. If one of them was brought in to the police, the KGB, whatever—they were all working together—there would be pressure to name the other people.

I'll tell you what they were afraid of. It's not just the terror of being sent to a Soviet labor camp and everything that entails. It would go on the records of the authorities that you were gay, a homosexual. It would be stamped in your little workbook, so if you do ever get out of prison and try to get a job, you would have that stamped in your papers —why you were arrested. It followed you for the rest of your life and made life in Russia impossible—they'd lose housing, lose employment. You would get out of prison and basically have nowhere to go. [15]

A cultural barometer once again, Nureyev, in effect, embodied the new state of gay sex in the wake of the sexual revolution of the 1960s and the birth of a gay rights movement before the same decade was over. In the late 1960s and early 1970s, gay men discovered the treasure the straight boys had guarded with such ferocity since the Sabine incident: not just the pleasure of male sexuality but its power. Gay sex went from being something you did when you could to something you did at every opportunity. The great gay capitals—New York City, San Francisco, and Los Angeles in the United States, Amsterdam, Paris, and sometimes London in Europe—became the longest ongoing parties since Messalina hit puberty. Handsome, rich, endowed with a gift that, had he opted for a career in pornography, would have earned him a double-digit nickname, Nureyev was lord of the land and more. He became the first gay hero everyone knew was gay— and having a very good time with what Edith Wharton called "the thing best worth knowing."

Like Marilyn Monroe, Nureyev developed a sexual perspective that, for all its vigor and conflicts, was surprisingly mundane. The earliest stories emphasize a taste for anonymity, distanced but to the point, with a taste for worship. Regular sex became as much a part of his regimen as a good meal at the right time. From most accounts, Nureyev's attitude toward sex was largely matter-of-fact. First bed and then dinner. A pattern was set for life. "You don't really expect me to go without sex for more than ten or eleven hours, do you?" Nureyev told director James Toback during negotiations for *Exposed*, clearly expecting that a steady flow of gentleman callers was part of the deal. Toback declined the arrangement but remembers that the stream of male company Nureyev managed quite well on his own were never an intrusion: "Sure enough, every now and again, Rudolf would disappear off into his trailer with one of his young men— he called them his 'butch boys'—and I'll tell you something, he always came back energized, ready to go. It was never a case of lethargy or torpor. He clearly used sex to inspire rather than dilute."[16] "Beauty," a friend remembers, "was not the priority in lovers." The signature feature was volume. "Rudolf liked big," a compatriot on the circuit remembers. "Big in everything. I don't think he was very inventive in what he did. He just liked a lot." He also let the world look on, in the proper setting. The late gay activist Michael Callen remembered an ecstatic evening at a New York City bathhouse watching Nureyev take on "four huge black men, one right after the other."[17]

There are two schools of thought on what position Nure-yev preferred in the act. The first is that Nureyev, as a veteran of the era remembers, was interested strictly in planting the seed rather than receiving it; the second, the exact opposite, that Nure-yev was, in the words of the writer Joel Rodham, "a notorious masochist. I remember one group scene at the Everard Baths. People wore only jockstraps, some naked with boots, and a cock ring Nureyev had been wearing."[18] A dancer with the Paris Opéra remembers a sterling instance of Nureyev's sexual practicality. Nureyev knew the dancer well after many a Nureyev and Friends concert tour, and one morning the dancer was summoned to Nu-reyev's apartment to run through a ballet Nureyev was soon to dance for the first time:

"So I go into the bedroom, and there they are—Nureyev, the boy, and one of those society women who were always around Rudolf. The breakfast table was on the bed and she was pouring out the tea for Rudolf and boy. And I taught him the ballet while the three of them had breakfast in bed together. You want to talk about surreal?"

For all the sense of sexual celebration Nureyev inspired, the bigger picture had its darker corners. Nureyev would never learn the lesson Paul Monette summarized in *Becoming a Man: Half a Life Story:* "When you finally come out, there's a pain that stops, and you know it will never hurt like that again, no matter how much you lose or how bad you die."[19] His greatest tragedy and only real defeat, Nureyev was never able to find the relief Monette describes. Instead, right down to the compulsiveness of his behavior, Nureyev became a classic example of the deadening closet sensibility. "Rudolf was tortured, tormented by his sexuality," Monique van Vooren explains. "He was ashamed of being homosexual. And I think he wanted to be degraded. He liked street boys, toughs, the lowest of the low."[20] The British journalist Lynn Barber recorded a telling incident in her memorial tribute to Nureyev in *The Independent on Sunday:* "The young Scottish dancer Michael Clark told me that he once went to a dinner at Nureyev's apartment in Paris with his boyfriend and at one point kissed him—Nureyev was furious and practically threw them out."[21]

Despite the fact that the majority of the inner circle was composed of women, beautiful women with position and wealth who were willing to brew Nureyev's tea and pick up his socks, Nureyev was also a dreadful misogynist: "I am probably a male chauvinist pig, but I consider men to have a better organized brain and better able to separate themselves from nature, from their own nature. They are the leaders in all the visual arts and in architecture. Men are better at the military. Men are better cooks, men are better at everything. You don't kneel to women. You mistrust them."[22] (To the end of his life, Nureyev's favored insult was "cunt.") When James Toback suggested to Nureyev that a little intimacy might charge his on-screen romance with Nastassja Kinski in *Exposed,* Nureyev's response was conditional: "Cut her tits off, sew on a dick, and then I'll think about it."[23] Had Nureyev lived a decade longer he might well have found himself involved in a sexual harassment suit. A principal male dancer with the Boston Ballet remembers that Nureyev's work with the company's male ensemble had its extradance elements: "Rudi made it very clear when he was interested in one of the male dancers, and it terrified the straight guys. When he didn't get the response he wanted, he kept pushing to see how far he could go. I never knew him to hold a grudge against any of the men who said no flat out, but I know he threatened to.''

Two incidents, both from the last years of his life, summarize Nureyev's complex and conflicted, celebratory and exhibitionist attitude toward the beast with two backs. The first was an exchange between Nureyev and a friend of many years that took place in the wings during an American Ballet Theatre performance of *Giselle* in the summer of 1988. Nureyev had not danced with ABT for more than ten years, and, in the intervening decade, his technique had deteriorated to the point where the ABT administration was reluctant to have him back. As part of a fiftieth birthday tour that Nureyev, according to an ABT colleague, ''managed to drag out for two years,'' he had finally returned for three performances of *Giselle*.

After the lengthy *pas d'action* that is the centerpiece of the ballet's first act, Nureyev returned to the wings, winded and worn.

''Rudolf came offstage,'' his friend recalls,

and he was just completely exhausted, covered in sweat, panting and puffing in a way that just didn't seem like Rudolf. So I went over, and I said, ''Rudi, are you okay?''

He was standing sort of bent forward, his hands on his knees, trying to catch his breath. He looked up and almost smiled.

''I am very tired this evening.''

I said, ''Rudolf, how long have you been dancing this ballet? How can you be tired already?''

''Different story tonight.''

I said I didn't understand, and besides it was really true—Rudolf danced better when he was tired. It gave him something to overcome.

''No, no. Different. I fucked all last night. I fucked all this morning, until rehearsal. I have no extra energy.''

I said, "Rudolf, don't you ever get enough sex?"
He looked at me and just said, "No."
I said, "But, really, Rudolf . . ."
"The difference is, last night I fucked and this morn-
ing I got fucked."

The concluding shot of Patricia Foy's 1991 documentary film, *Nureyev,* is as breathtaking a statement. Foy's account of Nureyev's life and career is a lucid, affecting portrait of Nureyev as he approached the end of his life. Drawn but tanned, Nureyev tells his version of events with wit, charm, and a brisk disregard for the facts surrounding certain key incidents, such as his defection. Clearly the version of his life Nureyev wanted to leave behind as an official record, the final credits of the film roll by as Nureyev sits naked on a slope of rocky beachfront on his island. Alone, content, gazing out at the ocean as he did often in the days after Fonteyn's death.

Two versions of the film were prepared. The first, made for a television broadcast, concludes with Nureyev still seated on the rocks. A second edition, for video release, continues long enough for Nureyev to stand up and face the camera.

And what does Nureyev choose as his farewell gesture for what he knows is his farewell film appearance?

For all the world to see, he just stands there, nude from head to heel, flapping in the wind but facing downstage.

The men in his life: Nureyev had three long-standing relationships. *Above,* the first and most passionate was with the great Danish danseur Erik Bruhn. *Left,* after Bruhn, Nureyev and Wallace Potts (to the left of Nureyev, in profile) lived together for seven years and remained lifelong friends. *Below,* Nureyev met Robert Tracy in the late 1970s. The relationship soured in the last years of Nureyev's life, and suits were threatened, although no suits ever went before the courts.

Long before leaving Russia, Nureyev was already a man of many moods. Here he is, *above*, as a modern-day Narcissus in what was then Leningrad, *right*, as the brooding young rebel, and *below*, as Adonis in first bloom.

ALL PHOTOS: SERGEI SOROKIN COLLECTION

Above, Nureyev with the man who changed his life, his ballet teacher at the Kirov academy, the great Alexander Pushkin. *Below left*, Nureyev's first role with the Kirov was in the Soviet repertory standard *Laurencia*. Here he partners the company's prima, Natalia Dudinskaya, in the ballet and wears the infamous "monkey wig." *Below right*, as a very young Albrecht in *Giselle*.

TWO PHOTOS: MIRA

UPI/BETTMANN

Nureyev's partnership with Margot Fonteyn generally is considered the high-water mark of both their careers. Here they are in three of their most famous vehicles: striking the ballet's signature pose in *La Bayadère* *(opposite top)*; completing the infamous "fish dives" in *Sleeping Beauty* *(opposite bottom left)*; as a besotted *Romeo and Juliet (above)* in the Kenneth MacMillan staging of Prokofiev.

Opposite bottom right, Fonteyn and Nureyev soak up the Mediterranean sun after their first concert tour.

Opposite, Nureyev's fire-eating performance in *Le Corsaire* was the most popular role in his early repertory.

Right, Nureyev scored a resounding personal success in Kenneth MacMillan's version of *Romeo and Juliet.*

Above, as a soaring Siegfried in *Swan Lake.*

MIRA

LOUIS PERE

JACK VARTOOGIAN

Although Nureyev began and ended his career a nineteenth-century artist, he spent a great deal of time experimenting with the twentieth century. *Opposite above and below,* as Vaslav Nijinsky's faun in *L'après-midi d'un faune;* in George Balanchine's neoclassic masterwork *Apollo; above,* performing for Martha Graham in *Appalachian Spring;* and *right,* for Murray Louis in *Moments.*

Top to bottom: the celebrity circuit was an integral part of Nureyev's life, and, as a founding member of the international jet set, he relished the high profile. Nureyev and Elizabeth Taylor at a benefit cocktail party; receiving the improbable combination of Shelley Winters and Alexandra Danilova after a performance; at a reception for the Pennsylvania Ballet with (left to right) Merce Cunningham, Suzanne Farrell, and Mikhail Baryshnikov.

Despite his avowed misogyny, many of Nureyev's closest, longest lasting friendships were with women, particularly women slightly older than himself. He poses here with two of his earliest friends in the West: Sonia Arova *(left)* and Maria Tallchief *(below)*. Tallchief introduced Nureyev to Erik Bruhn and later arranged his American debut on *The Bell Telephone Hour.*

THREE PHOTOS: LOUIS PERES

Opposite top to bottom: Nureyev dark and light: backstage before a performance and as a gregarious talk-show guest.

Above, Nureyev's followers were viligant and faithful. Here Nureyev attracts a crowd on the Lincoln Center Plaza and *(right)* accepts the birthday salute of his fans.

LOUIS PERES

With a few major exceptions, such as this notorious snakeskin suit and platform boots *(top left)*, Nureyev's wardrobe tended toward the simple and practical. "His clothes were expensive," one friend remembers, "but usually pretty simple. He'd buy a good leather cap, for example, and then wear it for twenty-five years."

JACK VARTOOGIAN

MARTHA SWOPE

Rebel with a cause: one of the key qualities in Nureyev's appeal was his ability to balance innocence and experience.

Nureyev in rehearsal: waiting his turn *(far left)* and a storm cloud about to blow *(left)*.

Nureyev's famous curtain calls—one arm sweeping over the house—were an integral part of his performances.

THREE

Rudolf

Everywhere at Once

Ten

"Freedom is not achieved simply by working freely."

—TENNESSEE WILLIAMS, *quoted in Ronald Hayman,* Tennessee Williams

From the moment of his defection, the new land Nureyev stood ready to storm was no more prepared for the Nureyev experience than the Soviets had been. The "leap to freedom" was less a case of Nureyev adopting a new homeland than his new world adapting itself to him. "He wasn't anything we considered a normal human being, you see," Nureyev's longtime friend and colleague from the Royal Ballet Antoinette Sibley once said. "He didn't look like one and he didn't act like one. He was born on a train and spent the rest of his life going one hundred miles an hour."[1] Nureyev didn't come West to slow down, and he certainly didn't come to learn a new set of rules. Consciously or not, he came to invent his own. He'd lived by his own priorities in Russia, and that is exactly what he did in the West. In fact, Nureyev's Russian career was a forecast of what was to come in the new world. His three decades onstage in the West were the rebellion of the Kirov years transposed to a higher key.

Time, circumstance, and Nureyev's selective memory eventually conspired to obscure the parallels between his Western career and his career at the Kirov. Even his defection was not quite the rift with the past enshrined by Nureyev's chroniclers, the most insightful of whom were still friends and advisors working from Nureyev's own account of his life. His break with the past was actually sharper back in the USSR.[2] During two open meetings within the Kirov company, the majority of dancers joined in his denunciation. An official trial by government officials was held behind closed doors in January 1962, and Nureyev was relegated to the uniquely Soviet status of a traitor and a "nonperson." His name was stricken from public records, his face cut from company pictures, his legacy reduced to whispers and underground bulletins. Nureyev was sentenced in absentia to seven years hard labor should he ever return to Russia. Despite all that, Nureyev remained ambivalent about a permanent home in the West until his purchase of a villa, La Turbie, above Monte Carlo, two years after Le Bourget; shortly before buying his Mediterranean pied à terre, a return to Russia was clearly still on Nureyev's mind when he and Alexandra Danilova engaged in a lively disagreement on the subject over borscht at the Russian Tea Room. The ever voluble assoluta of the Ballet Russe de Monte Carlo insisted to a disgruntled Nureyev that he not even consider the possibility he was obviously entertaining: "Danilova pounded the table . . . and shouted, 'You must not go back. . . . What kind of dancer will you be after five or ten years in jail?' "[3]

The question of a return was the great dangling proposition of Nureyev's early career. "The West and I have given each other a chance," Nureyev said in one of his first lengthy interviews. "If we don't succeed, I may—perhaps—go back."[4] Nureyev openly antagonized both the press and his public. "Western choreography is good—better, in fact, than the Russian," Nureyev told another reporter. "It has to make up for bad dancing." He complained to Life that "Western dancers are well-prepared technically, but they do not have on the whole the intellect the Russian dancers have." On the subject of the new cabals—the press and impresarios in particular—he told Time: "You must remember that you are giving food to people who would gladly cut you up and eat you. It's you who always pays. It's those others who eat and go to bed early."

Nureyev's durability as a public figure in the West finally obscured the fact that he took as much with him when he left Russia as he left behind, both professionally and personally. Nureyev's "Russianness" was right up there with his cheekbones as a premium stock-in-trade for the first decade of his Western career. At least professionally, his coup was to turn the past to his advantage. "When Nureyev comes out onto the stage," the influential American dance critic Arlene Croce wrote, "he brings this large, magical aura of freedom with him. It is greater than any gift he has as a dancer."[5] In terms of attracting—and holding—the public eye, Nureyev was smart enough to know that less can indeed be more. The Garboesque elusiveness he developed on the subject of Russia protected his family back home from any unexpected "accidents" but only whetted the appetite of his new following for any scrap of information they could find about him—and them, "the Reds." The ballet faithful came to see the new Nijinsky but, at least at first, the mass audience that soon followed came to see the Russian. Beginning with the Diaghilev era, international ballet had been linked so closely to Russians that, trying to form an American ballet in the 1930s, Lincoln Kirstein coined the term "Russianballet" as an explanation of the general public's idea of classic dance.

Nureyev was the first chance those audiences had had to see a real Russian, and they flocked to the theater for the spectacle. Perhaps the most ironic aspect of the leap to freedom was the value of the Petipa repertory Nureyev acquired under Pushkin. Nureyev was the first ballet dancer to grasp the meaning of the word "residual," and his stagings of the classic repertory, from his first *Bayadère* for the Royal Ballet in London to the last one for the Paris Opéra, guaranteed a steady cash flow for the remainder of his life.

The difference between Nureyev's life in Russia and his life in the West, in fact, was a shift in circumstance rather than a change in character. It's the same hero in another play. Nureyev began his Kirov career and his career in the West on the same cue and in the same costume. In both cases he appeared out of nowhere, on his own thousand of miles from what had once been home, driven by his hunger for ballet, with no money in his pocket and only the clothes on his back. The terms used to describe the Tatar urchin terrorizing the Kirov are exactly the terms that continued to describe ballet's first megastar to his dying day —restless, isolated, unpredictable, combative, always committed, for better or worse, to his own vision. The result was less an instance of then-and-now than an almost textbook portrait of the child as father of the man.

The rebel still kept to his cause. Although the most important European ballet companies are state-funded institutions, ballet in the West has never had anything like the political accountability dance has always had in Russia. Even the most adventurous Western ballet companies, however, still work within fixed frameworks, with rules that are broken at considerable risk. The choreographer is god. Management signs paychecks. Dancers do as they are told, onstage and off. Nureyev rewrote that scenario forever, just as he'd done in Russia.

Nureyev escorted HRH the Princess Margaret for a night on the town wearing an Yves St.-Laurent pony-skin jacket with matching thigh-high boots. He danced for Martha Graham, wearing a gold dance belt designed by Halston. He partnered Fonteyn and Miss Piggy. Even Balanchine—who worked on Broadway and for Samuel Goldwyn in Hollywood, who choreographed a ballet for forty Ringling Brothers elephants, and who got his New York City Ballet on television at every possible opportunity during its formative years—once referred to Nureyev as "the Liberace of ballet,"[6] a faux phenomenon, hooked on hype rather than the muse.

Nureyev's most telling rebellion was the one that eventually caused him the greatest personal pain. Traditionally, the life of a ballet dancer is a life spent on the road. The fabled ballerinas of the nineteenth century toured the great capitals of Europe year after year, and, as late as the 1890s, the reigning stars of the Russian Imperial Ballet in Romanov St. Petersburg were not homegrown dancers but a series of Italian guest ballerinas.[7] Ballet became an independent commercial enterprise with the arrival of the Diaghilev company in Paris in 1909, and touring became the bread and butter of the ballet companies that continue to proliferate across Europe and America to this day.

But the great ballet careers of the twentieth century were all built on a long-standing association with a single troupe, from Fonteyn with the Royal to Tallchief with New York City Ballet to Makarova and Baryshnikov at American Ballet Theatre. Nureyev, in contrast, reintroduced the freelance traditions of the great nineteenth-century ballerinas, averaging a minimum of two hundred performances a year with different companies in every corner of the globe for almost three decades. From the very beginning, his new life was spent en route: the first tours with de Cuevas and then the chamber quartet with Arova, Bruhn, and Hightower in 1961,[8] television performances in Frankfurt, London, and New York in 1962; and a five-week, nine-city visit to the United States and Canada with the Royal in 1963 that he and Fonteyn extended to the Mediterranean (at high summer) by organizing a concert tour that began with a gala in Nice, moved on to Israel and Lebanon, and concluded at the annual arts festival in Athens.[9] The pace was set for the remainder of Nureyev's career, and it didn't slacken until his last weary tours of Britain and Australia in 1991. In addition to an endless succession of individual engagements—dancing in Madison, Wisconsin, one night and Rome the next as a matter of course—Nureyev became a regular attraction with an unprecedented number of companies around the world. As a name guaranteed to fill a house, he was inevitably a welcome guest. The associations became a wildly complex but unbroken length of simultaneous associations multiplied into infinity with the Nureyev and Friends concert tours that began in 1974 and continued regularly until 1991. Until a five-month break from dancing in 1976 to make his feature film debut in Ken Russell's *Valentino*—prompted by a foot injury and a bout of pneumonia serious enough for him to spend four days in St. John's Hospital in Santa Monica—Nureyev was never offstage for more than two weeks at a time until the last two years of his life.

For thirty years, Nureyev was everywhere at once. With

himself as star, he staged his *Nutcracker* in Stockholm, his Byron ballet *Manfred* in Paris and Zurich, and his *Romeo and Juliet* in London. His first guest appearances with Fonteyn for the newly formed Australian Ballet in 1962 culminated a decade later with a feature film of his *Don Quixote* with the Australians, produced by Nureyev, directed by Nureyev, and starring Nureyev. He maintained on-again/off-again associations with the Vienna State Opera from the time of his first staging of *Swan Lake* there in 1964 until his debut as a conductor in 1991 and with La Scala in Milan from his first *Sleeping Beauty* for them in 1966 until the company added his *Don Quixote* to its repertory in 1987. In 1982, while his contract as artistic director of the Paris Opéra Ballet was being hammered out and as he was racing full-tilt toward his forty-fifth birthday, Nureyev was a one-man multimedia festival: a new full-length ballet based on Shakespeare's *The Tempest* for the Royal; a television version of the Diaghilev program he'd performed with the Joffrey Ballet three years earlier; four months of touring with the Boston Ballet; a month of work in New York and Paris on his second feature film, *Exposed*; his first commercial advertisement, Nureyev in black leather pants, black turtleneck, and fur hat as spokesman for Suntory, a Japanese vodka.[10] "Ballet careers that last," a great American ballerina once said,

> are not built on hopping from one company to another. Careers are built on working in the same place, day in and day out, with the same people year after year, and always having a place you can consider your artistic home. Look at the people who survive longest—there is always that place to go back to. The only exception I can think of to that rule is Nureyev, because, wherever he is, Rudolf works every day and always at the standard he sets for himself, which is very high indeed. It forces everyone around him to work at his level.

The years of touring set a deceptive precedent. They were as much about Nureyev the human being as they were about Nureyev the dancer. The final image of his life on the road is as much the portrait of a man without a country as a man who couldn't find a home to call his own. Nureyev clearly felt the absence. "All my life," he said late in his career, "I have been a gate-crasher."[11] One after another, his colleagues agree that no one company could possibly have satisfied Nureyev's appetite for dancing or for the spotlight. "I suppose it's a harsh thing to say considering the phenomenally important influence he had on the Royal Ballet in the long run," Georgina Parkinson, one of Nureyev's early colleagues at the Royal and a lifelong friend, remembers, "but Rudolf could be extremely greedy when it came to the number of his own performances. He felt it was his right to dance every night. All or nothing."[12] Nureyev's attitude spelled trouble. "Rudolf wanted to do all the performances," Dame Merle Park remembers about the Nureyev years at the Royal, "and you can't run any company that way."[13] Sibley concurs: "Rudolf was passionate about everything—he fitted in more in a day than most people managed in a week—but dancing was his life. He would have been perfectly happy dancing every night, at every performance."[14]

The ghosts of life in Russia were as important a part of the picture as the hunger for center stage. Like any eager, curious child forcibly kept too close to home too long, once Nureyev made the break to freedom a permanent home was both a need and a fear, security at the risk of another potential trap. The boy hounded first by his peers and then by the Soviet bosses was never able to stop running. "Rudi's driving force throughout his career, his paramount priority," according to an early Royal partner, Nadia Nerina,

was to make up for the lost years of his early training. It has always surprised me that this was not more evident to those persons, including critics, who knew him well. He was conscious that he had started his serious ballet training too late and he was too intelligent not to be conscious of it. Those years were lost irredeemably. They could never be recovered. To my mind, much of his eruptions and tantrums derived from a deep-seated anxiety and frustration, his insatiable desire to perform, to be onstage being an endeavor to overcome the "lost years."[15]

Nureyev still spent a significant part of his Western career looking
for a professional home and came close to finding one twice. In
both cases—with the Royal Ballet in the 1960s and in Paris during
the 1980s—the Kirov scenario repeated itself. A starburst debut.
Historic performances. Open warfare onstage and off. In each
case, Nureyev was finally forced to move on. In his own mind at
least, the move was forced on him by his enemies: "There is
always betrayal"[16] became part of Nureyev's code.

Nureyev's years with the Royal, of course, had at least
one significant contrast with his career at the Kirov. This time
the bosses were on his side. When Nureyev began his standing
association with the Royal Ballet after the first *Giselles* with Fonteyn in 1962, the Royal charter required that all resident members
of the company be native-born children of the British Empire.[17]
Nureyev was a complete break with the past. No other dancer in
the three-decade history of the Royal debuted in London in a
tailor-made Ashton original, and none of the subsequent Royal
guests, such as Chauviré from Paris and then Bruhn from Copenhagen, danced more than a handful of performances in London at
a time. By the end of 1962, Nureyev clearly was set for a longer
haul with the company, and, beginning with his status as "permanent guest artist," virtually every aspect of his Royal career was
unprecedented. Choreographers lined up to use him. By the end
of his first year of work with the Royal, Nureyev's repertory
already included ballets by the three most important British choreographers of the era—Ashton, John Cranko, and Kenneth Mac-
Millan. A year later he was adding his own ballets to the company
repertory: the *Bayadère* shades scene; a pas de six from *Laurencia*; the first full-length *Raymonda* in the West for the Royal's
touring company. Even more unusual, de Valois let Nureyev do
anything and everything he wanted in his performances of the
company's standing repertory, ballets that had gone unchanged
since the flood. "Madame de Valois at that point," according to
Sibley, "never let anybody change one step of any production to
suit themselves. The lighting never changed nor was any entrance
changed to make it better for a particular dancer. But Rudolf

wanted a different entrance. He wanted different lighting that Michael Somes had been asking for for years. He wanted to do different steps. Madam let him have everything he wanted."[18] When Kenneth MacMillan handcrafted his *Romeo and Juliette* on the specific talents of Lynn Seymour and Christopher Gable in 1964, the premiere performance still went to Fonteyn/Nureyev; Seymour/Gable were fifth cast.

The Soviets, however, were not letting Nureyev go quietly, and his early years in the West were spent in perpetual fear of the KGB. "Especially at the very beginning," the choreographer Glen Tetley remembers, "Rudi would fly into a panic at the sight of a man in a black raincoat."[19] Nureyev's KGB tormentors kept him in a constant state of anxiety. Years into his Western career, Nureyev was still receiving mysterious backstage telephone calls moments before he was to begin a performance. Some of them were threats. Even more unsettling, many of them were from his mother, who clearly was being forced to badger her son into a return to Russia. By 1963, Nureyev's presence in London was beginning to have larger political ramifications. The Soviets were ready to withdraw from a recent cultural exchange program with the British government in protest over Nureyev's association with the Royal. In February 1963 Sir David Webster, the head of Covent Garden, was forced to make a special trip to Moscow after the Soviets began threatening to cancel a month-long London engagement by the Bolshoi Ballet scheduled for June. The situation was serious enough that Sol Hurok, who was set to sponsor an American tour by the Royal later in the year, extended a business tour of Europe to include a pit stop in Moscow while Webster was there. The British held their ground, which is more than can be said for the French. A guest appearance Nureyev was scheduled to make in *Giselle* with Chauviré at the Paris Opéra Ballet in April 1963 was canceled by the Opéra's director, who, according to *Variety*, "gave in when it appeared that Nureyev's stint could endanger the good cultural exchange relationship between Russia and France. Many Russo singers and dancers have appeared at the Opéra, with others due, and Opéra ballet stars were due for a Russian tour when the *affaires* Nureyev came up."[20] Once again, the Soviet strong-arm was the wrong tactic. "I would not have courage to stay in the West unless provoked," Nureyev told an interviewer.[21] He was frightened into giving up all hopes of a return.

At Covent Garden, the free hand de Valois gave Nureyev did not endear him to the other Royal dancers. The fire and flamboyance of Nureyev's performance style was the complete antithesis of the neat, tidy, restrained English school of ballet. The British press took due note that Nureyev's stage manners could use a little polish, particularly in the company of his milder British brethren. No English dancer would, as Nureyev did on the first night of *Bayadère*, abandon a solo before its ending because he was unhappy with his performance up to that point. A British dancer would never, as Nureyev did at a gala matinee, suddenly throw his shoes into the wings and continue dancing barefoot. Even Sibley, who became a dedicated friend, remembers the general atmosphere as charged: "We were furious when we saw de Valois letting Rudolf make all these changes, but we sent him up as much as he sent us up. The dancers didn't let him get away with anything, and I think he knew what he was up against with us."[22]

Nureyev's example had a galvanizing effect on the fleet of up-and-coming young British danseurs. David Wall, who was a student at the Royal Ballet School when Nureyev came to London and went on to become one of the Royal's finest dancers, remembers the impact of seeing Nureyev for the first time: "His magnetism on the stage, his technical expertise, and his total commitment—at the age of sixteen, if you were near that, there was no way you couldn't be influenced by it."[23] Nureyev's impact on the senior men of the company, however, one longtime Royal follower recalls, "was devastating. It destroyed David Blair's career.[24] And some of the women came to hate him even more. Margot was finally on her way out. The others were finally going to get their shot and then—boom! Nureyev, and she's not going anywhere." Late in his life, Nigel Gosling remembered a friend's synopsis of Nureyev's impact on the Royal Ballet: "Nureyev was like the Great War. He wiped out an entire generation of dancers."[25]

Just as they'd been at the Kirov, Nureyev's offstage manners could be salt on an open wound. "It was hard for Rudi at the very beginning," Sonia Arova, an early friend and colleague, remembers. "He was in a totally different world in the West and didn't know how to function, what people were like here. He had a cunning kind of mind and kept his distance until he knew when someone was coming to him as a friend or coming to him to get something out of him."[26] A nervous Nureyev easily became a bitchy Nureyev. "You dance like you are wearing galoshes!" Nureyev yelled at the assembled corps of the Royal during an early *Bayadère* rehearsal, about the time he complained to a British journalist that the Covent Garden stage was "the best in the world. For fires. For dancing it stinks."[27] Relations remained tense until the success of *La Bayadère* in 1963, which, according to a Royal Ballet junior ballerina, Georgina Parkinson, "completely turned things around. After *Bayadère*, things changed. He worked more closely with us as a dancer and we learned that he could be extremely generous with his knowledge. Until then, however, his behavior was generally not the best. He had a temper, and he was certainly not afraid to use it. We had been brought up to do as we were told, and it seemed to us that Rudolf was not sufficiently respectful."[28] Parkinson also remembers that the Royal dancers, despite their onstage reserve, were less than afraid to hold their ground when Nureyev went too far:

I remember a stage rehearsal for *Daphnis and Chloë*. Margot was rehearsing with the company—I can't remember who her partner was—and, immediately after, she had a stage rehearsal with Rudolf for *Corsaire*. There is a large, isolated tree upstage in the *Daphnis and Chloë* set, and, with the full company working onstage, Rudolf walked out of the wings in his layers and layers of rehearsal clothes, took hold of the tree, and began giving himself his warm-up barre. It was absolutely mind-blowing. A group of the male principals—

the big butch boys, too—went over and bodily removed him from the stage. It was potentially quite violent.[29]

For the senior Royal ballerina Nadia Nerina, Nureyev's personal qualities left a lasting impression on the future course of the Royal's history:

Rudi was as cute as a baby cheetah. He grasped situations within seconds, intuitively guessing people's weakness and strengths. Madame de Valois had no child of her own. He sensed the void and set out to be the son she had never had. During rehearsals he would sit cross-legged at her feet, gazing up at her, chatting away and teasing her as would a naughty child. On one occasion he cajoled her into getting up and demonstrating variations on the *pas de bourrée,* which she did in high spirits. She was proud of the intricate, quick, neat footwork of the English school that she founded. She was proud of her own prowess. Only Rudi could have got her to "perform." Her discipline over dancers was rigid. No one would have dared to carry on as Rudi did. She behaved as if she were a doting mother with her favorite spoilt child, and Rudi played it for all he was worth. If he arrived late for rehearsals, a rare occurrence for any dancer, he would teasingly mimic her, completely disarming her. During the years that he was with the company, his wayward behavior and Madam's inability to come to terms with him not only demoralized the company, especially the male contingent, but put Madam in a somewhat equivocal position, to the extent, in my view, that, feeling compromised, she felt it necessary to retire far sooner than was necessary. Her sad decision is a point of historic importance in the history of the Royal Ballet company, for she retired far too early for the good of the company. If you question whether I believe that Rudi was to blame, the answer is yes.[30]

For all the Sturm und Drang, Nureyev established some of the most enduring friendships of his life during his years with the Royal, particularly among the emergent generation of ballerinas who were so much closer to his own age than Fonteyn. He developed a particularly devoted relationship with Lynn Seymour, the great dramatic dancer of the era and a woman whose outspokenness and flamboyance Nureyev appreciated. "He knew that I was ready for anything, really," Seymour remembers. "If he wanted to go to some dive or a strip show or something like that, I'd go."[31] Nureyev nicknamed Seymour Kabuki Lil. "Rudolf saved my life, over and over," Seymour recalls. "When times were hard and I couldn't find work, he'd find work for me. People love to go on about Rudolf's tantrums—I never once saw him lose his temper in a studio without good reason—but he was the most generous of friends."[32] The friendship only deepened with the passage of time. "We have shared secrets," Seymour wrote in her autobiography, "strolling arm-in-arm down Las Ramblas in Barcelona and swimming in the Mediterranean at Tel Aviv— nocturnal confessions before the sky is streaked with the light of a new day. Touring with the Royal Ballet or guesting with other companies in *Giselle*, *Swan Lake*, *Romeo* and *The Sleeping Beauty*, Rudi and I always managed to find ourselves with adjoining rooms and adjoining balconies, watching the sun come up with a bottle of champagne beside us. And slowly, as the sun overwhelmed the sky, we would polish off the champagne."[33] Merle Park has equally tender memories:

> Rudolf could be so generous. He was incredibly sweet and helpful when I was going through my divorce. "Come on, girl. Into the studio. We work." Five years later, when I told him I was going to remarry, he said, "I will ask you one thing. Does he make you laugh?" That's all. He didn't ask my husband's name, what he did for a living, how much money he made. Just, "Does he make you laugh?" He really was like a brother to me and I still find it quite hard to talk about him. He knew his life was going to be short, and he had to cram it all in. I'd say, "Rudolf, you'll kill yourself if you don't slow down. How can you go on like this?" His answer was simple. "Well, girl, what better way to die."[34]

"The Royal Ballet will be my permanent home," Nureyev told a British reporter in 1965, while remaining characteristically elusive about his actual plans. "I don't know what I have with them. I never sign any papers. They give me a timetable—timetable? is that right?—of what I am to dance. When I see a big window, two months maybe, I go somewhere else. They said at Christmas I am here and I am here."[35] Nureyev's only public reference to a permanent home, the comments were, in fact, an elliptical bulletin to the leadership of the Royal Ballet. By mid-decade Nureyev already was beginning to feel that changes in the administration of the Royal were edging him away from the center of the company's activities. His guest appearances elsewhere became more frequent, and the number of works he was making for other companies grew steadily: *Swan Lake* for the Vienna State Opera in 1964; *Raymonda* for the Australian Ballet in 1965; in 1966 his first original ballet, *Tancredi*, to a score by Hans Werner Henze, and his first *Sleeping Beauty*, at La Scala. Until at least the early 1970s he wanted a steady home with the Royal. After a series of rented apartments, Nureyev bought his first real home in 1967, a rambling Victorian estate in Richmond Park on the outskirts of London. Jerome Robbins remembers that, when he staged his watershed Chopin ballet *Dances at a Gathering* for the Royal in 1970, "many of the English felt that it was the first time [Rudolf] looked like a member of the company."[36] Comfortable or not, Nureyev still had his antennae up. He'd begun looking elsewhere as well.

By the mid-1970s, as she approached her midfifties, the number of Fonteyn's appearances at Covent Garden had been reduced drastically, and so had Nureyev's. "They always kept me only as partner to Margot," Nureyev later remembered, "and the moment she left they said, 'See you next year,' and they pushed me out."[37] For the rest of his career, Nureyev made only token guest appearances with the Royal.

The fresh exile left a scar.

"The moment [Margot] ceased to dance," Nureyev told the British journalist Mavis Richardson in a 1981 Thames Television interview,

> there was incredible urge to demote me, to turn me from identity into nonentity. Only thing I was serving was to fill

the house, to be tea cozy to keep teapot warm, and then get rid of as fast as possible. Clear the deck. Bring public in and then clear the deck. Go to America. Fill those theaters. Then kick in the ass. Out.

You don't wait around Covent Garden, begging for next piece of bread crumb. Or Kirov or Leningrad and waiting for whatever, waiting for party blessings. You just go and thank God West is still free. You go and organize your life. If Covent Garden can't provide you with work, you go and get it somewhere else. You get off your ass and go.

Eleven

The Nureyev
Industry

"I'll tell you how he made that much money. The man never picked up a check in his life."

—a Parisian who prefers to
remain anonymous

fter sex, money is the aspect of Nureyev's off-stage life that most often causes little beads of sweat to bubble across the foreheads of his friends and colleagues. Conversation comes to a withering halt, glasses of wine disappear in a gulp, and the subject is closed as soon as it's been opened. (I actually saw a veteran European choreographer—a man not known for keeping his mouth shut—turn sheet white at the very mention of Nureyev's vast financial holdings.) Everyone agrees that Nureyev was not a man to squander his cash—except on himself. "When Rudolf traveled," a colleague from the Opéra recalls, "he bought and bought and bought—never for anyone else, always for himself." Guests in his homes, however, wanted for nothing. Nureyev was a generous, gregarious host, and his table was consistently first-rate. In public, in nightclubs and restaurants, Nureyev became famous for an impediment in his reach. "Rudolf was not cheap in the way that very famous people can be," a second French friend explains. "He just never carried money on him." A third Opéra colleague is more blunt: "In a restaurant Rudolf considered it

178

your privilege to pick up the check, for the privilege of his company."

No one has a precise answer for how Nureyev became the wealthiest man in ballet, with an estate estimated in *Vanity Fair* of $80 million.[1] (The British estimate in *The Sunday Times* was noticeably less, between £10 and £15 million, or $15 to $25 million.[2]) "Do you realize the amount of money that is?" a prominent New York socialite and Nureyev friend for decades said not long after his death, still slightly stupefied by the sum.

> That's not the kind of money a person makes, unless, God forbid, you're Donald Trump. That's money someone is born into. Rudolf had seven homes. He had his own island, for God's sake. Do you have any idea how expensive it is to maintain seven homes? The overhead expenses have to be astronomical—the insurance, the staff, the upkeep. The taxes alone would kill you. A friend and I actually sat down with paper and pencil and tried to work out the figures. It's impossible. The most I ever heard of any ballet dancer making was ten thousand dollars a performance, back when people were flying to the Met to see Misha and Makarova. Even if Rudolf made that kind of money every night of his life, you're not talking anywhere near eighty million dollars. And for a ballet dancer! Someone was very smart somewhere.

In attempting to unravel the mysteries of the Nureyev Industry—and make no mistake, Nureyev was a one-man show business empire—the only verifiable fact is that the brains behind the operation belonged to Nureyev himself, a sharp, careful businessman with a close eye on the purse strings who hated taxes more than death. "Rudi," Nadia Nerina explains, "had his feet on the ground when it came to money: he knew what it was to have to survive and eat and was not going to throw his money around. He managed his own career well and was quite aware of his own financial value."[3] Sonia Arova, another of Nureyev's earliest partners in the West, agrees with Nerina: "Rudolf really knew what he was doing with his career. Nothing was done on impulse when it came to that."[4] Nureyev was also savvy enough to surround himself with world-rank financial advisors. His financial trust was not easily won. During his first months in the West, Nureyev insisted on being paid in cash. The spotlight on his defection made Nureyev as bankable a name as existed, and producers agreed to the cash payments. (There are reports as late as 1977, the heyday of the "dance boom," when the Kirov émigrés were making up to ten thousand dollars a performance, that Nureyev still demanded cash payments on occasion and still got them.) Despite the amount of money he was already making with the de Cuevas company and from his first television appearances —the largest sum of money Nureyev's dazzled eyes had ever seen—he kept such a tight fist on his income that he wouldn't even open a bank account during his first six months in the West. He finally did so only by default, when Arova refused to walk around any longer with sixty thousand dollars cash in her pocketbook. (Another old friend remembers going to the New York apartment Nureyev was renting during his first visit to New York. She tried to help Nureyev clean up a bit but had trouble with a floor rug with several odd mounds that would not flatten. When she finally pulled the rug back, she discovered that the mounds were piles of money Nureyev was hiding.) Arova opened a bank account on her own in the name of a mutual friend and told Nureyev about it only after the deed was done: "Rudolf was furious. He went green."[5] Once advisors were proven trustworthy, however, Nureyev stayed with them. Nureyev worked with the same business manager, a crackerjack Hungarian consultant named Sandor Gorlinsky, from 1962 until Gorlinsky's death in May 1990. His principal lawyer, Barry Weinstein in Chicago, was Nureyev's legal counsel for more than twenty years.[6]

Despite the amount of money he eventually accumulated —and the obvious pleasure Nureyev took in being rich, rich, rich —it's unlikely that avarice was a factor in his choice to remain in the West. Ballet dancers are not only cherished public figures in Russia, but they live in relative comfort and security—good clothes, the choicest of city apartments, summer dachas. (One of Nureyev's first purchases after joining the Kirov was his first automobile, the status symbol of choice in the Khrushchev era. His choice of vehicle was early evidence of the pennywise Nureyev: he opted for a Soviet make rather than the more expensive Western automobiles preferred by his friends.) Once he was on his own in the West, however, Nureyev caught on to his financial prospects almost immediately, and he quickly developed clear, considered opinions on how his new wealth was to be handled. The British merchant banker Charles Gordon, Nadia Nerina's husband, was Nureyev's first unofficial advisor in the West.[7] Gordon remembers a conversation over dinner with Nerina and Erik Bruhn in the early months of 1962: "Without any ceremony Nureyev immediately said to me in his halting English, 'Charlik, Erik say you help me. I am poor man—no money. I want to make money. Tax free!' The last two words somewhat startled me and I perceived that he was watching me closely to see how I would react to his use of a term with which even literate accountants were not then entirely familiar."[8] A comparable acuity and attention characterized Nureyev's financial dealings to his deathbed—literally. Under Gorlinsky's careful guidance, Nureyev had at some point established charitable foundations in Europe and America as a means of reducing his taxable income. The Rudolf Nureyev Dance Foundation in the United States owned his apartment in the Dakota in New York City as well as the majority of his financial concerns in America,[9] and his European interests were the property of the Ballet Promotion Foundation, based in Liechtenstein, the tiny European principality wedged between Austria and Switzerland. According to Jennette Thurnheer, "in legal terms, Rudolf himself owned practically nothing."[10] The arrangement had one final benefit for the beneficiaries of Nureyev's estate: since Nureyev was not the legal owner of his holdings, his estate was not subject to the standard inheritance taxes and remained intact.[11]

Nureyev's first great stroke of luck in stabilizing and extending his business affairs was Gorlinsky. According to Charles Gordon, who introduced the two men in 1962, Sandor Gorlinsky was "a gravelly-voiced, cigar-chomping Sol Hurok *manqué* with a heart of gold."[12] For Nureyev, he was the right manager at the right time with the right connections. The two men hit it off immediately. "Gorlinsky really helped Rudolf to make the right decisions from the very beginning," Sonia Arova remembers. "He really was there to help, and he did."[13] At the suggestion of Charles Gordon, Gorlinsky established Nureyev's first international tax shelter in 1962, a move that would serve his new client well for years and become a model for their future business activities. "In those days," Gordon explained in *The Spectator*, "for non-residents and off-shore investment, Luxembourg was very practical. I advised Sandor that unless he had already done so for his other clients . . . he should form a special Luxembourg company, and that this company 'owned by Rudi' was to have the sole right to receive any fees earned by him, that is, paid without any deductions. This essentially tax-free structure would secure Nureyev's cash flow and establish an increasing net worth. I told Sandor who to contact in Luxembourg and he did his stuff to perfection."[14] Gorlinsky remained on top of the game for the rest of his association with Nureyev and is regarded widely as the man who secured Nureyev's fortune. "I suspect Rudolf let Gorlinsky handle everything," Nerina, also a Gorlinsky client, suggests, "but part of Gorlinsky's success was due to the fact that, on major engagements and decisions, he always consulted thoroughly with his clients. With clients like Maria Callas and Tito Gobbi, Sandor was experienced in dealing with stars. Sandor and Rudolf got on well because there was trust. There were others who were sharper, but they did not match Sandor's integrity."[15] An influential French ballerina who was a long-standing friend of both Nureyev and Gorlinsky remembers a chance encounter she had with the latter in the late 1970s: "I met Sandor on the street one day and he was in an exceptionally good mood. I commented on his high spirits and he told me that it was because he had just managed to double Rudolf's money. There had been a fluctuation in the international market, some sort of very unusual shift in the price of gold at the Bourse for about forty-eight hours. Sandor noticed it immediately, knew what it meant, and doubled Rudolf's worth almost overnight."

Gorlinsky was also smart enough to realize that representing Nureyev was the opportunity of a lifetime, and the numbers were there to prove it. Nureyev was a top-dollar attraction from day one. Until his arrival in the West, the highest recorded salary for any ballet dancer was the $2,000 a week Sergei Denham's Ballet Russe de Monte Carlo paid Maria Tallchief in 1954. Tallchief, of course, had been a ranking star for almost a decade at the time, and her career as de facto prima ballerina of Balanchine's New York City Ballet in the early 1950s made her the most celebrated woman in American ballet, the first American-born ballerina to have her photograph on the cover of *Newsweek*. (Tallchief was literally Native American, the granddaughter of an Osage chief.) Nureyev was offered $2,000 a week for his first job in the West, the six months he spent touring with the de Cuevas company in 1961. In October of that year he received $4,000 for a twenty-minute guest shot on German television.[16] By the midsixties the money was rolling in from the constant guest appearances around the world at an estimated $3,000 to $5,000 each. Nureyev was receiving his first residual fees for his ballets—he received a fee every time the Royal performed his version of the *Bayadère* Shades scene—and a record $42,000 annual salary with the Royal.[17] (The sum is based on the approximate value in dollars of the sterling in 1965.) The list of Nureyev's acquisitions through the 1960s suggests a man with a solid sense of financial security: $100,000 for the La Turbie villa in the hills just above Monte Carlo in 1962,[18] at least $135,000 for his Richmond Park estate just outside London in 1967 (six bedrooms, four reception rooms, and a thirty-foot drawing room), and a Mercedes-Benz convertible.

With Gorlinsky at the helm, the Nureyev Industry was in full swing, as were the Nureyev Wars with tax bureaus on both sides of the Atlantic. Neither would abate. A full decade after the Rudimania phenomenon of the midsixties, a four-week Paris engagement by his Nureyev and Friends concert group at the six thousand-seat Palais des Sports played to 97 percent capacity every night. Although Nureyev's last sad tour of Britain in the spring of 1991 opened to a storm of demands for ticket refunds over the pathetic decline in Nureyev's dancing; the stormy confusion of the opening belied the fact that later performances were sold out at every stop on the three-week tour. Its closing night, in the very theater where the first protest had taken place, was completely sold out. As early as 1963, Nureyev was crossing swords with the English authorities over his tax status. The same year, after an audit Uncle Sam slapped him with a bill for $30,642.70 in overdue taxes from his American earnings. Nureyev paid the bill but subsequently informed the Internal Revenue Service that he had been overcharged $213 in Social Security deductions. Yet another record in a lifetime of precedents, Nureyev forced the IRS to give him back the money.[19] The disputes that led to his departure from the Paris Opéra Ballet in 1989 began with yet another skirmish in Nureyev's endless war with the French tax system. "Give money to the government," Nureyev told Arova his first year in the West. "Why? I do the work."[20]

Nureyev's introduction to Sol Hurok was his second stroke of good fortune. Nureyev and, as Edwin Denby called him, "Da Hurok," shared a considerable amount of common ground. They were both Russian émigrés who had grown up in bitter poverty. Masters of their respective fields, they both developed a taste for the lavish. They both knew how to work a cape in public. If Nureyev was the new Nijinsky, Hurok was the last Diaghilev, a master impresario of the old school. By the time he and Nureyev met in 1963, Hurok had been booking the best in the business for more than half a century, Melba and Chaliapin, Pavlova, Duncan, and Mary Wigman, Andrés Segovia, Artur Rubinstein, Van Cliburn, and Marian Anderson. Hurok had a particular fondness for dance and for dancers, despite the fact that, at the peak of the Depression, he lost seventy-five-thousand dollars on the first American tour of the Ballet Russe de Monte Carlo. According to John Wilson, a senior member of the Hurok staff for many years, "Hurok was the man who made ballet box office in this country. He brought the Royal Ballet to America for that famous first tour in 1949 and then he brought over all of the Russians—the

Moiseyev in 1958, the Bolshoi in 1960, and then the Kirov in 1961.''[21]

Nureyev didn't officially join the Hurok stable until 1965, but Hurok was clearly aware of his box office possibilities when he joined Sir David Webster on the 1963 visit to Moscow to straighten out "the Nureyev situation." As the man who sponsored the Russian tours to the West that were so lucrative for both sides, Hurok's presence in Moscow during negotiations added considerable clout to the British argument for keeping Nureyev at Covent Garden. When Nureyev joined the official client list of Hurok Concerts, his life changed once again, and not just because the Hurok organization created the "Rudi" phenomenon. Hurok knew how to keep a diva happy, and he was famous for the personal attention lavished upon his clientele. "If they're not temperamental," Hurok once said, "I don't want them. It's in the nature of great artists to be that way. There's something in them —some warmth, some fire—that projects into an audience and makes it respond. Give me the temperamental artist every time.''[22] Nureyev got the full Hurok treatment and loved every minute of it. Hurok insured Nureyev's legs with Lloyd's of London, and, according to Wilson, he bought José Limón's classic *Othello* quartet *The Moor's Pavane* for Nureyev and brought in Limón himself to teach it to him. "What Rudolf wanted," Wilson concludes, "Rudolf got.''[23] According to another former Hurok employee, the royal treatment included a tacit understanding that all of Nureyev's needs were to be met, sexual and otherwise: "The Hurok court included someone, an old Russian, whose job more or less was to make sure that Rudi was happy. Part of his job, as I understood it, was making sure there was a steady flow of boys."

Nureyev's life wasn't the only thing that changed when he hooked up with Hurok, particularly after Nureyev, headlining his *Don Quixote* on the Australian Ballet's first visit to America in 1971, sold out an eleven-week tour at every stop—without Fonteyn. The Australian tour also introduced another new development in Nureyev's career, the one Nureyev had been waiting for: the most important element in its success was the fact that Nureyev danced at almost every performance on the tour, thanks to the attentive scheduling by the Hurok office that allowed him the rest periods necessary to pull off this unprecedented feat. Light bulbs lit up in many a head. However ethereal, ballet is a business like any other, and, when Hurok was involved, it was big business. The Hurok organization, Clive Barnes wrote in the *New York Times* in 1975, was "almost unique in the large-scale arts organizations in that it needs to make a buck. It needs a profit and it is not subsidized."[24] When Hurok discovered that all he needed to rake in the cash was Nureyev—not a mammoth effort such as the Bolshoi or Royal Ballet tours, but Nureyev, dancing with anyone—the future of ballet companies around the world was written.

The North American tours of the Royal Ballet sponsored by Hurok Concerts through the sixties—first in 1963, on the wings of the "Rudi" mania the Hurok office had generated by 1965, and then once each in the last three years of the decade— always included stops in Canada, late of Her Majesty's empire. The links between the Royal Ballet and the National Ballet of Canada were strong; the National Ballet's founding director, Celia Franca, was a Royal alumna. Nureyev was a frequent visitor to Toronto through the 1960s—site of the Yonge Street arrest— particularly once Bruhn had signed on in Toronto as an associate artistic director in 1963. On a surprise jaunt to Toronto to visit Bruhn in January 1965, Nureyev made an unscheduled debut with the National Ballet when Bruhn developed a foot injury and was unable to dance his next performance of the *La Sylphide* he'd just made for the Canadian company. Despite a sprained ankle and a recent round in the hospital for tonsillitis, Nureyev went on as Bruhn's replacement with two days of rehearsal. "I don't care if my ankle is broken," he told his old buddy Lynn Seymour. "I've wanted to do this ballet for a long time and here is a chance to dance it—and with you, Lil."[25] Nureyev partnered his Kabuki Lil in Bruhn's *Sylphide* and got nineteen curtain calls.[26]

After his success with the Australians and *Don Q*, Nure-

yev approached Hurok about a new project—a touring version of
The Sleeping Beauty with the National Ballet of Canada. "The
idea was Rudolf's to a great extent," John Wilson remembers,
"but it struck Hurok favorably. For a long time he'd wanted a
Beauty that could tour. *Beauty* was a solid moneymaker, but the
productions Hurok had sponsored with the Royal and with the
Kirov were really too big for travel. Certain cities were especially
difficult to play because the sets were built in such a way that they
couldn't be reduced to accommodate smaller stages."[27] Hurok was
taken by Nureyev's idea. His involvement with the new *Sleeping
Beauty* Nureyev staged for the National Ballet of Canada in 1972
was even more hands-on than usual. "Until Rudolf's tours with
the Canadians," former Hurok publicist John Gingritch explains,
"Hurok essentially took existing productions and presented them
to new audiences. With Rudolf's *Sleeping Beauty*, Hurok moved
from a booking role to a role closer to that of a producer. It was a
shrewd move. Hurok went to a company that would be thrilled
to get to New York and the Met, and his professional stature
generated enough Toronto-based money to underwrite the production. Nureyev's *Beauty* became a new model for how to tour
a production. The production looked great, but it was portable."[28]
Designed by Nicholas Georgiadis and with a budget estimated at
almost $400,000—Nureyev made his entrance aloft, on a cur-
tained litter held by four serving men—Nureyev's *Sleeping
Beauty* for the National Ballet of Canada turned out to be a gold
mine for all concerned—Hurok, Nureyev, and the Canadians.
The production premiered at the National Arts Centre in Ottawa
on September 1, 1972, before moving on to the O'Keefe Center
in Toronto. It opened to ecstatic notices and then went on a five-
week North American tour that did record business at every stop,
the first of three Hurok-sponsored tours that turned the National
Ballet of Canada from a local company with a modest reputation
into a troupe of international standing.

    In an unprecedented marketing strategy, Nureyev and the
Canadians shared equal billing on all promotional material and
advertisements—the same typeface and exactly the same size.
Not everyone was thrilled by the idea of equal billing, and, by

1975, Nureyev was back in the vortex of a tornado. While he and the Canadians were in the middle of their third summer visit to the Metropolitan Opera House, the Toronto critic John Fraser, writing in the *New York Times*, published a scathing account of the Nureyev years at the National Ballet of Canada: "We have learned to cope with Nureyev's temperamental quirks—shouting at dancers onstage during performances, outrageous tantrums in rehearsals and during intermissions, and indifference to the national aspirations of the company. Such is the price a troupe pays when it hitches its lot to a passing star."[29] When the Toronto newspapers began making reference to "Nureyev's National Ballet," Nureyev refused to speak to the Canadian press for four years. However unhappy some of the locals, Nureyev's *Sleeping Beauty* for the Canadians also introduced two of his most important legacies to contemporary ballet companies. Over the next ten years, they would reshape troupes from Boston to Berlin, from Zurich to Paris. With Nureyev as their headliner, struggling regional companies suddenly found themselves in the exalted surroundings of Hurokland, performing in major theaters to huge audiences they could never have reached without Nureyev's name on a marquee. "By his very presence," Celia Franca concludes about Nureyev's time with the National Ballet of Canada, "we were given the opportunity for a kind of exposure we'd never known before. The tours were long, which meant steady employment, and the dancers got used to performing, and to performing often."[30] Most important of all, at Nureyev's insistence, a host of young dancers were thrust into an international spotlight. The unbroken line of Nureyev discoveries extends from Karen Kain and Frank Augustyn with the National Ballet of Canada—both of whom Nureyev yanked out of the ranks under much protest from administrators and company directors and set them on the path to world stature—to the fleet of ecstatic young star dancers Nureyev cultivated at the Paris Opéra in the 1980s.

His tenure with the Canadians established some important precedents for Nureyev's career as well. Until the end of the 1970s, Nureyev was an annual summer presence at the Metropolitan Opera House, contributing significantly to the financial health of the Met by filling the house for several weeks between the end of its spring season and the opening of the new opera season in the fall. At the same time, a new phrase entered the ballet lexicon: "Presenting Rudolf Nureyev and . . ." It would soon become familiar to audiences around the world, and one of the oldest traditions in ballet management disappeared. Until Nureyev and the Canadians, the ballet company itself was the event. Its stars were the icing on the cake. Nureyev and the Canadians shifted the balance of power. "We weren't selling the Canadians," a Hurok staff member explains. "We were selling Rudolf and the Canadians." (When Nureyev injured his foot on the last leg of the 1973 tour and could not go on, the final stop on the tour, an SRO engagement at the Kennedy Center, had to be canceled.) Nureyev found himself in the professional situation of his dreams: dancing his own version of the classic repertory and raking in an enormous personal salary as dancer, choreographer, and coproducer. Even better, his contract guaranteed his appearance at every performance, matinees excepted.

Nureyev's success with the Canadians led to the career move that would keep him onstage for the next sixteen years and expand his audience beyond measure. In the summer of 1974, Nureyev had performed a two-week chamber program with a group of seven other dancers at the Palais des Sports in Paris. The venture proved not only successful but, with only the barest overhead, lucrative as well. The day after Christmas 1974, Nureyev appeared on Broadway at the Uris Theater for three weeks with another concert troupe, this time sponsored by Hurok: Nureyev and Friends. Backed up by Merle Park of the Royal Ballet, the American dancer and choreographer (and sometime Nureyev flame) Louis Falco,[31] and members of the Paul Taylor Dance Company, Nureyev danced an eclectic program of short ballets—an extract from Balanchine's *Apollo*, Limón's *Moor's Pavane*, Taylor's *Aureole*, and the pas de deux from Bournonville's *Flower Festival at Genzano*. From a business angle, the idea was inspired. "The performance involved only a minimum overhead," John Wilson explains. "There were very few dancers, fourteen musicians, and no scenery. That's why it made so much money."[32]

Business only got better as the Nureyev and Friends concerts evolved into regular Broadway events. By the third season in 1978, three weeks of Nureyev and Friends raked in more than $500,000 in net gross, with estimates on Nureyev's take running as high as $45,000 a week.[33] The performances were also attracting an audience that would never consider sitting through a three-act ballet. "Merle Park—if they had her name plastered all over town I wouldn't go because I don't know her," Ben Weinstein, a clothier from Queens told the *New York Times* during the second Nureyev and Friends season at the Uris. "Generally I'm not fond of ballet at all. You may not like baseball, but when you know Babe Ruth is playing, you go. I wanted to see Nureyev."[34]

Nureyev had evolved from an industry into an institution.

Twelve

Who's Afraid of
Martha and George?

*"It took Martha Graham to finally give us Rudi
in the nudi."*

—ARLENE CROCE, After-Images

On Sunday, March 14, 1971, Nureyev quietly but firmly added another notch to the bedpost of his professional conquests. No quickie, this one would alter the scope and length of his career and help rewrite the future of dance. Along with Tom "It's Not Unusual" Jones and Barbra Streisand, Nureyev appeared as a guest on a Burt Bacharach television special, dancing with the Paul Taylor Dance Company in Taylor's Armageddon comic strip, *Big Bertha*, which Taylor had reworked to the theme music from *Butch Cassidy and the Sundance Kid*, no less.

For a night, there was a truce in the Arab/Israeli conflict of the dance world—the war between ballet and modern that had waged unabated for half a century. Twenty years later, when the former combatants are such dependable—and lucrative—friends (how else could there be a Mark Morris?) it's easy to forget that that first liaison between Nureyev and the Taylor company was, for its time, the equivalent of blasphemy. Ballet dancers did not mingle with those barefoot people—and vice versa. "Nureyev must get a great deal of credit for building the bridge from ballet to modern dance," the American choreographer Murray Louis wrote. "He took the plunge, he took the largest gamble, he had the most to lose. He saw this other movement vocabulary as something he had to try, and above all he had the courage to do it, not as an experiment with one choreographer, but a steady development with several. He saw it too as an investment in his future. It was inconceivable for him to retire from dancing at the height of his prowess and he had no intention of doing so. The modern dance promised longevity to his performance career."[1] Nureyev's lucky star had made an unexpected appearance. Contemporary dance offered Nureyev two welcome, and well-timed, surrogates. It presented a vast field for exploration as, through the 1970s, Nureyev's appearances at Covent Garden diminished in number and his technique began to show strain. By the time of the first Taylor interlude in 1971, Nureyev was already thirty-three years old. It's the age when male dancers begin to consider their options.

Nureyev also loved a good fight, and the tenacity with which he explored the dance world outside ballet thrust him straight into the front lines. The standoff between the champions of classic ballet and the pioneers of a modern dance was more than a matter of competition. On both sides, these were believers, and the lines of battle were drawn with the kind of fervor that inspires crusades and ritual sacrifice. (The early modern dancers, in fact, won the rabidity sweepstakes. Simply studying with a second teacher was considered grounds for excommunication.) To the adherents of Mary Wigman's *ausdruckstanz* experiments in Weimar Germany and Martha Graham's dialogue with her soul in America, the artifice of ballet was evil incarnate—shallow, trivial, the last desperate link to a ruling class that was better dead and buried. For ballet dancers, the new barefoot dancing was the same vision of hell—incoherent, strident, and, most offensive of all, ugly. From the moment Isadora Duncan declared herself "an enemy of the ballet," the leaders on both sides reveled in shock tactics. The Rosetta Stone of modern dance, Graham proclaimed that movement was a product of the genitals, setting many a repressed swan aflutter. No slouch in the broadside department, her arch rival, Balanchine's champion Lincoln Kirstein, predicted that, were Graham to give birth, her only possible offspring would be a cube. The closest ballet and modern had ever come to a truce was the clearest evidence of how wide a bridge Nureyev had to build. Barely two years before Nureyev arrived in the West, Balanchine and Graham created a new work together, *Episodes*, for New York City Ballet. The meeting of the two masters was a ceasefire in name only. Balanchine and Graham did not so much work together as work in tandem. Balanchine did his section of the ballet, Graham did hers, and never the twain did meet.[2]

Enter Nureyev, the man who wanted to dance everything —and did. Onstage and off, Nureyev was a walking set of contradictions—generous and tightfisted, violent and endearing, funny and cruel. The most surprising incongruity of all is the fact that a man who spent a lifetime pummeling his stubborn body into the outline of a premier danseur invested as much time and focus as Nureyev did in realigning his body into its exact opposite— the angular, temporal, earthbound dimensions of a modern dancer. Over the course of his Western career, Nureyev worked with more choreographers than any other star dancer in the history of ballet. The majority of them were not ballet choreographers but choreographers working in the grittier territory of a modern dance.

The Royal, as things turned out, was the ideal place to get his bare feet wet. Although, technically, Taylor's truncated TV edition of *Big Bertha* was the first time Nureyev danced without ballet slippers (excepting, of course, the famous performance of *Bayadère* when he ripped off his shoes midvariation and threw them into the wings), the range of the Royal's original repertory during the 1960s introduced Nureyev to a group of choreographers who were attempting to redirect the vocabulary of classic ballet into a new idiom, something darker and more driven, closer to the cutting edge of reality, a danced argot that dealt less with the otherworldly than with the needs and neuroses of a continent ravaged by World War II.

The shift began in France in the first decade after the war, with a new wave of choreographers led by Roland Petit and

Maurice Béjart, both of whom would be working with Nureyev before the end of the 1960s. The landmark success of Petit's *Le jeune homme et la mort* in 1946 and Béjart's *Symphonie pour un homme seul* a decade later introduced the tone, establishing a new set of terms and a new set of characters. Sex ceased to be a metaphor for the sublime and became instead one of the powers of darkness. The questing ballet prince became a loner caught in an existential trap. His heroine lost her rank as ideal and became Pandora on pointe. The frank new emphasis was instantly appealing to Nureyev, an arresting fusion of personal concerns on both sides. "Modern and contemporary dances," Nureyev told the American dance journalist Kitty Cunningham, "have more audacity in their themes." His interest was primed from the start, and for a variety of reasons. He also had a slight edge. All of the contemporary choreographers with whom Nureyev worked until dancing for Taylor—Béjart, John Cranko, Kenneth MacMillan, Petit, Rudi van Dantzig—received their first training as classical dancers.

By the time Nureyev reached the Royal, the company's emergent generation of choreographers, led by Cranko in the fifties and MacMillan in the sixties, were edging the company's repertory toward this complex new world of conflict and *musique concrète*. Nureyev's first attempts at their choreography—Cranko's *Antigone* and MacMillan's *Diversions* and *Images of Love*—were tentative but promising. (All three productions were out of the Royal repertory after a single season.) Nureyev made at least three important discoveries. As the headstrong Eteocles, one of the two adversary brothers in *Antigone,* his innately dramatic stage presence was on fertile new ground. In the role of the tortured poet/hero in *Images of Love,* MacMillan's setting of Shakespeare's Sonnet 144, "Two loves I have, of comfort and despair,"[3] Nureyev found a new outlet for his sexual urgency in performance. According to Lynn Seymour's autobiography, "Christopher [Gable] was the comforting angel (sacred love) and I was the despairingly Dark Lady (profane love). We struggled for possession of the 'poetic' Rudi. Our threesome was a lightning

flash of arms and legs, reaching ravenously towards some cease-
less pleasure."[4]

The combination of unexpectedly complementary assets—
Nureyev's drive and modern's drama, his hips and the thrust of
the dances—opened a whole new world of possibilities, particularly after Nureyev's enormous personal success in Petit's *Jeune
homme et la mort* on French television in 1966. The image of
Nureyev as Petit's doomed rebel hero that was used to promote
the broadcast—Nureyev on his knees, his arms aching forward,
his chest bared, and in jeans tighter than tights—became one of
the signal images of a decade in heat.

He also discovered that the new idiom was tougher than it
looked. Nureyev scored another huge personal success in 1969
with his first performance of van Dantzig's popular ballet, *Monument for a Dead Boy*. The acclaim, van Dantzig still feels, was
more for Nureyev's idea of the ballet than for van Dantzig's: "A
dancer like Rudolf was not exactly what I had in mind when I
made the ballet. The role was for an antihero, a shy boy who
didn't know exactly who he was or where he was going. That is
hardly what Rudolf was, and it required a less powerful man.
Rudi was too much of an emperor. He reigned in his world and
onstage."[5] Van Dantzig's next encounter with Nureyev, when he
was invited to stage a new ballet for him at the Royal the following year, is a telling portrait of Nureyev at his most contradictory,
as well as a glimpse into why he never really mastered the contemporary idiom: "He was so eager to work on *Ropes of Time*.
He really wanted to do it and to be as good as he could possibly
be. But he did not follow obediently. He resisted. He'd say, 'This
step is not good for me' or 'I can't do this jump if you make me
stand too long first.' I finally had to draw the line and there were
steps I would not change. Then onstage he would do what he
wanted."[6] However disrespectful of a choreographer, the distance
was only part of a larger intent to learn summarized by Ninette
de Valois: "He was never too proud to learn."[7] The American
choreographer Glen Tetley has vivid memories of Nureyev's efforts when Tetley made *Field Figures* at the Royal in 1970, the

work critic Nigel Gosling described as Nureyev's "baptism of fire" into an unsparingly modern idiom. (The aural accompaniment is by Stockhausen.) "Nureyev begged to be in *Field Figures*," Tetley remembers, "and he learned the movement extremely well. He seized on it totally, instantly, and went deep into the movement. It was a total, concentrated performance."[8]

Although European choreographers virtually lined up to work with him—in the late sixties, Petit made three new ballets for Nureyev in two years—Nureyev had to work harder to get to the Americans, and he got through to a lot fewer of them. In contrast to the host of Europeans he worked with in his modern mode, Nureyev worked with only three resident contemporary companies stateside through the seventies and early eighties— the Taylor troupe, the company run by Alwin Nikolais and Murray Louis, and, most famously, the Graham company. Nureyev came to Martha the Mighty as part of a package deal for a gala fund-raiser, but both Taylor and Louis he pursued—assiduously. For years, both men resisted his entreaties to work with their companies, however much money he might have raked in for them at the box office. The man who had five original roles created for him during his two years with the Royal Ballet had a repertory of only five works created specifically for him in the United States over a thirty-year career—three by Louis and two by Graham (teasingly enough, in the title role of *Lucifer* and then as the adulterous Reverend Dimmesdale in her version of *The Scarlet Letter*). According to Louis, "Rudolf was not an easy dancer to choreograph on. He was brought up on ballet patterns and was comfortable with putting those patterns together. It was unnatural for him to go against certain time patterns, for example. He wanted to lock things in and it was very stressful for him to learn the importance of keeping himself open to unfamiliar beats, new rhythms."[9]

Nureyev's association with the Taylor company was especially good news on both sides. Taylor's ecstatic romp to Handel, *Aureole*, was a dependable high point of the early Nureyev and Friends concerts, and the residual payments from many a Nureyev *Aureole* didn't hurt the Taylor company. "He used me," Taylor explains, "and I used him."[10] Nureyev first saw Taylor's dancers perform at the Spoleto Arts Festival in the summer of 1964, when he staged his first *Raymonda* there. The two men met by chance. "His company had just finished a rehearsal and mine was about to start," Taylor remembered later. "He was alone looking at the set and he wasn't altogether pleased about it. I liked it—nothing but scrims and lights. So I said, 'Well, if you don't like it, I'll take it. I like it.' I don't think we were even formally introduced."[11] Nureyev took an immediate liking to Taylor and his elliptical directness. "He was wiry, but I had the bulk,"[12] Taylor explains. "I was bigger and older." Taylor enjoyed the fireworks of the Nureyev persona, particularly once he'd caught on that Nureyev's "reputation for temperament (his 'red light') is based more on his bark than his bite. He [knew] that Spoletini adore temperament, always expect it from artists and would feel gypped not to witness any. Invited to a jet set–type dinner party for the Royal Ballet given at Gian Carlo [Menotti]'s after the opening,[13] Rudi takes a while to towel off and dress and arrives at the party a little late. He's famished, but the food has already been eaten, so he generously gives everybody an extra performance by smashing several wine glasses against the wall—stylishly Russian and the only courteous thing to do."[14]

Taylor could also see that Nureyev was smitten with his dances. Thirty years after their first meeting in Spoleto, he still has clear memories of Nureyev

> standing in the wings during performances and trying to imitate the steps. I put him off for years but he never let up. Our paths didn't cross often, but, every time they did, the subject came up again. I told him it takes years to make a modern dancer, just the way it takes years to make a ballet dancer. Ballet dancers sometimes think they can just step right in, but it's actually harder for them because ballet is so ingrained in their muscles. They can't help doing their grandeur number, the prince thing, which was, of course, what had gotten Rudolf where he was. He finally convinced me that he wanted to do the dances because he wanted to do

the dances. He knew perfectly well I wasn't pleased with *Big Bertha*, or, actually, the Rudolf version of my poor dance. Even that didn't stop him. He was always willing to try again.[15]

Taylor's willingness to let Nureyev try and Nureyev's determination to get it right changed the course of dance in the United States. Ballet and modern were not mutually exclusive territories anymore. The Taylor/Nureyev association through the 1970s—a Hurok tour to Mexico, seasons at the Sadler's Wells Theater in London, a week together at the Alvin Theatre on Broadway—was the long-awaited armistice. "Rudolf did not come as a temperamental star," Taylor remembered. "He came as a dancer, as an instrument. And he just drove himself. I was always saying, 'Don't you think you ought to rest a while?' But he was all for going through it again. He wanted to do it exactly as it should be done."[16]

If Nureyev's association with the Taylor company was the de facto peace treaty between ballet and modern dance, his work with the Martha Graham Dance Company was the victory celebration—on both sides. But for the personalities involved, their first outing together, *Lucifer*, which Graham created for Fonteyn and Nureyev in 1975, could have been much less—a one-shot PR extravaganza. Nureyev and Fonteyn as guest artists with the Martha Graham Dance Company was the kind of inspired mix-and-match that screams big money. The potential value of the idea is as clear as the amount of effort that was extended in pulling it off: the complexities of the combined Graham, Fonteyn, and Nureyev schedules were such that Graham had to create Nureyev's role on him with one of her dancers substituting for Fonteyn, repeat the process for Fonteyn with a proxy Nureyev, and then fine-tune the piece only days before the first performance. The premiere of *Lucifer* at the Uris Theatre on Broadway on June 19, 1975—with Nureyev in the title role and Fonteyn barefoot as Night—was, in fact, the fund-raising event of all fund-raising events. The honorary chairperson for the gala premiere was First Lady Betty Ford, escorted by Woody Allen in tuxedo and sneakers, and the audience, who'd paid up to ten thousand dollars a ticket, included Paul Newman and Joanne Woodward, Andy Warhol with Paulette Goddard, two Kennedy sisters, and Diane Keaton chaperoning Allen and Mrs. Ford. Insuring that the focus of the evening remained clear—i.e., on herself, no matter who was waiting in the wings—Graham opened the program with a twenty-minute preperformance speech saluting her audience and "reminiscing about her life and her commitment to art."[17] The evening was everything Graham could have hoped for. The proceeds wiped out her company's $75,000 debt with money to spare: the net proceeds of the evening approached $200,000 and guaranteed the company a winter season in New York.

Despite her insistence upon dancing barefoot like everyone else, *Lucifer* was, at best, a glancing experiment for Fonteyn. "Through it all," Arlene Croce wrote in her *New Yorker* review, "one could almost hear a sweetly confident little voice saying 'I've been angular' in the same way that Barbara Stanwyck in *The Lady Eve* says 'I've been British.' "[18] For Graham and Nureyev, it was considerably more. However discordant their movement idioms, bottom line, Graham and Nureyev spoke the same language, the diva dialect that has moved a little closer to extinction with their deaths. Both were given to pronouncements in the grand manner; both had built secondary careers on their explosiveness; and, as performers, both finally had to be forced off the stage. (According to Graham's biographer, Don McDonagh, a Brooklyn Academy of Music engagement by the Graham company in 1970 was contingent upon a season of repertory including "precisely those works that Graham had no intention of reviving because they no longer afforded her the opportunity to perform."[19] At seventy-six, Graham had gotten the hook from her own company.) Graham, whose choreographic output had been prodigious when she was making ballets for herself, had made only four short pieces in the six years since she'd been retired from performance. Contact with a performer of Nureyev's electricity was exactly the tonic she'd been needing. "He embodied for Martha," Graham principal dancer Christine Daikin explains, "everything her art embodied—great passion, attack, ferocity."[20] He also, characteristically, made a few tentative efforts to test the waters of authority. "Rudolf was a Russian," Graham wrote in her autobiography,

> but I began to realize that he had an Irish tongue. . . . The only real problem with Rudolf was early in our *Lucifer* rehearsals. He kept coming later and later to rehearsal. Finally when he ambled in a full thirty minutes late, I looked up and said, "I think I am going to be angry. I am angry." With that the dancers scattered. I went up to Rudolf and let him have it. I don't know if I would have had I known his reputation for talking back. But then again, I probably would have, with my black Irish temper. I told him he was a great artist but a spoiled, willful child. And that was just for starters. He only stammered and apologized. It must have done some good. He was never late again.[21]

Nureyev bowed to the master—happily. He *wanted* to dance for Graham, to learn her technique, to do things her way. According to Janet Eilber, the Fonteyn substitute for the initial *Lucifer* rehearsals, "Martha enjoyed herself working with Rudolf. She could relax, let her hair down, and he was generally a very good boy. Rudi teased Martha and she loved flirting with him."[22] She also loved being the boss. "I didn't approach Rudolf," Graham told Anna Kisselgoff in the *New York Times*, "but I felt that as long he wanted to do something, it should be centered around him rather than for someone else. He was at the moment in his life when he needed to be centered. I'm not saying I was altruistic. He came and worked on the technique and then he went away. It was stop and go. Then I thought of the thing he is, and I started with the idea 'Tyger! Tyger! burning bright/In the forests of the night.' "[23] For one veteran Graham follower, "*Lucifer* was minor Graham, but it gave Martha and her company a second wind, a new era of vitality that continued right through to the end of her life."

The effect on Nureyev was equally vitalizing, and his association with the Graham company continued intermittently over the next ten years. His Graham repertory eventually included some of her few master roles for men: Oedipus in *Night Journey;* the Preacher in *Appalachian Spring;* the title role in *El Penitente;* and a second Graham original, the male lead in her telling of *The Scarlet Letter.* "Rudolf's level of commitment in rehearsal was astonishing," Eilber remembers. "In performance, someone could have set my hair on fire, and no one would have noticed. Nureyev went to Graham to learn and he did."[24] Christine Daikin agrees: "Nureyev's efforts to master the Graham style were all-consuming. He was doing it for himself and for Martha. As great as he was in his field, it was impossible for him not to know how different and difficult the modern dance is. He knew it was an entirely different technique, physically and intellectually, and he worked until he got it right. This was not a lark."[25] A remark Nureyev made to Fonteyn during a *Lucifer* rehearsal reflects the thoroughness of his attempt at grappling with the Graham technique. According to Eilber, "Fonteyn was having a great deal of trouble with a side fall next to Nureyev. It was a completely Grahamesque movement, and she just couldn't get it right. She wanted to stay upright, and Martha agreed to change it for her. 'Alright,' Rudolf told Fonteyn with a sniff. 'Be comfortable.' And so she did the fall exactly as it was supposed to be done. The story became one of Martha's favorites."[26]

In the final analysis, Nureyev never quite crossed the finish line into a dancer of genuine contemporaneity. Ballet was too deep in his blood, and even his own ambitions proved a liability. Nureyev's constant roundelay from company to company, from ballet to modern and back again, left him without the time to reinvent his body one more time. "He did whatever he could," van Dantzig concludes, "but modern was not his language. You could always hear his ballet accent."[27] Despite the problems—Murray Louis eventually learned to work out Nureyev's original roles on his own dancers and then teach them to Nureyev later—his interest was genuine. "And even when he sought out other techniques," Arlene Croce wrote in *The New Yorker,* "as when he danced with the companies of Martha Graham and Paul Taylor, he was plainly not on holiday; he was merely exchanging one hair shirt for another."[28] Nureyev put his money where his mouth was. Not only did he secure commissions for unknown young choreographers such as van Dantzig to create *Ropes of Time* for as established a company as the Royal, but, as van Dantzig explains, "just by working with me, he put my company on the map."[29] When Hurok refused to add Tetley's *Field Figures* for a Royal Ballet tour to America, Nureyev made inclusion of the ballet a condition of his own contract and forced Hurok's hand. Over the course of his associations with the Taylor, Niko-lais/Louis, and Graham troupes, Nureyev worked without ever taking a cent in fees from any of the companies involved.

In 1979, out of the blue, Nureyev finally bagged the chore-ographer who had almost gotten away: George Balanchine, the greatest choreographer in contemporary dance—the man who made ballet move like New York City. When Nureyev first ar-rived in the West, an encounter between the new Kirov émigré and the first one seemed an inevitability. A meeting was certainly high on Nureyev's itinerary. He was talking about tentative ar-rangements for an introduction during the first week after his defection, before he could possibly have had any communication with the master choreographer in New York. The two men were not to meet for more than a year, until a visit Nureyev made to New York City in 1962. He was invited to attend a New York City Ballet program during the company's fall season at City Center. After the performance, Nureyev, Balanchine, and Barbara Horgan, one of the City Ballet's administrators, went out for a drink. Balanchine's reaction was cordial and comradely but did not include the anticipated offer of a contract. It did include one of Balanchine's most misunderstood one-liners: "Come back when you are tired of dancing the prince."

According to Horgan, Balanchine's response was more complex than has been generally assumed:

> Balanchine, quite rightly, told Rudolf, "If you come here, you have to relearn everything you've learned. You have a choice now. You have a choice in the sense of doing

what you're familiar with, which you do very well, and being successful, being a star, getting it out of your system, if you wish, and then coming back."

Now, it's a little more complicated than that because what a lot of people don't understand about Balanchine's words to Rudolf was that Rudolf first came to him as a perfected dancer. He arrived with what he had learned fully formed. Now, there have been some dancers with New York City Ballet who have arrived fully formed and have had to remake themselves. And some of them have and some of them haven't. . . . It's a very risky business. Dancers don't like to take chances like that. Because it's like being reborn. You have to give up everything and start all over again. . . . What I truly believe Balanchine was saying to Rudolf was, in essence, "You're already where you're going to be. And if you want to work with me, you have to be someplace else. In other words, you may have to go back to come forward again." And Rudolf may not have really been able to understand that, but, I think, he was smart enough to comprehend that and really think about it and decided, "I really can't do that. My body won't be able to do that. My age won't be able to do that." And he was smart enough to understand what he would give up. I don't think money, for example, had a thing to do with it. . . . It was more than Balanchine saying, "You cannot have the role of the prince here." It was much deeper than that: "You will have to start all over again."[30]

Nureyev got a clearer idea of Balanchine's meaning when he danced his first Balanchine ballet soon afterward. Nureyev's performance of the dizzying male lead in *Theme and Variations* during his brief-lived career with American Ballet Theatre was not his finest hour. ("All I can say is that it was strange," the American ballerina Eleanor d'Antuono, one of the four demi-soloists in the performance, remembers. "Very slow, really slowed down almost beyond recognition, and . . . well, just very strange."[31]) With rare excursions—*Prodigal Son* and the *Agon* pas de deux for the Royal and the Paris Opéra—Nureyev steered clear of the Balanchine repertory for the next decade, until he went to the choreographer for permission to include *Apollo* on his first Nureyev and Friends concert. Balanchine was amenable to the idea and sent his longtime associate John Taras to teach Nureyev the role. "New York City Ballet is very practical," Horgan remembers.

> We were going through some very difficult problems at the school [the School of American Ballet, New York City Ballet's affiliate academy]. Particularly the school. We were having some problems ourselves here because, without getting too technical, our Ford Foundation grant had run out. And so the school was actually in a much more perilous situation than we were with regard to the continuation of funding. So Balanchine sort of nodded, and he said, "Well, you know, how many weeks?" It was five weeks, so he asked for five percent of the [box office] gross, because that's what [Balanchine] used to get as a choreographer for the Broadway shows he did. I think it came out to about twenty-five thousand dollars, which was more money than you could possibly imagine in those days, which went right to the school as a contribution.[32]

Apollo was clearly of great personal importance to Nureyev. "*Apollo* to [Nureyev]," Arlene Croce wrote of his performance, "is obviously a great and exalted ritual whose mysteries must be unfolded at maximum leisure. . . . Nureyev is not actually bad as Apollo, and he might be fine if he quickened his pace, relaxed his oversculpted phrases, and cut loose with some of the swinginess of [Paul Taylor's] *Aureole*. . . . *Apollo* has succumbed to misplaced reverence in the past, but never had it taken so long to die."[33] However shaky his efforts, by the time of his first *Apollos*, Nureyev had added Balanchine to the list of contemporary choreographers he was determined to master. "Whenever Rudolf worked with a company that included former Balanchine people," a dancer colleague recalls, "he would virtually corner them to talk about Mr. B. He wanted to know everything. It was as if he wanted to suck up as much as he could because he couldn't get to the source. I remember when we worked together in Zurich that he was especially fascinated with the way Balanchine 'presents' the foot, the formal presentation. Something as simple and essential as that. When it came to Mr. B, Rudolf was quite humble."

His patience was rewarded with Balanchine's antic setting of Molière's *Bourgeois Gentilhomme* in 1979. "It was Balanchine's idea to use Nureyev," Horgan remembers. "The whole idea was a collaboration between the New York City Opera and New York City Ballet. The curtain-raiser was the Purcell *Dido and Aeneas* and the second act was *Bourgeois*. I don't know how Balanchine got the idea of Rudolf, but he called me up at home one morning and said, 'You know, maybe you can find where Rudolf is.' "[34] However long he waited before acknowledging Nureyev and his contribution to ballet, the ballet Balanchine finally made for Nureyev has the evanescence of a champagne toast. With a keen eye to the specialties of the house—Nureyev is never offstage—Balanchine celebrates the common ground between them—their Kirov training in the chiseled academicism of Nureyev's first solo and, in particular, their mutual regard for showmanship. The ballet's wily hero, Cléonte, is a jokester with a disguise for every occasion and his eye on his target, the lovely Lucile. His resourcefulness never wavers and his dreams come true. Nureyev's partner in the ballet, the great Patricia McBride, remembers the entire experience as a pleasure for all concerned: "Rudi worked so hard. He wanted to do everything Mr. B wanted and more. He kept wanting to put in more technique. I think Balanchine was surprised at how easy it was to work with him. Mr. B wasn't well at the time. When he came back to finish the ballet, all I can remember is Rudi's warmth, so warm and so funny."[35] Nureyev learned the essential lesson of modernism, what he called "a lesson in simplicity. [Balanchine] employs bare essentials to tell the highlights of a story. He goes to the top of the mountain only when he can't avoid it. In the pas de deux, there suddenly comes a big dynamic in the music. I expected a lift, the girl up in the air. But suddenly I am only putting the girl down slowly on the floor. So simple and unexpected."[36]

Thirteen

Valentino and Beyond

"Oh, some day I know I'll be an actress. Rahlly, I do."

—*KATHARINE HEPBURN in* Morning Glory

*B*y the time Nureyev reached the Kirov in the mid-1950s, he was a member of a rebel generation that had been developing in the Soviet Union for almost a decade. Like their contemporaries around the world during the restless late 1950s, they were instantly identifiable in any crowd—by their clothes, by their hair, and by their defiant attitude. By the final years of the Stalinist era, the youth movement in the USSR already was widespread enough to have earned a name of its own. The rowdy young rebels—teenage girls in tube miniskirts and major lipstick, their escorts in the local equivalent of zoot suits—were known as the *stilyagi*, a term that combines the Russian words for style and the lower reaches of a woman's sexual anatomy. By the Khrushchev thaw, the *stilyagi* not only had their own coded slang but they had splintered into subgroups such as the *tarzanets*, the young men who went ape over the Soviet release of *Tarzan Goes to Manhattan*. One former *tarzanet*, Mikhail Gorbachev, would later reminisce about how much he and his comrades "enjoyed the Tarzan movies shown in their dorm at Moscow University and filled its corridors at night with ape-man howling."[1] The appetite for things American was voracious, music and movies in particular. Despite a Stalinist ban on alien musical forms, especially jazz, the musical idols of the *stilyagi* were Duke Ellington, Louis Armstrong, and Dizzy Gillespie. Among vocalists, Miss Peggy Lee was the queen. (Gillespie and Lee were the student Nureyev's special favorites.) Khrushchev lifted the ban on foreign music, with reservations: "When I hear jazz, it's as if I had hard gas on the stomach."[2] Despite the impact on the big boss and his considerable abdomen, the rebel generation went into full swing just as Nureyev reached Leningrad—part beat, part bop, part Elvis. (On assignment in Tashkent in 1956, an American journalist spent an evening in a *stilyagi* club with a horde of junior Soviets stamping to "Stompin' at the Savoy," as an incensed security officer wailed over the speaker system: "All this energy could be invested in building a hydro-electric power station, rather than wasted here on a dance floor."[3]) American movies had the same energizing kick. In spite of official attempts to politicize American films—the Frank Capra classic *Mr. Deeds Goes to Town* reached the Soviet Union as *The Dollar Rules*, the James Cagney/Humphrey Bogart gangland epic *The Roaring Twenties* as *A Soldier's Fate in America*—the heroes of choice among the men and women of Nureyev's youth were vintage, if slightly eccentric, Hollywood—Sonja Henie, Deanna Durbin, Cagney, John Wayne, and, top of the line, Johnny Weissmuller.

American music and American movies were already an integral part of his perspective when Nureyev reached the West, and they remained two of his great lifelong passions. By the time he'd become a fixture with the Royal in the 1960s, Nureyev already had accumulated a collection of more than four thousand recordings, as heavy on jazz as on the classics. He became famous among his new friends for seeing as many as two or three films in a single evening, and Michel Canesi, Nureyev's doctor during his final illness, remembers that there was little Nureyev enjoyed talking about more than the classic Hollywood films of the 1940s and 1950s.[4] *All About Eve*—the great Bette Davis vehicle that gave the world "Fasten your seat belts, it's going to be a bumpy night"—was a special favorite (not to mention that his delight in it was certifiable proof of Nureyev's homosexuality). From his earliest years in the West, Nureyev gave evidence of a more than peripheral interest in a career as an actor, and as a film actor in particular. By the mid-1960s Nureyev already had had some effective film performances to his credit: a vibrant *Corsaire* in *An Evening with the Royal Ballet* in 1963; an impassioned Romeo in a BBC version of Kenneth MacMillan's *Romeo and Juliet* in 1964; the doomed hero in Roland Petit's *Le jeune homme et la mort* in 1966. He was clearly after bigger game. "Let's be honest," Nureyev said when he finally got his shot at Tinseltown in Ken Russell's star-crossed *Valentino*. "Everybody wants to be a movie star. It's time to do it before . . . they have to photograph me through a mattress."[5]

By the time filming began on *Valentino* in August 1976, Nureyev had been in active pursuit of a film profile for more than a decade. In 1964, after dancing the title role in Robert Helpmann's ballet version of *Hamlet* with the Royal, Nureyev told *Variety*, the film industry trade paper, that his real interest was in performing the Shakespeare original.[6] In the summer of the same year, Italian film producer Dino de Laurentiis announced that he had signed Nureyev to make his big-screen debut in a forthcoming de Laurentiis epic, *The Bible . . . in the Beginning*—as the snake in the Garden of Eden. De Laurentiis had seen Nureyev perform at Spoleto in 1964, and, when his original choice for the role didn't work out—a thirteen-foot, one-hundred-pound python with no respect for lighting cues—de Laurentiis thought of Nureyev. "He will slither down the tree," John Huston, the film's director, explained. "He will be a man serpent, a kind of hybrid, homo-reptile."[7] De Laurentiis got more specific: "Special makeup will be created on Nureyev's body by the painter Mirko, and he will not use a costume as such."[8] Nureyev demanded more money than de Laurentiis was willing to shell out, and the deal fell through. Barely a year later—at the height of his celebrity with the Royal Ballet—Nureyev had another film project in the works, once again in big-time company. Nureyev, Franco Zeffirelli, and Edward Albee met in Rome early in 1966 and announced plans for a film that would star Nureyev and be directed by Zeffirelli from a script by Albee on "the emotional and spiritual life of a dancer."[9] Once again, the project evaporated, as did a third in 1970—a film of Nijinsky's life. "Everything was set," Albee remembers about the Nijinsky project. "I wrote a complete script, Tony Richardson was set to direct, and Paul Scofield was set to play Diaghilev. At the last moment, the producer—Albert R. Broccoli of Broccoli and Saltzman[10]—began negotiations to buy the Technicolor Corporation, and there went the money. The film never happened."[11]

After three strikes in a row, Nureyev took matters into his own hands—and came up a winner, twice. Nureyev eventually disowned the 1972 documentary *I Am a Dancer*. "Originally," he said just before the film's London premiere, "it was intended as a film for French television. Then they decided to expand it for the cinema and somehow I became entangled in the developments. We shot two and a half weeks in Paris, and then two more sequences in England. You work so hard on a film and at the end only a few sequences are tolerable. At one time I said I would pay thirty thousand pounds to have the whole thing destroyed. I still would."[12] However unhappy he may have been over the finished product, *I Am a Dancer* was just the kind of upscale success Nureyev needed to prove his potential as a big-screen attraction. In both London and New York, the film was released in only a few select theaters on a limited-run basis, generating an aura of "special event" that brought audiences in in droves. One British critic's response to the vérité portrait of Nureyev's driven, solitary pursuit of his muse was typical: "Whether *I Am a Dancer* ultimately tells anything more about him personally than *Elvis . . . That's the Way It Is* did about Presley is debatable."[13] In spite of the uncertain notices—and Nureyev's refusal to make personal appearances to promote the film—the London premiere of *I Am a Dancer* in July 1972 did fourteen weeks of SRO business. Its American release at the Ziegfeld Theater in New York City in March 1973 was such a commercial success that a return engagement was announced within less than a week.[14]

I Am a Dancer did the trick. Barely six months after its London release, Nureyev had completed his second theatrical film release—a big-screen version of the full-length *Don Q* he had made for the Australian Ballet. Nureyev was star, director, and coproducer.[15] Budgeted at $1.5 million, *Don Quixote* was released through the Walter Reade Organization, one of the last projects initiated by Reade himself. Nureyev justified Reade's gamble. He brought the project in on time and under budget and took to the multiple responsibilities like a duck to water. When Nureyev returned to England, he had an editing machine installed in his bedroom at Richmond Park, and he would work on the film in the early morning before rehearsals and when he returned home after the evening's performance. Smashingly photographed by Geoffrey Unsworth, the cinematographer of *2001: A Space Odyssey*, with lots of juicy close-ups of Nureyev as the cutup hero Basilio, the release of *Don Quixote* in 1973 brought Nureyev some of his most ecstatic notices yet. Judith Crist called Nureyev's *Don Q* "one of the loveliest renditions of the Cervantes work on film and one of the best ballet films to date."[16] Writing in the *New York Times*, Anna Kisselgoff gave *Don Q* the review of a publicist's dreams: "[*Don Quixote*] is a film that takes the dangerous risk of wedding cinematic realism with formal ballet conventions and triumphs as a genre of its own. The result is a dance film for all audiences, an exciting, intelligently conceived spectacle."[17]

Nureyev had made his point. He could fill a movie house too.

Every great career has at least one bomb.

Nureyev's had two.

Not many actors are asked to carry a major Hollywood release their first time out, as Nureyev was with Ken Russell's 1977 portrait of the silent film legend Rudolph Valentino. Although *Valentino*'s budget seems tiny today, in 1976, when Nureyev signed onto the project, five million dollars was a lot of money to risk on a man whose stardom was based upon not speaking. A shrewd negotiator as always, Nureyev agreed to a screen test, but only to be done after contracts had been signed. The after-the-fact screen test turned out to be a sharp move on

Nureyev's part, because he had finally found something he could not do—act on film. He could never manage the transition from the presentational acting required by the dimensions of an opera house to the internalized technique demanded by the close quarters of a motion picture camera. (Ethel Merman had the same problem.) "Rudolf was a stage animal, theatrical to the bone," New York City Ballet principal dancer Heather Watts explains. "That's why he never worked well on film. His impact was in the flesh."[18] Nadia Nerina of the Royal Ballet agrees: "Nureyev was first and foremost a stage presence, [which] explains his lackluster performances in front of the camera. His film career was a failure because in an arid studio bereft of his sustenance, his audience, his performances were wooden and two-dimensional."[19]

Nureyev and Russell had first met when Russell was considered briefly for the Nijinsky project in 1970. The introduction was unhappy on both sides of the table. Nureyev felt patronized by Russell, and "while I admired his work, I did not like him personally."[20] The *Valentino* experience did little to change Nureyev's opinion. "You know I did one film that I regret having done," Nureyev said when he was approached about a second feature film project a full six years after *Valentino*, "and I detested the director."[21]

The combination of a nervous, uncertain Nureyev, away from ballet for the first time in twenty years,[22] a director who'd made a career out of Glenda Jackson's bared breasts in *Women in Love*, and a crew of more than three hundred people wedged between them was an explosive mix. The British actress Felicity Kendal has only glowing memories of working with Nureyev on *Valentino*. Nureyev was in the initial stages of planning his own danced version of *Romeo and Juliet* for London Festival Ballet, and the two had endless conversations about the play: "There were a lot of difficult people on the film, and personally I didn't find him one of them. He had absolutely no presumptions to being a great actor. He was himself. He didn't pretend to be the best actor in the world, but he was the best dancer and that was what they wanted him for."[23] The American actress Carol Kane agrees: "Working with Rudolf was a kick, a ball. He was so attractive, so mischievous, so game, willing to try and fail. Alive! Alive! He was not one to waste a moment of life. He seemed to eat it up, an artist, an aristocrat."[24]

Unfortunately, theirs is the minority opinion. When the company and crew first assembled in Almería, Spain, for the first read-through, Nureyev refused to participate. He returned to his hotel instead, and the rest of the actors read the script for the first time without the title character. At his first costume fitting, Nureyev became so irritated by the buttons on a jacket that he ripped them off and flung them at the costume designer, Shirley Russell, Ken Russell's wife. He also arrived in Spain with shoulder-length hair that he would not allow to be cut. After protracted arguments among Nureyev, Russell, and the producers, Nureyev agreed to have his hair cut but on a condition: that the company hairdresser, Colin Jamison, come to his hotel suite. The first foot went down, the battle was on, and Nureyev lost the first skirmish: he went to Jamison.

Nureyev's most famous battles on the set of *Valentino* were with his leading lady, Michelle Phillips, late of the Mamas and Papas. Phillips still has vivid memories of "the most miserable working experience of my life. It was so awful that near the end of filming I finally told one interviewer that I couldn't understand how anyone had even imagined that a gay Slav could play a Latin lover.

Rudolf was so insecure about film acting that he was transformed into an insecure, mean-spirited person, a very mean guy. From the moment he arrived, everything was wrong—the dialogue, the wardrobe, everything—and it never ended. He was nasty and abusive to everybody. Three different dressers were fired or quit before they found someone who could handle him. He slapped a tech assistant across the face, and, one day when Ken Russell and I were sitting outside on the set having a meal and Rudolf saw that there was a bottle of wine on our table but none on his, he became so enraged that he grabbed our bottle and threw it into the sand. The worst was the morning I arrived on the set and Rudolf and Ken were already deep into a screaming match over the script, in front of the entire crew. "I will not say these stupid words!"[25] My chair was right next to where this was going on, so I sat down and listened a while, and then finally made the mistake of chirping in, "Well, what would you like to say, Rudolf?" Rudolf shouted, "This is none of your business," slapped me on the hand—hard—and then whirled back to face Ken so that his butt was virtually in my face. I smacked him flat on his bottom—hard—and the surprise of it sent him reeling across the room. That's when it really got ugly. "You cunt! You little cunt!" He stormed off the set and we were all dismissed for the day.

The strange thing is that he could be a very sweet guy when he chose to be. The night before filming began, I was in a restaurant with my daughter and my niece. Rudolf was also there, and we invited him to join us for dessert. He talked to the girls about when he was growing up, about how lucky they were to have food, and they were just enchanted. And then, when the girls were gone and we were alone, he turned to me and said, "I hope you understand that I have no interest in women." I was flabbergasted that he felt the need to say that. He hated the fact that he had to kiss me. Anything we did together in the film in that regard, he was forced to do.[26]

Fifteen years after the fact, it's hard to say which aspect of *Valentino* is more notorious—the filming or the film. The idea for *Valentino*, Russell told the *New York Times* shortly after its release in October 1977, originally came to him "out of the blue."[27] Unfortunately, the year that elapsed between the time the project was first announced in August 1975 and the first day of filming in August 1976 gave Russell lots of time to ruminate on what had first attracted him to a Valentino film: "I was interested in what happened to a personality destroyed by the press and public opinion."[28] (Russell had gotten nary a good review since *Women in Love*, six years earlier.) By the time production was underway, Valentino was a secondary character in his own life story, second fiddle to Russell's fixation on impending apocalypse.

In the annual *Variety* report of the top-grossing film releases of the year, *Valentino* ranked ninety-eighth,[29] tied with Disney's rerelease of *Alice in Wonderland*.[30]

Martha Graham said she saw it twice.

James Toback's espionage thriller *Exposed*, released in 1983 with Nureyev second-billed to Nastassja Kinski, was also born bad. An American auteur in the tradition of the French New Wave, Toback was a scriptwriter turned director whose first film, *Fingers*, was a failure *d'estime* in 1978, a box office disaster that earned flights of praise from, among others, Orson Welles, François Truffaut, and Rainer Fassbinder. (Truffaut included *Fingers* on his list of all-time favorite films.) The front offices were less impressed. Once it finally made its way into release in 1982, Toback's second feature, *Love and Money*, also went nowhere in the cash department, forcing Toback to spend a full year of "nonstop humiliating rejection" before he could find funding for *Exposed:* "Anyone in the world who finances movies turned it down because it wasn't like any other movie. Luckily Nastassja Kinski wanted to do it, and she stuck with it against the advice of her agent, her lawyer and her boyfriend at the time, Paul Schrader, who told her that *Cat People* was going to make her the biggest star in the world."[31] Postproduction on *Exposed* took another year after the distributor of the film, MGM-UA, lost confidence in the project. Filmed in New York and Paris in the winter of 1981–82, *Exposed* didn't make it into theaters until April 1983, and then only because Kinski loaned Toback seventy thousand dollars to complete the final editing.[32]

It's easy to see why the moneymen balked. Toback brought in some of the best in the business for *Exposed*—the original score is by Georges Delerue and the cinematography by Henri Decae, the man who shot Truffaut's landmark *The Four Hundred Blows*[33]—but the film also has the most improbable casting since the remake of *Lost Horizon* as a Liv Ullmann/Sally Kellerman musical. Kinski is cast as a Wisconsin farm girl, Nureyev as a concert violinist waging a one-man war against an international terrorist cartel, led by Harvey Keitel. Nureyev is first seen at a cocktail party sheathed in black and smiling like a Cheshire Lucifer. He spends a great deal of his subsequent time brooding and staring out of icy windows. Coals to Newcastle in such a setting, he is also given cryptic, elliptical dialogue on the order of "Every man is his clock. Ticktock. He may rise by the sun and go to sleep with the stars. Ticktock." In perhaps the coldest love scene ever filmed, he seduces Kinski by "playing" her body with his violinist's bow. A musician with a handgun, Nureyev finally shoots Keitel, who then shoots Nureyev, and *Exposed* ends in a bloodbath.

According to Toback, the four weeks of filming on *Exposed* saw a kinder, gentler Nureyev. Toback got the idea of casting him as an urban guerrilla as the result of a long-standing fascination with the Nureyev persona: "It wasn't just that he was this great artist, which, of course, he was. It was because he'd always seemed to be witty, dry, intelligent, without any of the sentimentality of a 'dance artist.' "[34] Negotiations were simple and direct, with a single last-minute snag. Toback first contacted Nureyev through Lester Persky, one of the backers on *Valentino*, and, when Nureyev expressed interest, flew to London with a print of *Fingers*. The two men met for dinner, Toback read Nureyev the script of *Exposed*, and "by five A.M. he'd pretty much agreed to do it." Nureyev's salary was to be $200,000 for three weeks of work. A week before filming was set to start in December 1981, Nureyev telephoned Toback: "He said, 'We have one loose end to fix—my money. It's not $200,000. It's $350,000. MGM has a lot of money. They can pay me.' I explained that the only way I could get the extra money was to take it out of my salary. He said, 'Fine,' band that's what happened. It was the only disagreement we ever had. He was very cooperative, not temperamental at all, and everyone liked working with him. He didn't like to improvise and wanted things explained, but he never took an aggressive stance."[35]

According to Toback, the easygoing Nureyev on the *Exposed* set exhibited another uncharacteristic tendency. Plagued by a cold and bronchitis throughout the midwinter shoot, Nureyev "was always putting down his appearance. He kept referring to himself as an old man, 'old and decrepit.' He called Decae the Maestro, and was always saying, 'Maestro, please—make me look young. Make me look beautiful.' "[36]

The Manhattan offices of Jim Henson Productions might seem the last place to find another detour in the career of Rudolf Nureyev. Nestled in an Upper East Side town house worthy of an Edith Wharton short story, the Muppet headquarters are in a neighborhood Nureyev knew like the back of his hand—the territory of the wealthy and the privileged, Swellsville. Like the fantasy environment Nureyev created in his New York and Paris apartments with countless antiques, tapestries, and objets d'arts, the world behind the heavy oak door of the Muppet town house is an exquisitely appointed, self-contained universe. A hand-carved circular staircase climbs four flights to a stained-glass vision of Kermit the Frog's pond. Calder on pixie dust, a bubbling mobile in grays and rose and tiny Muppets dangles from Kermit's cutglass haven right down to the reception area. In "Jim's office," Kermit stands sentinel over a scrolled mantel piece, as Gainsborough's "Blue Boy."

Nureyev's guest appearance on *The Muppet Show* in November 1977 is more than just his happiest moment on film. Television was a medium Nureyev understood and enjoyed. He made his first guest shot on what he called "that little black box" less than six months after his defection, and his American debut was, in fact, the *Bell Telephone Hour* appearance with Tallchief. Perhaps because so many of his early guest appearances on television were before live audiences, like *The Ed Sullivan Show* or the *Hollywood Palace* variety hour, the camera became largely irrelevant, just another face in the crowd. The showmanship that was half Nureyev's dazzle jumps right through the screen. (A risky bit of arts programming for the time, the PBS broadcast of Nureyev's *Sleeping Beauty* with the Canadians on December 17, 1972, drew the highest Nielsen rating for the evening, and, according to *Variety*, "wiped out the Julie Nixon Eisenhower special."[37]) And Rudi the Elusive was, of course, the dream guest of the new television interview industry. Nureyev did his fair share, always with the big leaguers. He was at his least effective in a "canned" format—brusque and uncomfortable with Mike Wallace, vague to the point of evasion with David Hartman—but in high gear with David Letterman and a laugh fest with Dick Cavett, in snakeskin from head to toe.

From his graduation performance with Sizova through the glory days with Fonteyn, Nureyev was always at his best in worthy surroundings, especially in situations and company characterized by irreverence, wit, imagination. The stand-up sketches and musical numbers Nureyev performed with the Muppets—and Miss Piggy in particular—are the most relaxed he would ever be on film. Nureyev clearly was having the time of his life, and he gave his audiences a rare glimpse of the quality that most often moistened the eyes of his friends and colleagues in the months immediately after his death—a wonderful sense of humor. "He was a very witty man," Jerome Robbins remembers. "He knew how to make sparks happen," an assessment that's easy to accept about a man who once explained his sartorial eccentricity to *GQ*: "I probably developed double-breasted-suit poisoning back in Russia in that period when Khrushchev and everybody else looked like walking refrigerators."[38]

Legends to the contrary, Nureyev was also a man who knew how to laugh at himself, surely one of the reasons his appearance on *The Muppet Show* is so endearing. One afternoon in 1982, during a series of guest performances of *Don Quixote* in Los Angeles with the Boston Ballet, Nureyev found himself embroiled in a disagreement with a stagehand that quickly developed into a shoving match. During that evening's performance, after his first solo, Nureyev returned to the comfort station always kept waiting for him in the wings—a chair, a side table with a thermos of tea (Earl Grey, five sugars), his clogs positioned directly in front of his seat. Nureyev took a sip of tea, slipped his feet into the clogs, and crashed face first onto the floor. The stage crew had nailed his clogs to the floor. No one laughed harder than Nureyev.

The Muppets gave it to him right between the eyes—with both barrels. The program is both an exhilarating, on-the-money satire of the uptown arts and a sly assessment of the Nureyev persona, with a special wink to Nureyev the international sex symbol. The evening opens with an ecstatic paean by Sam the Eagle about how honored the Muppets are to engage a class act, a "man of dignity and culture on this weird, sick program," particularly an artist as esteemed as "the great Rudolf Nureyev, my favorite opera singer." ("Ballet? Are you sure? Well, six of one, half dozen of the other. Culture is culture.") When Nureyev finally arrives, late as always—excepting dance class and performances, punctuality was never a Nureyev trademark—he turns up in tight, tight jeans revealing *mucho* crotch, and a tighter leather jacket. While multiple Muppets scurry to accommodate their star, Miss Piggy, as Brunhilde, performs an excerpt from *The Barber of Diefledermoose* by Giuseppe Wagner.[39] The swipe at grand opera is only a warm-up for the extract from *Swine Lake* with Nureyev and a six-foot Miss Piggy,[40] on pointe and in a tutu made from forty yards of tormented tulle. Set to a dazzlingly astute recension of the Tschaikovsky score, their knockdown, drag-out White Pig Adagio is one of the great sparring matches of all time, and Nureyev lunges at the pas de deux with the vigor of a man who's been waiting for years to squeeze a ballerina's snout. The best is yet to come. Nureyev's final duet with La Piggy is set in a steam room. He enters in a hooded caftan and strips down to a towel to an enthusiastic response from Miss Piggy: "Holy maracas!" Joining her sauna-side, he gets the come-on of his life. Miss Piggy addresses him in her most coy contralto: "Helll—oooo! Oh, what's the matter? Don't you talk to strangers?" Nureyev's uncertain response—"Depends how strange the stranger is"—elicits a burst of giggles: "Oh, you have a wonderful sense of humor and a marvelous mind. And [dropping her voice an octave] the other parts of you ain't bad either." Their duet rendition of "Baby, It's Cold Outside" descends into an all-out campaign by Miss Piggy who does things with her snout few people could manage with both hands in order to remove Nureyev's towel.

Miss Piggy could not be reached for comment.

Fourteen

Back to Paris

"And Paris! Paris!
City of light.
City of the tough customer.
City of the first-class subway token."

—BETTE MIDLER, A View from a Broad

wo developments in 1983, one planned, the other a fatal surprise, changed the course of Nureyev's life. After two years of wrangling over contractual details, Nureyev assumed the directorship of the Paris Opéra Ballet with the company's 1983–84 season, his first bid for a place to hang his beret since the Royal Ballet all those years ago. The three-year contract between Nureyev and the Opéra was a masterpiece of thrust-and-parry, each side getting as much out of the arrangement as the other would allow. The Opéra insisted that Nureyev spend 180 working days per year in Paris, the longest amount of time he was to spend in any one city over the full course of his Western career. Nureyev agreed to the six months on the Seine, but got two important concessions. The time did not have to be consecutive and was one day short of the period that would have kicked his salary into a higher tax bracket.[1] The Opéra picked up the clout and cachet of Nureyev's name on its roster. Nureyev was guaranteed a record forty performances of his own at the Garnier during those six months (the maximum for any of the other Opéra dancers was seventy a year), although Nureyev was not allowed to dance opening nights. He was also guaranteed the opportunity to stage at least one new production of his own every year.

In the weeks just before becoming, as he was soon designated, "the tsar of the Opéra," Nureyev began having new physical problems in addition to the standard round of sprains, strains, and bruises. As a result of the decades of malnutrition in Russia, Nureyev always had been particularly susceptible to infections, respiratory infection in particular. By the time of his move to Paris, however, the colds and bouts of bronchitis were more than chronic. They were constant. For the first time in his life, Nureyev's weight began dropping below his normal 160 pounds. There were other peculiarities as well—unexplained fevers and severe, recurrent night sweats. Only a handful of French and American doctors, and a terrified gay world, knew in 1983 what the puzzling symptoms meant. If Nureyev sensed something might be seriously wrong with his health, he turned a blind eye, writing off the sweats and weight loss as just another variant on the pattern of aches and pains he'd danced through year in and year out.

At the time, the move to Paris seemed the more serious event, a completely uncharacteristic choice for Nureyev to make. The decline in his dancing—the strain of his performances, the struggle and unsteadiness—already had critics everywhere lunging for their Roget's to find yet another synonym for "Stop!" But the demand for Nureyev's name on a marquee continued unabated. At forty-five and despite the onset of what would turn out to be AIDS, he was still capable of the pace. Nureyev celebrated New Year's Eve 1983 by dancing every ballet on a Diaghilev program in Monte Carlo, and by the end of January had begun a three-week run of his *Don Quixote* on Broadway with the Boston Ballet, dancing at every performance, matinees included. In March he returned to Japan for the first time in twenty years to partner Yoko Morishita with the Matsuyama Ballet before moving on to a series of *Giselles* in San Juan and then the American premiere of his Byron ballet *Manfred* with the Zurich Ballet in Washington and Chicago, dancing at every performance, matinees included. Summer was nonstop: the eighth consecutive Nureyev Festival at the London Coliseum in the first week of June; *Don Quixote* and *Swan Lake* with the Boston Ballet from June 27 through July 9; the next two weeks of July with the Ballet Théatre de Nancy in two wildly divergent programs, a Diaghilev evening of Massine's *Boutique fantasque* and Fokine's *Le Spectre de la rose*, *L'après-midi d'un faune*, and *Petrouchka*, and then a program of contemporary European ballets—Béjart's *Song of a Wayfarer* duet, Hans van Manen's *Song without Words*, Jiři Kylián's *Symphony in D*, and, most aggressive of all, Birgit Cullberg's *Miss Julie*. By the end of July it was back to New York to dance Petit's *Notre-Dame de Paris* at the Met, partnering Makarova—their first and only American appearance together and their first performance together anywhere since the row at the Cour Carrèe a decade earlier. Nureyev was scheduled to dance ten more *Don Q*s with the Boston Ballet in mid-August but tore his left calf muscle during an early preview, went on that night anyway, and was then forced to cancel the rest of his performances, which canceled the season. Between the Boston injury and September 6, his first day on the job in Paris, he still managed more performances with Petit's Ballet de Marseille and danced in Spoleto, Vienna, and London as well.

From the start, Nureyev and the Opéra were a volatile mix, and the explosions began even before he'd started work. By the terms of his contract, Nureyev was triple-salaried, as premier danseur, as choreographer, and as director, for an annual total estimated at $150,000;[2] before Nureyev had warmed the director's chair, Paul Paix, the government official in charge of the National Lyric Theatres, the umbrella organization that includes the Opéra Ballet, resigned in protest over the size of Nureyev's salary. Paix's resignation was the first storm in the six most tempestuous years of Nureyev's life since his six years in Leningrad. Nureyev knew what he was getting into when he agreed to take charge of the company. He'd been a regular guest at the Opéra throughout his Western career and staged the *Bayadère* Shades scene for the company in 1975. He also knew that the Opéra is a notoriously difficult organization, top-heavy with bureaucracy and perennially subject to the tides of national and local politics. He was its fourth ballet director in a decade. The turnover rate, however, had as much to do with the complexity of the Opéra's administrative structure as with the skills of any single director. The Paris Opéra is, in effect, a mammoth national corporation. (When Nureyev arrived in 1983 the company was receiving fully half the French government's annual budget for dance —more than $12 million.[3]) It employs more than 150 dancers and has a vigilant network of unions famous for holding their ground. The backstage intrigues are legendary. The root of Nureyev's difficulties, one longtime Opéra veteran explained on condition of anonymity, was a bedrock clash of perspectives, Nureyev's vision of "his" company versus the Opéra's traditional vision of itself: "It is very difficult for a foreigner to understand. The Opéra is not just a company. It is *l'Opéra de Paris*. The Opéra Ballet exists on its own, as *l'Opéra de Paris*, whoever the director is. The director is nominated for three years. With or without the director, the company goes on. Bonjour, Mr. Director. Good-bye, Mr. Director. The company that is created by the director goes when the director does, but the ballet continues to exist by itself."

Predictably, Nureyev's manner did not soothe taut French nerves. "It is better to work with a company one can transform rather than one that is in good shape," he announced in one of his first interviews. "You can leave your stamp on this kind of company. I will attack on all fronts." He was true to his word, but Nureyev lost the first skirmish. Clearly evincing a Wagnerian *gesamtkunstwerk* approach to his new job, Nureyev immediately expressed an interest in becoming involved with the company's affiliate dance academy. He met a worthy opponent in the director of the Opéra Ballet school, the formidable former French ballerina Claude Bessy, who let him know that the school was her territory.

Nureyev's second assault was on the Opéra's antiquated physical facilities and was a triumph of logic and vision. "Before Rudolf arrived," remembers Patrice Bart, a longtime Opéra principal dancer and one of Nureyev's two chief administrators during his last years in Paris, the company's main rehearsal space was a great big studio beneath the central cupola at the very top of the Garnier. It was basically a reproduction of the stage, the same size and dimensions, complete with an orchestra pit. Rudolf thought it was a waste of space. He hired an architect to break up the big studio into three spaces on two different levels. The larger new studio remained the one directly beneath the *coupole*, but below that he built two medium-sized studios with a movable wall between them that could be removed to make one big room if necessary. Suddenly, everything was much more convenient than it had ever been before.[4]

The threat of impending change was not met with *gentillesse*, particularly among the company's dancers. Despite 1789, 1848, and Coco Chanel, France is not a country fabled for embracing radical change, and, according to Patricia Ruanne, an early Nureyev partner from London who became one of the Opéra's chief ballet mistresses at his invitation, "the Opéra is French and French and French and more French."[5] The company's dancers are also civil servants, with steady paychecks, comfortable lives, and the security of a pension after twenty years of service. The majority of them were less than thrilled with the prospect of a new routine, particularly once the work on the new studios required that the dancers travel twenty minutes in both directions to the rehearsal spaces rented for the interim. The mere fact of Nureyev's presence was a threat to many of the Opéra's principal dancers, most of whom already had worked with him and knew his black days. With Nureyev as a full-time presence, the senior Opéra dancers saw a cloud over their own number of performances in the new boss's forty guaranteed nights on stage. Adding to their suspicions, at least at first Nureyev clearly saw the Opéra as a replay of the "Rudolf Nureyev and . . ." relationship he'd had with the Canadians. The prospect of perennial second billing generated widespread resentment among both the dancers and the staff of the Opéra. "Rudolf wanted control over everything," one administrator remembers. "He wanted to be everywhere and that was his first mistake with the Opéra. People were afraid he would eat the company, and he certainly wasn't diplomatic about what he wanted, that's for sure. He didn't understand the way the Opéra is organized. He would say, 'I am the director. I have the title.' But here at the Opéra, you also have a second director and a third director and a fourth and so on. It's why it finally didn't work. He wanted to put his nose everywhere."

Thierry Fouquet, Nureyev's chief administrative liaison during his first two years at the Opéra, remembers the early Nureyev years as "exciting but not easy. It was a time of creative agitation. Rudolf wanted a lot from everybody, and he had very strange working hours, until one or two in the morning, or between one and three. He didn't understand the rules—the bureaucracy, the administration, and, in particular, the union regulations you have to understand in order to run as large a company as the Opéra. He could never understand something like the dance promotion jury that decides which dancers are to be promoted to the next highest level. The jury has twelve members, and Rudolf resented when the vote went against his choice. I don't think he was fond of democracy."[6] Patrick Dupond, who was to succeed Nureyev as head of the Opéra ballet, remembers crossed swords at the Garnier: "Even Rudolf, with his strong personality, was not really the boss, and that was a problem. The boss was the administration—the general director, the president. I saw Rudolf hand in his resignation more than once."[7] For Nureyev the problems were not of his making. "I was abruptly dropped into a surrealist setting," he told *Le Monde* after two years on the job. "I worked for a long time without a secretary, office, telephone, or even a chair. The Opéra has its rites. You feel the administrative side is invading everything. Administrative cumbersomeness results in delays and constraints unthinkable in a normal company."[8]

Matters came to a head in 1984 with what became known as the *Swan Lake* Wars. For a quarter century the famous Soviet staging of *Swan Lake* by Vladimir Bourmeister had been one of the Opéra's most dependable attractions, a guaranteed crowd pleaser and, by the Nureyev era at the Opéra, a national institution. First staged in Moscow in 1953, the Bourmeister *Swan* was one of the major hits of the first Russian seasons in Western Europe in 1956. Response to the ballet was particularly strong in Paris, and it entered the Opéra repertory in 1960. The Paris petite bourgeoisie adored the audience-friendly novelties of the Bourmeister *Swan*, such as the interpolated character of a Court Jester whose pyrotechnic displays juiced the ballet's generally staid first act.[9] The Paris critics cherished the staging for its restoration of Tschaikovsky's original musical sequence. Dancing the ballet year after year after year, the Opéra dancers came to depend upon the Bourmeister *Swan* as the next best thing to a night off. Nureyev hated it and made his objections clear. The new finale Bourmeister tacked onto the ballet to stroke the Soviet taste for sappy endings —Odette and Siegfried live happily ever after—was a worst-case example of the "Soviet realism" he had loathed in Leningrad. Even worse, according to Patrice Bart, "he thought the Bourmeister, with things like the *bouffon* in the first act and all that, was not true to the purity of *Swan Lake*. He thought it was a third-rate conception of the ballet and called it 'ersatz *Swan Lake*.' "[10]

Although Nureyev's staging of the full-length *Raymonda* for the Opéra in 1983 was generally well received, his announcement of a new *Swan Lake* in the spring of the following year— with choreography by Rudolf Nureyev—was the local equivalent of spitting on the *tricolore* and about as popular. With an untimely television broadcast of the dense, psychologically complicated *Swan Lake* Nureyev had made for the Vienna State Opera in 1964, unilaterally despised by the local critics and public, *les guerres des cygnes* went into full swing. The French dance press was livid, the Opéra administration became visibly nervous, and the corps de ballet quickly evolved from a company of swans into a flock of fledgling Mesdames Defarges. With scant days before the premiere of the new *Swan Lake*, the dancers flung their final gauntlet and threatened a strike. Nureyev turned the resistance to rubble with the master's instinct—and nerve—he'd been honing since his fainting spells back on Rossi Street. He finally agreed to divide the season's twenty-five performances of *Swan Lake* into fifteen of his own and ten of the Bourmeister (although the ratio eventually shifted further in favor of Nureyev's version).

The concession came with a reminder that Nureyev could play hardball with the best. Scant days before the prospective strike, two of Nureyev's colleagues arrived in Paris. Antoinette Sibley had ended her three-decade career with the Royal Ballet two years earlier, but, with Nureyev's vigorous support, was in the process of making a return to performance. She was scheduled to make her Covent Garden debut in Ashton's exquisite rendering of the Turgenev *Month in the Country*, partnered by Mikhail Baryshnikov, who was also making his first appearance in the ballet. Nureyev offered the two dancers a place to rehearse in Paris. On the morning the Opéra dancers were scheduled to meet for the final vote on whether or not to strike, Nureyev, in practice clothes, went to the studio where Sibley and Baryshnikov were about to begin working and asked them to accompany him to another studio, where they would do their morning barre *à trois*. "Please," Sibley remembers Nureyev saying. "We must do this." They went straight to the studio where the dancers were meeting for their vote and chose an isolated corner of the barre to begin their warm-up exercises. The sight of three of the world's most accomplished dancers, going about their daily work as any other responsible professional, had exactly the impact Nureyev planned. "Rudolf was so shrewd," Sibley remembers. "He knew exactly the effect the three of us would have. All talk of a strike simply evaporated."[11]

The remainder of the Nureyev saga at the Paris Opéra could be subtitled "The Two Faces of Rudolf"—Nureyev the Tatar warrior and Nureyev the miracle worker. The Terminator Nureyev was someone the Opéra already knew well. "For some reason," choreographer Glen Tetley recalls about Nureyev's guest appearances in Paris during the 1970s, "the Opéra always seemed to bring out the worst in Rudolf. When I made *Tristan and Isolde* there for him and Carolyn Carlson in 1974, he threw some outrageous fits and threatened not to go on until I helped him realize how good his understudy would be."[12] The understudy was the beautiful young Vietnamese dancer Charles Jude, who bore a striking resemblance to Nureyev in his youth. A staple of the Nureyev and Friends tours, Jude would become Nureyev's first protégé in Paris, one of the Opéra's most valued *étoiles*, and with his wife, Florence Clerc, a close lifelong friend. Late in his life, Nureyev reportedly said that, after Fonteyn, Jude was his favorite partner.

By the time Nureyev took over the directorship of the Opéra, his offstage performance of Rudolf Nureyev was the last vestige of the stagecraft and dramatic power that had first made his name. The completeness of the characterization—royal even in practice clothes and the last person to cross—recalls Lydia Sokolova's description of Pavlova, in her ecstatic autobiography, *Dancing for Diaghilev:* "The only time Pavlova wasn't acting was when she was asleep. I never saw her sleep. I wish I had."[13] Explosions were a requisite part of the picture, and Nureyev did not disappoint, particularly when confronted with his two *bêtes noires*, both French specialties—resistance and professional ineptitude. The Opéra dancers learned quickly that, when the volume of Nureyev's voice began to swell and his hand moved toward the thermos of tea or soup always at his side during rehearsal, the moment had come to duck. (Green beans were another popular projectile.) During one early rehearsal, Patrick Dupond remembers, "Rudolf was working with Jean-Christophe Paré[14] and slapped him. Nobody moved. Everyone just looked away, like it hadn't even happened."[15]

The flights of Nureyev's temper were rarely gratuitous, and even Nureyev's distaste for Dupond began with Nureyev's opinion of Dupond as a crowd-pleasing *demi-caractère* dancer rather than a classic danseur noble. (The extremity of Nureyev's response to Dupond, though, was another story. His reduction of the most popular dancer in France to a nominal position as guest artist with perhaps barely a dozen performances a year was a rare lapse in his otherwise sound business sense.) The battle royals of the Nureyev era in Paris were also indicative of the strengths that made him the first director in fifty years to energize the Opéra.

Two incidents were particularly telling. Nureyev's regard for his Kirov heritage, and the training he received under Pushkin in particular, had intensified with the years. By the time he reached Paris, he was acutely aware of a successful ballet company's need for a consistently high level of daily training. Throughout his tenure as director of the Opéra, Nureyev took classes regularly with the company of teachers who worked day after day with the Opéra dancers. The daily classes were as much for his own physical maintenance as for the opportunity they provided for a quality check on the level of classroom instruction. Nureyev's penchant for offering classroom corrections, even when he was only an observer, led to one of the greatest standoffs between rival divas since Maria Montez confronted herself over the cobra jewels. "The Day Rudolf Slugged Renault" made every paper in Paris and resulted in Nureyev's only public apology. Michel Renault had been a fixture at the Opéra for more than forty years, first as a valued principal dancer and then as one of the company's long-standing instructors.[16] A symphony of scarves and flying port de bras, he was also the kind of old-school *reine soleil* who could kick a door closed behind him in midsentence without losing a syllable of what he was saying.

One summer morning in 1984, shortly after the local press reported that costume fitters at the Opéra were refusing to dress Nureyev because he'd thrown a bottle at one of them for being too slow, Nureyev passed the studio where Renault was teaching class and dropped in for an update. After a short time, he began to offer Renault his own suggestions for what to emphasize, and all hell broke loose. Renault and Nureyev began screeching at one another at a volume to rival Jane and Blanche Hudson on a bad day. Renault used one insult too many, and Nureyev struck him flat across the face. Renault went straight to the press. By the time the story hit the stands, Renault's impassioned account of his injuries was running from a bloodied nose to a displaced jaw. Neither was true, but Nureyev had, in fact, inflicted a more painful wound. The force of his slap sent Renault's wig sailing straight to the floor, directly in front of a studio filled with dancers who could not get to a telephone fast enough after class. Nureyev was forced to make a public apology and received a fine of six thousand francs for physically abusing a member of the Opéra.

Never one to be completely undone, he got the Opéra to pay the fine for him.

Nureyev's brawling went tabloid again two years later. In 1986, Nureyev invited the controversial French-born choreographer Maurice Béjart to stage two new works for the Opéra. For a quarter century, Béjart, whose black eyes and clipped beard are most kindly described as Mephistophelian, reigned supreme over his Brussels-based Ballet of the 20th Century, one of Europe's most popular pacesetters.[17] The premiere of the two new Béjart ballets was an enormous success, and, during the ovation that greeted them, Béjart stepped forward to announce that he was promoting one of the evening's dancers to the highest level in the Opéra hierarchy, the rank of *étoile*. The promotion was news to Nureyev, who made an announcement of his own the next day— the decision to advance a dancer to *étoile* status was the sole priority of the director and guest choreographers had better attend to their own business.[18] Béjart went straight to the press. In an appearance on French television, he accused "Mr. Nureyev of having lied, of having deliberately organized this affair so that his name, absent from the evening, would be quoted in the press. . . . I am asking that an intruder get out. *Au revoir*, Mr. Nureyev." This time, the Opéra administration stood behind Nureyev and issued a statement of its own, disavowing the promotion. Béjart, it read, "seems to be going through a difficult psychological period where he mistakes desire for reality and which it is hoped he will pass through quickly."[19]

In the final analysis, the scrapes and screaming of the Nureyev years at the Opéra were a secondary feature of a much larger accomplishment, one that many of his colleagues now consider the great achievement of Nureyev's career—his transformation of a tired ballet company into a troupe of international rank. The history of the Opéra until the Nureyev renaissance was, at best, an erratic one. Ballet was born at the court of Louis XIV, and the Opéra today is a direct descendant of the Académie Royale de la Danse that *le roi soleil* established in Paris in 1671. The house that premiered *Sylphide, Giselle,* and *Coppélia* (on the eve of the Franco-Prussian War), the Paris Opéra was the center of international ballet until the Imperial Russians took control at the end of the nineteenth century (under the leadership of a Frenchman, Marius Petipa). French ballet had been pretty much on the decline ever since, despite a brief surge in the decades between the First and Second World wars, the Opéra's last glory days until the Nureyev era half a century later.[20] The star presence of Serge Lifar, Diaghilev's last protégé, as director, premier danseur, and chief choreographer guaranteed a hold on the Paris spotlight through the 1930s. In the following decade, however, despite the (mysterious) popularity of Lifar ballets such as *Les mirages* and *Suite en blanc* and the emergence of a glittering new ballerina, Yvette Chauviré, charges of collaboration with the Nazis leveled against Lifar cast a cloud over the Opéra and initiated a period of decline and isolation.[21] "The Paris Opéra has its own view of what a performance is about," Edwin Denby, the poet laureate of American dance criticism, wrote in 1950.

> The dancers do not present the ballet as a stage drama. The ballet is a ceremony which offers them an occasion for the exhibition and the applause suitable to their various ranks. The excitement of the official ceremony is in the suggestion they individually convey of being people it would be delightful to know at home. And that is perhaps why the dancers scatter in all directions a great many of those little shakes, peckings, and perks of the head that look so pretty around a Paris dinner table, though coupled to the foot activity of ballet they unfortunately give an effect of witlessness.[22]

Enter Nureyev, the man with a plan. "I respect what he did for the Opéra immensely," says the choreographer Jerome Robbins, not a man known to lavish praise. "I think he pulled that whole company right up out of the doldrums and gave them a discipline. . . . He gave them a goal to go after. He was interested in the dancers, and he really made them into quite a good company. . . . Anyone who stood up to the Soviet Union would not be afraid of anything—and he wasn't. He carried that audaciousness right through to the end of his life. What he wanted he wanted, and what he didn't like he didn't want."[23]

What Nureyev wanted for the Opéra was some fresh air —and fresh faces. Bringing in the latter was an uphill battle with a company as rigidly hierarchical as the Opéra. "Rudolf was firmly of the belief," an Opéra ballet mistress explains, "that if a dancer who is very talented has to wait until he is thirty-one for someone to retire before he can become a premier danseur, the moment is gone. It's too late. They've lost heart, they've lost hope, and they've lost their best years. He believed that, if the talent is there and it's ready to go, then it's got to go. That's why he pushed the promotions through faster, and it was not a popular move."[24] The generation of dancers who had dominated the Opéra for more than a decade—Ghislaine Thesmar, Noëlla Pontois, Michaël Denard, Cyril Atanassof[25]—were all approaching the age of retirement, as were a significant number of the corps de ballet dancers. Nureyev seized the opportunity, and, according to Dupond, "the average age of the company changed completely."[26]

"The new generation," the exquisite Opéra étoile Elisabeth Platel remembers, "was ready to go,"[27] and the result was the first revelation of Nureyev's Paris period. In less than two years, audiences were being treated to a new Paris Opéra Ballet. Nureyev transformed a sluggish, too-secure corps de ballet into a vigorous, streamlined ensemble of women pawing for their next opportunity, and the male ensemble was refashioned on the Bruhn paradigm—clean, long-limbed, precise, and finished. He brought on an exuberant fleet of new étoiles, all of them under twenty-five—Manuel Legris, Laurent Hilaire, Isabelle Guérin, and, most spectacular of all, a former gymnast named Sylvie Guillem, who became the most acclaimed young ballerina in Europe.[28] Nureyev's stormy association with Guillem is powerful proof of his commitment to the development of new talent. In 1982, before Nureyev was director of the Opéra, he gave Guillem her first major role in his Paris staging of Don Quixote—the elegiac reigne des dryades that was tailor-made for Guillem's endless floating extensions and became the talk of the town. In 1984, when Guillem was barely nineteen, Nureyev made her the youngest *danseuse étoile* in the history of the Opéra, despite a temperament to rival his own. A notorious squabble during a European tour provides a telling example of the leeway Nureyev allowed Guillem. After a head-on confrontation in rehearsal, Guillem refused to dance at that evening's performance. The curtain was held for almost half an hour, according to an eyewitness, while Guillem stood her ground. She developed a sudden desire for the taste of fresh strawberries. (Richard Crookback uses the same routine in Shakespeare's *Richard III*.) The strawberries appeared, Guillem took a single look at them, and proceeded to the stage.

The new Opéra looked as good as it did because Nureyev kept his dancers busy. They not only had plenty to do but plenty to see and assimilate. "He really showed us a new way of dancing the classic style," Elisabeth Platel explains. "It was a contemporary approach, not old-fashioned, but also *royal—du vrai style classique, du vrai Petipa pur.*"[29] In addition to streamlining the Opéra's approach to the traditional classics, Nureyev also introduced a host of new influences. Less than six months after he took control of the Opéra, the Martha Graham Dance Company became the first modern dance ensemble ever to dance on the stage of the Palais Garnier. The engagement was an unqualified success (and a particular triumph for Graham, who had been crucified by the French critics on her first visit to Paris exactly thirty years earlier). In addition to Nureyev's own stagings of the Petipa standards—among them the new *Raymonda*, the notorious *Swan Lake*, and his versions of *Nutcracker* and *The Sleeping Beauty*—the Paris dancers soon were faced with an unprecedented range of contemporary styles. Nureyev brought on the newest of the new names in choreography—Maguy Marin, William Forsythe, Karole Armitage, David Parsons, Michael Clark—as well as works by the great contemporary masters, from Merce Cunningham's *Points in Space* to Paul Taylor's *Aureole, Sacre du printemps: The Rehearsal*, and *Speaking in Tongues*. (The chief administrator of the Graham repertory, Ron Protas, refused Nureyev access to Graham masterworks such as *Appalachian Spring* and, in 1987, paid for his resistance in public, when Nureyev, unhappy over the seating plan at a Graham gala, poured an icy cocktail over Protas's head.)

The influx had the impact Nureyev planned. The Opéra woke up. "Rudolf got rid of the French cream," Patrice Bart concludes.

> He got rid of all the decoration that people used to have here and made them cleaner and more classical. He gave a discipline to the company and a more modern look with all the choreographers he brought here to work. He was always trying to give the dancers contemporary influences. "You should use your body for breathing, like Graham," he used to say. "Use everything you can take from the moderns in the classic ballets." That sounds like a contradiction, but it's not. There can be a very stiff side to classical dancing. You can get stuck. No movement in your dancing, no breathing. Rudolf made the company not only more beautiful but stronger, because he gave them all this information. They looked more modern, more alive, and that was Rudolf. [30]

In 1986—the year Nureyev's contract was up for renewal[31]—he took the plunge and brought the Opéra to America for the first time since 1948. The three-week debut engagement at the Metropolitan Opera House in New York City was an unqualified critical and commercial triumph. Once again, a Nureyev season was the hottest ticket in town—but with a crucial difference. This time he'd ceded center stage to his creation, the new Paris Opéra Ballet.

Fifteen

"I Cannot Have AIDS"

"Unclean, unclean! I must touch him or kiss him no more."

—MINA, *in* Bram Stoker's Dracula

T he Opéra's triumph in New York was Nureyev's last smash hit until *La Bayadère* in 1992. Other imperatives, such as the approach of his fiftieth birthday, were taking over his life, and, for once, there was nothing Nureyev could do about the situation. But Nureyev already had performed a miracle. His achievement with the Paris Opéra Ballet was his unsigned letter to the world, one accomplished in the shadow of a plague. According to Michel Canesi, Nureyev's physician from the time of his diagnosis with HIV, the alleged AIDS virus, in 1984 until his death in January 1993, Nureyev's illness spanned more than twelve years. He stopped working barely three months before his death.

For any number of reasons—the bitterness of his child-hood, the fear of KGB reprisals, the voracity of his appetites—Nureyev was never a man to dwell on the past. "Never look back," he told interviewers at the drop of a hat. "That way you fall down stairs." If he had been the type to ruminate on days gone by, Nureyev surely would have noticed that his life had been spent in intimate proximity to the great events of the day, almost in spite of himself. The great events of Nureyev's life inevitably occurred next door to the watershed events of his time. Nureyev was never a political person, but his defection—to him, an apolitical move—was one of the defining moments of the Cold War. Drawn irresistibly to the alternative adventures of bohemia, he arrived in London just as it was becoming the center of international hipdom.[1] The ur-love child, Nureyev reached the West just as the sexual revolution got underway. The rest is history. By the 1980s, Nureyev "shared with the athlete-kings what Joan Didion calls the conviction that the lights would always turn green, wherever they traveled."[2]

On July 3, 1981, the *New York Times* ran a small item deep in its national section on the emergence of a new "gay cancer," more than a year after the first reported cases of what the world would come to know as AIDS. The disease already had claimed the lives of eight homosexual men in New York City, San Francisco, and Los Angeles,[3] and reports of new cases were increasing at an astronomical rate. The brutal symptoms of the new disease—a disfiguring form of cancer known as "Kaposi's sarcoma" that had been seen before only in geriatric wards, and a virtually unheard of strain of pneumonia, *Pneumocystis carinii*, that could kill in a matter of days—ignited a panic in party town, particularly since its targets seemed to be the men driving through the fastest lane at the highest speed. By 1982, Nureyev was already so acutely aware of the chilling new rumors that he was ready to jeopardize his $350,000 salary for *Exposed*. "The insurance company required a blood test and Rudi flat out refused to have one," the film's director, James Toback, recalls about contract negotiations with Nureyev in the summer of 1981. "He really held his ground about it, too, and the only way he would agree to any kind of blood test at all was if it were done by his own doctor. I explained to him that the test had to be done by the doctor assigned to the film by the insurance company. He refused to go along with that and finally said, 'My doctor will send you a paper for the insurance company.' That's exactly what happened, and for whatever reason the report from his own doctor was acceptable. We shot in New York and Paris in December and January, and he was not feeling well most of the time—colds, chronic bronchitis, things like that."[4]

By the time Nureyev had taken on his new job in Paris in September 1983, his physical problems were assuming an ominous pattern, such as the weight loss, unexplained fevers, and recurrent night sweats that were already synonymous with the onset of AIDS. According to Nureyev's lover Robert Tracy, who went with him to Paris, the night sweats would leave him "drenched in the morning but he wouldn't mention it. That was another way to avoid acceptance of what he had."[5] Matters didn't improve with the new year. When Nureyev went with the Opéra for guest performances at the Edinburgh Festival in the summer of 1984, according to Patrick Dupond, "he was not well at all. He had pneumonia and then, on top of that, he had hepatitis too. He was green and he couldn't breathe, and we all said that he should go back to Paris, go to a doctor. But he did all of his performances anyway, every single one of them. It was beyond courage."[6] Not long after the Opéra returned home, Nureyev contacted Canesi, a young Paris doctor specializing in venereal disease whose offices he'd first visited a year earlier for an unspecified problem:[7] "It was at the beginning of 1983 [that I first saw Nureyev]. Charles Murdland, one of the directors of London Festival Ballet, I think, whom I had just met, telephoned me one evening to ask if I could immediately see Nureyev, one of his best friends. I asked Nureyev to see me for a blood test. I gave him the test but there was nothing significant."[8]

When Nureyev made a second visit to Canesi in the autumn of 1984, the results were different. Canesi sent him to Dr. Wily Rozenbaum for blood tests. Rozenbaum was an early hero of AIDS research in France, and his laboratory at the Pitié-Salpêtrière hospital in Paris was one of the few French medical centers with the facilities to administer the new blood test for the presence of HIV. In November 1984, Nureyev made his first visit to Salpêtrière. According to Canesi, the test results suggested that Nureyev already had been HIV-positive for "three or four years."[9]

■

The word "victim" was never in Nureyev's vocabulary. His first response to the test results was a slightly anxious optimism. The idea that his condition might kill him simply was not within the realm of possibility. "'I know I am going to be a very, very old man,' " Canesi remembers Nureyev telling him more than once. "Yes, we knew that there was something wrong, but at that time we thought only ten percent of seropositive people were going to develop the disease. He was not anxious at first, not really, especially since his health quickly became much better. He thought that it was something that would not cause him really serious problems."[10] Nureyev made himself available to whatever treatments Canesi suggested, and, in consultation with Rozenbaum, began receiving daily injections of a promising new drug, HPA-23. The American movie idol Rock Hudson, who had received a diagnosis of AIDS in June 1984, came to Paris to begin treatments of HPA-23 in the autumn of that year. After a short round of injections, Hudson soon was told that the signs of HIV infection were no longer evident in his blood. Unfortunately, the results of "short-term treatments were flawed. Although HPA-23 might halt the replication of the virus, as soon as the patient was off the drug, viral reproduction began anew, ravaging the patient's immune system. This would not be clear for several months, however, so Hudson left Paris convinced that he was cured of AIDS."[11] Also, as both Hudson and Nureyev would learn, the secondary effects of HPA-23, according to Canesi, were "very, very toxic."[12]

The initial treatments of HPA-23 stabilized Nureyev's health. "He thought he was cured," Robert Tracy remembers, "and for a long time it seemed as if he were."[13] A good boy for once, Nureyev began a diligent routine of visits to Canesi for daily injections. At the same time, he turned to his traditional cure-all—work—with a vengeance. In January 1985 Nureyev took a troupe of twenty Opéra dancers on a two-week tour to India. After that, the number of his solo guest appearances kept to the breakneck momentum of old—Spain, Germany, a return to the Edinburgh Festival, a sold-out appearance at Valence in the south of France with "an endless line of people queuing around the theater in a terrible downpour to get a ticket."[14] Before the end of the year, he'd staged his *Don Quixote* in Peking and two new productions for the Opéra, his version of *Nutcracker* and an original full-length ballet based on Henry James's *Washington Square*, to music by Charles Ives. December found him in Florence, partnering Sylvie Guillem in her much-anticipated debut as *Giselle*. The treatments and the pace seemed to do the trick, and Nureyev's relief was palpable. "I don't know whether it was the injections or psychological, but he was really in good form," Canesi remembers. "Perhaps, also because things were going very well at the Opéra. He felt well again. Seeing that he was fine, that he could dance and handle his choreography, he rather forgot about his illness. He performed all over the world with no problems."[15]

By 1987, with his fiftieth birthday just around the corner, Nureyev was anxious again as his health became more and more erratic. Early in the summer, his old pal Lee Radziwill made a trip to Paris to visit Nureyev "because he was looking so terrible. I knew he was sick, and I thought this would be the last time I'd see him. I think when I left the apartment he did, too. But then when I came back in September, he looked so well I said to him, 'What have you done to yourself?' He held his head high and, looking very proud, said, 'I've danced every night.' "[16] Whatever the restorative powers of performance on Nureyev's health, within weeks of Radziwill's visit Nureyev had contacted Canesi with an urgent demand: "AZT was just beginning to be used in France. I didn't want to give it to him straight away because I was worried that the side effects would hamper him. Rudi lost his temper and said, 'I want this medicine.' I replied that I didn't want to give it to him because there hadn't been long enough to judge the results. At the time very high doses of AZT were being used, which was quite dangerous. But I had to give in to him and prescribed it in about 1988—he was so insistent. But he didn't take it regularly. He just did whatever he felt like. He went off every time with tons of drugs, and every time I went to see him I found unused packets all over the place."[17]

■

Thirteen years and counting into the AIDS epidemic, the most ironic advice an AIDS patient can receive is to look on the bright side. (It's also the most annoying.) However well intended, the sentiment is only a reminder that there is no bright side to AIDS. It's a lesson Nureyev's generation of long-term survivors learned in the fire. Those lucky enough to last through the early years of the most stigmatized disease of modern times saw the nightmare unfold—the criminal negligence of the Reagan administration, the murderous policies of the blood industries, particularly in both the United States and France, the witch-hunts of a so-called moral majority exultant at a disease killing all the "right" people. The history of the AIDS epidemic has been minutely, movingly chronicled by gay authors driven to their best work by a need to make sense of—and warn the world about—a disease racing out of control, then and now—Randy Shilts's masterful *And the Band Played On: Politics, People, and the AIDS Epidemic;* the brimstone rhetoric of Larry Kramer's *Reports from the Holocaust* and his play *The Normal Heart;* Michael Callen's practical, poetic *Surviving AIDS.* Unfortunately for patients when Nureyev received his AIDS diagnosis, forced to cope with the disease before there was an effective body of AIDS literature, the available information was scattered, incomplete, and contradictory (much as it is today, unless you've got a really good doctor).

Nureyev was well read. He was aware of the yellow journalism invoked by AIDS, the sensationalist approach of most of the media. The ugly projections, and their potential impact on his career in the hands of the press he already hated so much, could hardly escape him. The complexity of his response to the presence of HIV in his blood—initial optimism, fits of panic, and, finally, bedrock denial—is a textbook study of the emotional and psychological roller coaster that parallels the bitter assault AIDS makes upon the human body. AIDS also induces "an opportunistic infection of the spirit," Paul Monette wrote in *Borrowed Time: An AIDS Memoir.* "It comes like a slowly dawning horror. At first you are equipped with a hundred different amulets to keep it far away. Then someone you know goes into the hospital, and suddenly you are at high noon in full battle gear. They have neglected to tell you that you will be issued no weapons of any sort. So you cobble together a weapon out of anything that lies at hand, like a prisoner honing a spoon handle into a stiletto. You fight tough, you fight dirty, but you cannot fight dirtier than it."[18]

As Nureyev would come to learn, there are good days and there are bad days and then there are terrible days. Particularly for someone such as Nureyev, whose image was built upon his physicality—his beauty, his stamina, the limitless resources of strength and physical facility—the corrosive effect of AIDS on his person would have been bitter enough. The games AIDS plays with the mind are every bit as cruel, waves of hope—a good doctor, a good day, a good night's sleep—crashing against the black rock of despair on a daily basis until a person becomes "soul-weary of AIDS—of having it, fighting it, or hearing and thinking about it."[19]

Nureyev found out immediately what the societal aspects of AIDS can mean to a man who'd spent twenty years cultivating a high public profile, or to a gay world that had spent almost as long forging a place in the sun. Nureyev's visit to Salpêtrière, with the Pasteur Institute where HIV was first identified, the center of AIDS research in France, did not go unnoticed. Salpêtrière is located in the center of Paris. In no time the rumor was everywhere: "Nureyev has AIDS." The Paris grapevine is thorough and, as soon as the rumors of his AIDS diagnosis hit the local circuit, word also began to spread that Nureyev was experimenting with a procedure known as plasmapheresis, a controversial and extremely expensive treatment in which the blood is "washed" clean. The patient's blood is removed by transfusion in measured quantities and then replaced with fresh plasma. (Canési still denies the talk of the blood cleansing: "Someone told me that in New York they were saying that I gave him my own blood, which made him look like a vampire. No, the stories about the blood transfusions were completely—it's a fantasy. [AIDS] doesn't work this way.")

The backlash was instantaneous. Nureyev was soon meeting people who would not shake his hand. Nureyev proceeded about his business as usual and began to construct a wall of silence around the facts of his illness. "The disease was never discussed," Patrice Bart, a close Opéra colleague, remembers,[20] and even his closest friends were kept in the dark about the reality of Nureyev's condition. The choreographer Rudi van Dantzig was an old and valued colleague of Nureyev since his days at the Royal. Van Dantzig was a frequent visitor to Paris during the 1980s and always stayed at Nureyev's Quai Voltaire apartment. "Even on those last visits to Paris," van Dantzig recalls, "I didn't know that Rudolf had AIDS. I'd heard the rumors like everybody else but could not believe them. It just seemed impossible that he could work as hard and as much as he did with AIDS. I could not combine Rudolf's capacity to work with the idea that he had AIDS. I wish now that I had known because I would have understood his behavior at the time better. He seemed so afraid to go to sleep at night. Now I understand why."[21]

Once again, he was at the epicenter of a social earthquake. According to Paul Monette, the issue of privacy—whether or not to publicly acknowledge an AIDS diagnosis—"engages vectors of the nightmare that make it different from every other medical crisis,"[22] particularly for a celebrity. Unlike the response to his defection, however, the apolitical attitude Nureyev maintained about his illness was at critical odds with the most important advance against the epidemic to date—the epidemic's empowering effect on the gay world literally fighting for its life. If you weren't part of the solution, you were part of the problem. Nureyev, despite the contribution he could have made (in visibility as well as cash), let the parade pass him by. The gay icon who never once said the word AIDS in public, he became part of the problem. The angry repercussions were far-reaching. "Nureyev's silence about his illness shows that AIDS is still in the closet," the *Los Angeles Times*'s art critic Christopher Knight told *Newsweek* shortly after Nureyev's death. "You still run up against the sissy factor: culture is only paid lip service because it's considered the insignificant province of women and gays, which is what allowed Patrick

Buchanan and his ilk to beat up on the NEA [the National Endowment for the Arts]. AIDS is not a gay disease, but because it first showed up in the gay population it's bound up with the gay-rights movement."[23] For Paul Monette, Nureyev's silence on his AIDS diagnosis right to the end was a disservice both to the gay world and to himself:

> I think it's perfectly appropriate to keep something like an AIDS diagnosis to yourself. Why set yourself up for a backlash? But people are dying in droves because of the ignorance of the general public, who seem to exist in a void on the subject of AIDS. It's true that Nureyev was a great artist, a very great artist, but great artists also owe a great deal, and their notoriety also includes the harder stuff, like a responsibility to the world around them. The worst thing that those of us have to fight is the shame of it. I did feel shame at first, and my lover and I both kept our condition a secret for almost two years. That choice alone almost killed us.[24]

For all its legitimacy and logic, the anger leveled at Nureyev for his inaction must be balanced against the fact that AIDS is also an illness suffered by individuals. Nureyev clearly missed his chance to serve a greater good for once in his life, to lend his inexhaustible resources to a cause other than Rudolf Nureyev. Even his will made no provisions for a bequest to AIDS research until a few short months before Nureyev entered the Notre-Dame du Perpétuel Secours hospital in the Paris suburb of Levallois for the last time, when, according to Canesi, he finally acknowledged that "I must do something for all those people."[25]

The length of time Nureyev lived and worked with AIDS is among the longest on record. The physical feat alone is the most staggering tour de force of his career. AIDS, like all illnesses, reverses a critical balance of power in the human body: you don't tell your body what to do—it tells you. It drains the body not only of energy and strength but of hope and will. According to Wallace Potts, Nureyev "did everything he could to fight [the disease]. His whole life was dancing and being onstage. For the longest time he thought that if he fought hard enough he

could beat this thing. Toward the end he was reconciled. He was
not a sentimental person. He never complained. He didn't show
any signs of pain. But at the end, the fevers took their toll."[26]
The Opéra *étoile* Elisabeth Platel agrees with Potts's assessment
of Nureyev's determination to keep his condition at bay: "He
never worked as a sick person. He was always in the studio every
day—pushing, dancing, working."[27] As Nureyev proved for all
the world to see, the will is the way. The long-term survivors
Michael Callen interviewed for *Surviving AIDS* led him to conclude that their common ground was "grit. These people were
all fighters: skeptical, opinionated, . . . passionately committed to
staying alive. They have worked hard to stay alive."[28] A fighter
from day one, Nureyev stayed alive by working hard, until the
very last. He conducted the final rehearsals for the Opéra *Bayadère* in October 1992 from a reclining position but didn't miss a
single rehearsal.

Nureyev also was following the instincts that had determined the course of his life since that first blinding glimpse of
ballet at the Ufa Opera House all those years ago. The loner kept
to himself. Acknowledging his condition would have invoked his
two most dreaded demons. It would have necessitated a public
admission of his homosexuality, which Nureyev's formative
years in the shadow of Stalin could never allow. And it would
have been tantamount to suicide, because Nureyev's dancing career would have been over. The length of time he continued to
perform, aware of what he looked like onstage, is the definitive
statement on Nureyev's equation of life and dance. An official
announcement of his AIDS diagnosis would have complicated his
life impossibly. For one thing, Nureyev would not have been
allowed reentry into the United States. For another, he knew that
the audience that had once come to see Nureyev, the god of the
dance, would now come to the theater to see the dancer with
AIDS.

Elena Tchernichova, a friend and confidante of Nureyev
since their days together as boarders at the Kirov school, remembers a comment Nureyev made during their last evening together
in 1991. A colleague of theirs from American Ballet Theatre, the

beautiful American danseur Clark Tippet who was on his way to becoming a major choreographer, had just been diagnosed with AIDS. Tippet's name came up over dinner.

Nureyev's response to the news of Tippet's condition was simple and telling.

"Tell him never to stop dancing."

Sixteen

The Fat Lady Sings

DAME EDNA EVERAGE: So, who was your favorite partner?
RUDOLF NUREYEV: Miss Piggy.

—The Dame Edna Everage Show.

Near the end of *Valentino*, for reasons that are never fully explained, Nureyev finds himself involved in a professional boxing match before a vast, jeering crowd. Rudi/Rudy cannot be dissuaded from head-on battle against an opponent twice his size, and he takes a merciless pummeling. With unholy relish, Russell charts blow after blow after blow to Nureyev's glistening face and body—flat against his face, deep into his belly, even a double-fisted punch onto the top of his head—until our hero upchucks a stream of rich red blood. Still undaunted, Nureyev refuses to stop fighting and, with one final burst of yes-I-can, sends his nemesis straight to the floor.

Although it is, as Googie Gomez would say, "a stretch" to imagine *Valentino* bearing any relation to life as we know it— the idea seems antithetical to Ken Russell's entire body of work —the boxing match is the only scene in *Valentino* that finds anything in Nureyev other than a handsome man with a foreign accent who moves beautifully. Granted, Nureyev looks smashing in the ring. The lighting emphasis on his pouty mouth, all red and ripe, gives the scene a sense of roughhouse and romance, and the formfitted boxing shorts adds a steamy sense of S & M. In retrospect, however, Nureyev in boxing gloves is a snapshot synopsis of his lifelong war against the world. Nureyev the pugilist was as much a part of his public and private persona as Nureyev the prince.

Nureyev never had greater need for boxing gloves than during the last five years of his life. From a twelve-hour return to Russia to visit his mother's deathbed in 1987 to his final entry into the Perpétuel-Secours hospital just outside Paris in November 1992, Nureyev's last years were a series of body blows. He lost his mother and, in February 1991, Fonteyn lost her long battle with cancer. Then, in barely two years Nureyev would also say good-bye to his job at the Opéra, see the last shreds of his ballet audience disappear, and, most brutal of all, finally relinquish all hope that he could continue to dance. Instead of defeating him, the last battles gave Nureyev his last signature role, onstage and off—the phoenix. Over the last months of his life, the world saw a new Nureyev, a softer, warmer Nureyev. There was the promise of a new career as a conductor and then his swan song to ballet, the Opéra Bayadère, waiting in the wings.

The onslaught of ill fortune in the late 1980s, underlined by the increasing intrusions of AIDS, did little to curb Nureyev's temper. During the final years of his performing career, Nureyev's hostility toward the dance press reached proportions of genuine ugliness. In a 1990 interview for Esquire, he referred to the Soviet critic Inna Sklarevskaya as "that Yiddish bitch."[1] In March 1991, Nureyev made a personal attempt to keep the New York Times away from a performance he was scheduled to give on Long Island. He telephoned Anna Kisselgoff, the chief dance critic for the Times, and informed her that she was not to attend the performance. When Nureyev was informed that the Times makes its own decisions, his response was direct: "Then I will have to resort to violence."[2] (Kisselgoff attended the performance without incident.) Barely a month later, during a Nureyev and Friends performance in Verona, Italy, Nureyev became so irritated with a young

Italian danseur that he kicked him in the rear with enough force to send the young man to the hospital. In December of that same year, Nureyev was the storm center of a furious scandal in Vienna. When his offer to conduct a special gala performance received a "thanks, but no thanks" response, the rejection was both a professional insult and a personal affront. Not only was Nureyev an Austrian citizen,[3] but his quarter-century association of convenience with the Vienna State Opera had been good news for both sides. According to an eyewitness, "Rudolf went wild." The charges and countercharges flooded the Vienna press.

Nureyev had valid reasons to rail at the winds of fate, and AIDS was only one of them. The two trips he made to Russia in the late 1980s—the first to visit Farida's bedside, the second two years later for guest performances with the Kirov—were both harsh disappointments. Nureyev had worked diligently since his defection to get his mother out of Russia, the reason he never once went on record with criticism of the Soviet government. (As a result of Nureyev's rare tactfulness on any subject, Sir David Webster, the head of Covent Garden, once called him "the best public relations the Kirov could have.")[4]

Farida was, in effect, a hostage, the Soviets' trump card in their game with Nureyev. She was used with merciless mastery: both of Nureyev's surviving sisters, as well as his niece and nephew, were allowed to visit him in Monte Carlo and in Paris, but never the visitor he wanted most—his mother. Nureyev's efforts to bring her to the West became most determined in the mid-1970s, when Farida's health began to falter. In 1976, a host of his highest ranking colleagues formed a special committee to assist Nureyev in bringing Farida to the West. The committee eventually compiled a list of 107,000 signatures in support of Nureyev's letters, and the names involved included Edward Albee, Ingrid Bergman, Leonard Bernstein, Helen Hayes, Katharine Hepburn, John Gielgud, Paul Newman, and Andy Warhol. This, in turn, prompted forty-two United States Senators to make personal appeals to Soviet Prime Minister Aleksey Kosygin. Nureyev made direct appeals to both Britain's prime minister, Harold

Wilson, and U.S. President Gerald Ford, both of whom promised to make appeals to Moscow; the following year, he took his request to the United States Commission on Security and Cooperation in Europe, a committee organized by Congress to monitor compliance with the recent Helsinki Conference accords.

The massive effort was to no avail. Just before Farida's death in November 1987, the Gorbachev government allowed Nureyev an in-and-then-straight-out return to Ufa to say goodbye. When Rudik finally saw his mother again for the first time in twenty-seven years, the dying old woman didn't recognize the son who'd traveled more than five thousand miles to see her. According to one of Nureyev's closest Russian friends, however, when Nureyev had gone, Farida turned to her nurse and said, "That was Rudik, wasn't it?"

The return to the Kirov was no happier. Nureyev's performances in the theater of his youth in November 1989 were anything but a triumphal reintroduction. In addition to the standard fevers and exhaustion of AIDS, Nureyev performed with more than his usual number of injuries, including a torn calf muscle in his left leg. His partner, the exhilarating young Russian ballerina Zhanna Ayupova, was thirty years his junior. And, at fifty-one, Nureyev chose the grueling role of James in *La Sylphide* as his return vehicle. True to form, he passed up few chances to shock the natives offstage as well. "Not everyone waited for him with love," a local critic wrote of the prodigal's return.

> Many anticipated disappointment, having heard that Nureyev "arrived lame" and generally "can't do anything anymore." . . . What upset people [at rehearsal] was his shuffling little walk, his unconcealed distortions of the choreography (which left his partner at a loss), and, to top it all off, his bright yellow outfit, with thick plastic clogs worn over his ballet slippers. . . . At the performance everything became strangely muddled; we tried to look through time to see the dance as it would have been thirty, or even twenty years ago. Our ovations were addressed to the past.[5]

Nureyev danced all five of his scheduled performances. "I don't know why I did it," he confessed to the journalist Luke

Jennings not long after. "It's probably a very childish thing, but I'm of the school of Margot Fonteyn, who never could cancel a performance. If you could stand you could dance."[6] The ironic last scene with Farida and then the inevitable defeat at the Kirov left Nureyev with a bitter aftertaste: "I don't miss Russia and it doesn't miss me either. I went back there and it didn't make a dent. My last trip there—the people who came, the fans, they looked like people who came out of the Gulag. Strange, worn, shabby old people, like in one of those science fiction films. It frightened me. Depressing. Those were my fans. They came out of thirty-three years ago."[7]

Matters were not much better back in Paris, where Nureyev's more frequent absences were becoming a problem for the administration of the Opéra. According to Nureyev's own count, he spent 80 rather than the requisite 180 days at the Opéra during the company's 1988–89 season.[8] Meanwhile, Nureyev was embroiled in the last great *scandale* of his years at the Opéra. He was determined to name his latest protégé, Kenneth Greve, a strikingly handsome twenty-one-year-old Danish corps de ballet dancer from American Ballet Theatre, to *étoile* status with the Opéra. The very idea was a direct assault on the cherished Opéra hierarchy, and Nureyev was intransigent on the subject.[9] "You can imagine what a revolution that caused," the *danseuse étoile* Elisabeth Platel remembers about the Greve impasse. Nureyev was so enraged at Platel's refusal to dance with Greve that he threw a glass of wine in her face at a public dinner party and refused to address her for a year. Patrick Dupond still rankles at the subject:

> People have been suffering for years to get a role and then out of the blue some corps de ballet boy comes in and is dancing the prince in *Swan Lake*. It's simply impossible, unless he's a genius, which, unfortunately for Kenneth, was not the case. The administration finally said "No," and Rudolf was furious. To him he was the boss and he found out he wasn't. I think people finally came to feel sorry for poor Kenneth. He couldn't breathe, couldn't dance, couldn't do anything he was so scared. He'd go onstage shaking.

The confrontation brewing between Nureyev and the bosses, Opéra president Pierre Bergé in particular, came to a head in August 1989. His contract as ballet director was to expire at the end of the month, when Nureyev announced his imminent departure on a nine-month North American tour of his first musical comedy, *The King and I*. Protesting perhaps a tad too much, Bergé denies the rumors of acrimony over Nureyev's contract negotiations: "I never, never, never had a fight with him. The truth is that his contract was over, and he came to me and said, 'I don't want to renew, because I want to play in *The King and I* and do movies and other things I feel I have to do.' I said, 'Rudi, I understand completely.' We never had a fight. Never!"[10] A final decision was postponed but, by October, two of Nureyev's associates, Patrice Bart and Eugène Poliakov, had been named interim directors. (According to many Opéra dancers, Bart and Poliakov already had been the de facto directors of the company for two years.) By November, tempers were going public, as were reports of a $270,000 balance on a $600,000 French tax bill that Nureyev insisted be reduced.[11] Complaining about Bergé, he told the *New York Times*, "It is easier to speak to God."[12] As tough as Nureyev, Bergé, complaining about Nureyev's frequent absences, told French television, "The Paris Opéra Ballet does not give sabbaticals."[13] On November 21, the day Nureyev returned from the Kirov fiasco, he and Bergé released a joint statement:

> The Paris Opéra and Rudolf Nureyev have reached the mutual decision to terminate the latter's function as the director of dance at the Paris Opéra.
> However, in order to maintain a close relationship between the Paris Opéra and Rudolf Nureyev, it has been decided to create the post of principal choreographer, to be henceforth occupied by Rudolf Nureyev in order to insure that his productions will remain with the Paris Opéra.
> The Paris Opéra would like to express to Rudolf Nureyev its gratitude and its esteem for the exceptional work he has accomplished during his years as director of the company of dancers.

Nureyev was on his own again. But by 1989 Nureyev's technique had long since deserted him. There was nothing left. The first warnings had sounded in the press as early as the first Nureyev and Friends concert at the Uris in 1974, when Arlene Croce wrote in *The New Yorker* that Nureyev was "no longer the bounding Tartar, nor at age thirty-six could he be, although audiences still gasp hopefully at his every jump."[14] His shaky classical solo at the start of *Swine Lake* on the Muppet program only three years later, however enjoyable it was, is evidence that Nureyev had reached the downhill slope: clearly underrehearsed, he is tense, forced, and strained; his dancing is unsteady to the point of desperation. By the early eighties, when AIDS-related complications were adding to his chronic physical problems, Nureyev was showing decline in every technical regard but stamina. Typically, Nureyev exacerbated the situation by refusing to scale down choreography to compensate for his reduced capacities. "No matter what physical problems Rudolf had," an Opéra colleague remembers, "he danced every step." Gallant as Nureyev's fidelity to the choreography may have been, the choice only made him look worse. The first demands for ticket refunds surfaced as early as 1985, when two British patrons of the Palace Theatre, Manchester, reported Nureyev and the management of the theater to the local Office of Fair Trade for misrepresentation. "When he did dance in the first ballet," their complaint read, "all [Nureyev] did was wave his hands and arms. . . . He did none of his famous leaps at all."[15] The lion's leap, as Fonetyn once described Nureyev *en l'air*, was by now long gone. But Nureyev still went on, and on and on, damn the torpedoes.

Even after his unceremonious exit from the Garnier, the thought of retirement—what Nureyev called the "Hiroshima question"—was still beyond the realm of possibility. By the fall of 1989, with the contract dispute at the Opéra still unresolved, he was on the road again for the next nine months with *The King and I* tour. Once again Nureyev made some major noise over insurance company demands for a blood test—with good reason. The American government, then and today, forbids foreigners with HIV from entering the United States: "I think he refused,"

Canesi remembers. "But the tour went ahead all the same. The contract was enormous, and he made a fortune."[16] (Word among *The King and I* company was that Nureyev was pulling in fifty thousand dollars a week.) As always, quick guest shots elsewhere were worked into Nureyev's schedule, such as the return to the Kirov in November and overnight appearances from Washington, DC, to Thunder Bay, Ontario, but he missed not a single performance in nine months on the road with *King and I*. The tour received uniformly unhappy notices, particularly for Nureyev, whose "singing" was more *sprechstimme* in the Rex Harrison style. Still it managed to pull in close to $11 million.

From all accounts, Nureyev enjoyed his shot at being a song-and-dance man, although the constraints of his illness were becoming more serious: Nureyev would not allow any theater on the tour to use its air conditioning during performances, for fear of developing a chill. At the first rehearsal, after his big solo "Is a Puzzlement," Nureyev walked directly over to a corner and buried his head in a garbage can out of mortification. He hosted a Christmas party for the cast when the company played Miami at Christmas and was still in high gear when the tour reached British Columbia near the end of the run. Nureyev was in a Vancouver restaurant after a performance when he was confronted by a gushing fan, a woman of a certain age who had also been at the theater that evening. Unfortunately, her ecstatic litany of praise opened on the wrong note: "Oh, Mr. Nureyev! Mr. Nureyev! Everything was just wonderful, and the children . . . Oh, the children!" Nureyev's response, according to a company dancer, was vintage stock: "Fuck the children. What did you think of me?"

Nureyev went straight from *The King and I* into a Nureyev and Friends tour that played a dozen cities in Mexico, the United States, and Canada. At the Edinburgh Festival in August 1990 Nureyev received his last favorable notices as a performer —and among his most impassioned. Flemming Flindt's dance account of Gogol's *The Overcoat* cast Nureyev as a beleaguered office clerk in old Petersburg. "Nureyev abandons all pretense of youth and glamour," Judith Mackrell wrote in *The Independent*.

The Overcoat . . . extracts from him a performance of un-
questioned greatness—utterly unfaked in its characterization, lacking any face-saving tricks in the movement. In his
dusty trousers and flapping coat, making no effort to conceal
his thinning hair, Nureyev allows himself to look much older
than he really is. And far from trying to gloss over the
decline of his technique, it is out of the ruin in Nureyev the
dancer that he creates the character of Akakyevich the social
misfit.[17]

Despite the enthusiastic response to *The Overcoat,* Nureyev knew the end was approaching. In the winter of 1990, for the
first time since *Valentino* fifteen years earlier, he went forty days
without a single performance.

Assaulted on two fronts, age and AIDS, Nureyev's determination to continue performing is the last great enigma of his
career. It contradicts his most fundamental signatures—not only
the energy of his prime but the pride in his physical powers
that got his audiences panting. "I think he could never have not
danced." Sibley concludes, "I cannot even imagine Rudolf not
dancing every single day of his life. I don't know what he would
have done without dancing."[18] Early in his Western career, Ninette de Valois described Nureyev as "a man with no illusions—
absoultely none," and the wry realist in him has to have known
what he looked like onstage at fifty-one—enervated, broken,
balding. "It makes me so angry that he let himself look that
way," Maria Tallchief said not long after Nureyev's death. "That
he let himself be photographed that way."[19] In 1990, the Balanchine Trust, which supervises the performance level of Balanchine's ballets, withdrew permission for Nureyev to perform
Apollo any longer. "Rudolf was not dancing well," Barbara Horgan, the director of the Trust, explains:

George had died and there are three heirs to *Apollo.* They
certainly weren't complaining about Rudolf in the sense of,
"He can't do this any more." But we started to get really
very bad reviews that were embarrassing to Rudolf and, we
felt, embarrassing to the Balanchine name. So I called An-

drew Grossman [Nureyev's representative at Columbia Artists Management] and I said, "Look, we have a real problem." Andrew said, "We'll give you more money." I said,
"You know it's not about the money. It's about Rudolf. And
I'm going to tell you something, Andrew—you'd be doing
him a favor by taking it out of his repertory and getting him
something else to do. If you're a friend, give him a break." I
know Rudolf was very bitter about it, I was told, and very
angry. We were referred to as "those awful ladies who do all
these awful things." But you know what? It had to be. It
just couldn't go on like that.[20]

And it didn't, not after Fonteyn's death in February 1991.
There are those who feel that during Fonteyn's last years Nureyev did less than he could have to relieve the astronomical cost of
the medical care for Arias and then, after her cancer diagnosis,
for Fonteyn herself. Nadia Nerina and her husband, Charles Gordon, are among those who question Nureyev's behavior. "Rudi
may well have been in contact with Margot until she died," Nerina explains, "and he had apparently helped her financially at
times. But she died destitute and her final misery could easily
have been avoided if Rudi had helped her to sort out her financial
problems. His early fame as a dancer was very substantially due
to her. He was much in her debt. He could easily have afforded
the help she needed."[21] Gordon agrees: "As someone who indi-
rectly, though only at the very beginning, was responsible for
helping him to establish his net assets on a proper basis, I have
some ground to upbraid him for not having been more generous
towards Margot Fonteyn during her last wretched years, for after
his escape to the West he unquestionably owed far more to her
than to anyone else."[22]

Word that Fonteyn's death was imminent, however,
brought out the devoted, teasing Nureyev she had known three
decades earlier. Nureyev began making regular trips to her bedside in Panama, lavishing her with gifts—teddy bears, *I Love
Lucy* videos, and, on his last visit, a Dior dressing gown that sent
Fonteyn into gales of her famous, high-pitched giggle. When
Fonteyn died on February 21, 1991, Nureyev went into isolation

on his island. "She was suffering a lot," Nureyev told his friend Luke Jennings, "so it was good for her, I think. It was a release."[23] He spent days staring out into the Tyrrhenian Sea.

Nureyev's farewell tour of Britain two months later was the low point of his career. His choice of venues had been on the decline for some time. In 1987, a Nureyev and Friends tour did two shows a day for two days in the Circus Maximus at Caesar's Palace in Atlantic City; his final New York–area appearance in March 1991 was not at the Metropolitan Opera House but at the Tilles Center for the Performing Arts at C. W. Post University in Brookville, Long Island. The final tour of Britain was managed by a B-circuit promoter whose "roster of superstars" included Bill Haley and the Comets and Pat Boone. Performed to taped music, the month-long tour opened at the Sunderland Empire, a suburban London variety theater that had known better times. Nureyev's friends were horrified by his concession to the third-class conditions. The British designer Tessa Kennedy went to see him perform at the three-thousand-seat Wembley Conference Center, Nureyev's last appearance in London: "It was tragic, horrible. . . . There were these rows of nasty chairs covered in hideous material, and fluorescent strip lighting. . . . The audiences were often ghastly, too. The whole thing was an uncharacteristic relaxing of control on Rudolf's part."[24] Nureyev was booed, patrons sued for refunds, and the notices in the press were the worst yet, under headlines on the order of RUDOLF IS BALLET AWFUL and FLAT-FOOTED NUREYEV LEAVES THEM SHOUTING FOR MONEY BACK. Irritated all the way to the bank, Nureyev wrote off the protests —"Your newspapers," he told the London *Times*, "are edited by Kitty Kelley"[25]—just as he did when the whole unhappy scenario was repeated on his final Australian tour later in the year. In February 1992, Nureyev made his last two appearances as a dancer—*en travesti* as the evil fairy Carabosse on the opening night of his *Sleeping Beauty* at the Deutsche Opera in Berlin and as an angel in Gabor Kavahazi's *Christoforo* in Budapest.

Demon and angel. The circle was complete.

By the early years of the 1990s, the punches were still coming hard, fast, and below the belt—Nureyev was bitterly hurt when the Royal Ballet announced that it would stage Mikhail Baryshnikov's version of *Don Quixote* rather than Nureyev's.

In March 1991, less than a month after Fonteyn's death, Nureyev began to study orchestral conducting with an old and trusted friend, Wilhelm Hubner of the Vienna Academy of Music.[26] Nureyev's knowledge of the international music repertory was encyclopedic, and the possibility of a career on the conductor's podium already had been suggested to Nureyev by, among others, Karl Böhm, Leonard Bernstein, and Herbert von Karajan. (In 1988, at Bernstein's suggestion, Nureyev briefly considered entering the course for conductors at the Juilliard School of Music in New York City.) Within three months of his first lessons with Hubner, Nureyev had begun what he would call his "third walk to Golgotha," conducting his first recital at Vienna's Palais Ausburg. The prospect of a whole new career—and one he could extend indefinitely—seemed to bring back that old-time feeling—and attitude: "Now I know how those bastard conductors feel. You have this fantastic struggle with the orchestra to keep the tempi up. The brass is heavy, the contrabasses are heavy. To keep them together with the violins, you have to goose them all the time."[27] By autumn, with more concerts under his belt in Vienna as well as in Deauville, Ravello, and Athens, the fledgling maestro already had amassed a repertory that included Beethoven, Haydn, Mozart, Prokofiev, Stravinsky, and Tschaikovsky. On May 6, 1992, Nureyev made his last New York appearance, appropriately enough, at the Metropolitan Opera House—conducting a performance of Prokofiev's *Romeo and Juliet* by American Ballet Theatre.

"Very few professional musicians would have attempted to do what Rudolf did that last evening—the guts that it took and the stamina," Charles Barker, ABT's principal conductor, remembers.

Yes, Nureyev was already more than familiar with the score, but getting through three hours of *Romeo and Juliet* under the pressure of a performance at the Metropolitan Opera House is altogether another story. The proper cues have to be there and the beats have to be right, or the musicians will cut a guy's legs off. It's a grueling task, physically grueling and emotionally taxing.

He arrived in New York about two weeks before the performance to begin working with the company pianist. He looked pretty tired and dragged out, but he was very willing to work as much and as long as necessary. The first work session was supposed to be for three hours, and, about midway through, I suggested that maybe we should take a break. Rudolf insisted on working the whole three hours, and we actually ended up going into overtime. He had one three-hour rehearsal with the orchestra, with a few of Rudolf's friends in the house for moral support—Jessye Norman, Jackie Onassis. Nureyev was lively and upbeat all through the orchestra rehearsal, making jokes from the podium. In performance there were a few minor snags, and musically he was very conservative, which is something a young musician will do in general. As far as the guts department goes—just getting up there and doing it—he was totally A-1.[28]

By the time of the Met farewell, Nureyev's medical status had become critical. In September 1991, in Bucharest to conduct performances at the local opera house, Nureyev became so ill that he was forced to return to Vienna for treatment. Nureyev's doctors decided to operate, and surgeons discovered a kidney condition. Nureyev was given a catheter, and recovered. The following March, while back in Russia to conduct performances in St. Petersburg, Kazan, and Yalta, Nureyev became dangerously ill once again. He was hospitalized in St. Petersburg for pneumonia, and, for the first time in his life, was genuinely afraid. Douce François, who accompanied Nureyev to Russia, remembers that "he was in despair. 'Like my father,' he kept saying. And when he was afraid like that, he was hard to calm."[29] After a week in the Petersburg Hospital, Nureyev was well enough to return to Paris, where he received a diagnosis of pericarditis, a viral infection of the heart. A second round of surgery at the Ambroise-Paré clinic in the

Paris suburb of Neuilly-sur-Seine drained a full pint of fluid from around his heart. "His condition was catastrophic," Canesi recalls. "I thought he was going to die. I explained the situation to him and we started to treat him with Ganciclovir. Rudi knew how serious his condition was and said, 'So what are we going to do?' I said we were going to try this treatment. And things turned out well."[30] Two weeks later, Nureyev was in New York City working on *Romeo and Juliet.*

By the time the Opéra began its annual summer break in August, Nureyev had completed most of his work on his staging of *Bayadère.* Despite the standard Opéra inanities—the dancers threatened an "eco strike" over the stuffed parrots sewn to the sleeves of one set of costumes—Nureyev was ready and eager to mount the classic ballet that had eluded him his entire career. Before the summer break, he choreographed two new suites of dances for the male corps—who are, in the standard staging, spear-carriers par excellence—while keeping an eye to the finer points of the ballet. "He did some embroidery in the first act pas de deux," one of his closest assistants, Patricia Ruanne, remembers, "and helped clarify things that had become muddied."[31]

Ruanne also remembers that things had changed by the time the company reassembled for final rehearsals:

> It was difficult when we came back in September because he had lost quite a bit of ground. Kurgapkina [the Russian ballerina Ninel Kurgapkina, a lifelong friend and ally of Nureyev] was there to help and we sat down with the tapes. If there was a discrepancy, we would ask Rudolf. Some days he stayed for quite a long time, for most of the call, in fact, but as time went by that became more and more difficult. Finally, he could only stay for an hour or two. But he was there every single day. On the good days and the bad days and on the weekends. He was still fixing things after the premiere. It wasn't over just because it was on.
>
> It was very difficult for everyone. There would be moments when it was all fine because everything and everyone was so busy. But there were times when you would turn

'round—and it sounds ridiculous but there were times when one could forget the changes that were going on inside him —and you just cried at the sight of him, looking so sick and so frail. But he did not get weak-spirited, and so we couldn't. He stayed with it and remained as he always was. He wasn't at all tragic about what was happening to him.[32]

The *Bayadère* triumph was Nureyev's last successful treatment for his failing health. John Taras, the American chore-ographer Balanchine had sent to teach Nureyev his first *Apollo* all those years ago, visited the Quai Voltaire two days after the *Bayadère* opening night, and found an "apartment full of people. Douce [François, Nureyev's amanuensis], Charles Jude, Canesi. I was told, 'Rudolf is asleep,' and then suddenly his bedroom door opens and in walks Rudolf, talking about the choreography school he wanted to open in Petersburg. He had just bought a huge new dog."[33] The two-week excursion to St. Bart's was a wise move. According to Jude, who went with Nureyev to the Caribbean, "he lived normally. He ate. He watched television. And then after he would say 'Let's go bathing' and we would leave for the beach. It was beautiful there. It was hot. And he was fine."[34]

Through the first weeks of November 1992, after his re-turn to Paris, Nureyev was in and out of the hospital with bouts of severe thrush infections, and finally, on November 20, he entered Perpétuel-Secours for the last time. "It was difficult to feed him," Canesi told *Le Figaro*. "He couldn't swallow anything and it was decided to feed him on an intravenous drip, even though we knew there was an enormous risk of infection, as with all patients whose immune system is breaking down. From then on he declined steadily."[35] Shortly after Christmas, Nureyev's sisters were sum-moned to Paris, which may or may not have been the wisest move. "I learned more about Rudolf in the last ten days than in the ten years I had known him," Canesi explains. "When I saw his family. The sisters would be together and they could not accept that he was going to die, and they did not understand it very clearly."[36] There were reports that their behavior was disruptive.[37]

On the morning of January 6, Russian Christmas Eve, with his sister Rosa and a staff nurse in the room with him, Nureyev died. Canesi's official release cited the cause of death as "a cardiac complication following a grievous illness."[38]

It was over. Perhaps.

Epilogue
À distance

"In Xanadu Did Kubla Khan . . ."

—SAMUEL TAYLOR COLERIDGE, Kubla Khan

The grand foyer of the Palais Garnier is a movie set waiting to happen. The confectionery exterior of the Garnier—all those cupolas, caryatids, and cornices curving into the Place de l'Opéra is actually just a prelude to the real drama, which is inside.

That was certainly the case with Nureyev's funeral service in the foyer of the Garnier on January 12, 1993. The several hundred invited guests entered the Garnier with dark storm clouds massing overhead and left the service as the winter sun finally broke through. Nureyev's mahogany coffin was carried into the foyer by six of the Opéra's ranking dancers and placed on the central plateau of the Garnier's Grand Staircase. The stairs leading up into the theater were filled with the Opéra's company of dancers; those leading to the chamber orchestra, speakers, and audience seated below were flanked on both sides by students from the Opéra school and bundles of white chrysanthemums. The forty-five-minute service was an aptly Nureyevesque combination of the secular and the divine. No mention of a religious god, only his earthly spokesmen: extracts from Pushkin, Byron,

Michelangelo, Goethe, Rimbaud, selections from Bach and Tschaikovsky.

The White Russian cemetery of Sainte-Geneviève-des-Bois, where Nureyev chose to be buried, is an anomaly among the great Paris cemeteries. Centuries of Paris literally lie at your feet in the Montmarte Cemetery. The vast, rolling expanse of the Père Lachaise cemetery has the edge in clientele: a cross between a theme park and celestial Las Vegas—Abélard and Héloïse, Colette and Wilde, Edith Piaf, and, the most popular of all, Jim Morrison. Sainte-Geneviève-des-Bois is located in a suburb just south of Paris, its cemetery right across the road from an expanse of public space that's been known to host a French circus. The last-century romanticism of the Montmarte Cemetery seemed a more logical last stop for Nureyev, particularly as it would have placed him in the company of the first two "gods of the dance," Nijinsky and Vestris. Beginning in the late 1980s, the construction of a conspicuous, unmarked, and decidedly homoerotic tombstone in Père-Lachaise was rumored to be in preparation for Nureyev's grave. But at Sainte-Geneviève-des-Bois a sense of correctness, propriety, and attention begins with a wall of blanched stone that stands between the cemetery and the outside world. Behind the wall is a parallel universe—literally. Everything is order, even spaces, immaculate angles. Green is everywhere but never random or wild. The great, sighing boughs of pine only emphasize the harmony and restraint in row after ordered row of headstones and monuments.

Sainte-Geneviève-des-Bois is locally unique in that it is dominated by a single group, the community of White Russian exiles who settled in Paris between the world wars. You can all but hear the balalaikas—and not playing "Lara's Theme" but "God Save the Tsar." Whole units of White Russian officers are buried in Sainte-Geneviève-des-Bois—as military units. Although it has only one Romanov, a first cousin of the last tsar, the cemetery has some major in-laws, among them Prince Felix Yussupov, the man who dispatched Rasputin. It also has the world's most select company of Imperial Russian ballerinas: Vera

Trefilova, allegedly the Aurora of the age; Mathilde Kschessin-skaya, the woman who relieved Nicholas II of his virginity; Olga Preobrajenska, who became Paris's most revered ballet teacher. They are exactly the women Nureyev would have partnered at least once, probably in his own staging of a White ballet.

The bus chartered to transport the majority of the Opéra dancers to the funeral site lost its way, and the service was over before they got there. But what some people most remembered about the graveside scene was Nureyev's sisters. "And then there were the sisters," William Chatrier, the Opéra's general secretary, recalls. "The most elegant women in Paris and then those two babushkas. Even at the luncheon after at the Meurice—the most exclusive, expensive place in Paris—they wouldn't take those damned things off."

Six months later back at the Garnier, in a quiet, comfortable dressing room that hardly could be more distant from the gilt and glamour of Nureyev's last rites, it is another working day, just like any other. It's late in the afternoon and things are winding down. There's no performance tonight. A sense of the daily, of the anonymous, hangs over the backstage area. Out in the hall, a pair of wardrobe women who've had far too long a day are cutting the corners of every *couloir* in pursuit of a lost tutu, arms and accusations sailing in all directions. A lone stagehand is embroiled in a serious struggle with a recalcitrant cable, a few feet away from a cluster of corps dancers huffing up a storm over when the damned elevators will finally show up.

Manuel Legris, the youngest of the Opéra's principal men, is just back in his dressing room from a rehearsal for the male lead in Balanchine's *Theme and Variations*. Legris knows the role is a handful, and his eyes are less than ablaze with inspiration. Barely twenty-five, Manuel Legris hadn't been born yet when Nureyev decided to leave Russia. It's hard to imagine that the two men, not just generations but worlds apart, could ever have had any common ground. They hardly could be more different, either in temperament or physicality. Onstage and off, Legris is diffidence itself, a polite, deferential paradigm of the well-brought-up young Frenchman, with blinding batterie and a jump like a javelin.

Leaning back across his dressing table, Legris is, in fact, a summary of Nureyev's accomplishments. Legris wouldn't be sitting where he is, preoccupied with *Theme and Variations*, if Nureyev had gotten on that plane back to Moscow all those years ago, and the reasons run deeper than six years under Nureyev's tutelage at the Paris Opéra Ballet. To be sure, Legris benefited from the Nureyev revolution at the Opéra through the 1980s. When Nureyev went after the Opéra's stifling hierarchy, Legris was one of the figures yanked from obscurity onto center stage. When Nureyev decided that dancing more and more of the full-length nineteenth-century classics was exactly what the Opéra dancers needed to develop a lasting technical base, Legris was one of the dancers who suddenly found himself a baby-faced Siegfried. When Nureyev needed dancers to fill out his Nureyev and Friends tours, the core group he turned to most often regularly included Legris, who picked up a world of practical experience in the process. "I think I have some gifts and maybe they would have gotten me somewhere," Legris explains, "but, basically, Rudolf gave me everything I have.

"I think about Rudolf all the time now," Legris concludes. "Everybody does. It is very strange how we all think so much about Rudolf, now. Every day someone remembers something else. 'Oh, you know, Rudolf used to say that this step was . . .' His corrections, the things he tried to get us to do. I don't just mean that I think about him in rehearsal or when I see something that reminds me of him. I mean, when I am just sitting here. When I am by myself. Maybe putting on my makeup before a performance."

There is a long, surprised pause, and then a slight, surprised smile.

"Rudolf, he knew a lot."

APPENDIX ONE

The Ballets

1963

The Shades scene from *La Bayadère*, after Petipa. First staged for the Royal Ballet. Staged for Paris Opéra in 1974.

1964

Raymonda, full-length, after Petipa. First performed by the Royal Ballet second company. Staged for the Australian Ballet in 1965, for the Zurich Ballet in 1972, for American Ballet Theatre in 1975, for the Boston Ballet in 1979, and the Paris Opéra in 1983.

The Pas de Six from *Laurencia*, after Chabukiani. Staged for the Royal Ballet.

The Grand Pas de Deux from *Paquita*, after Petipa. Staged for La Scala, Milan, in 1970, the Vienna State Opera in 1971, and American Ballet Theatre in 1971.

Swan Lake, full-length, after Petipa/Ivanov. Staged by the Vienna State Opera. Staged for the Paris Opéra Ballet in 1984 and La Scala, Milan, in 1990.

1966

.*Don Quixote*, full-length, after Petipa. First performed by the Vienna State Opera. Staged for the Australian Ballet in 1970, for the Zurich Ballet in 1977, for the Paris Opéra in 1981, for the Peking Ballet and the Matsuyama Ballet in Tokyo in 1985, and La Scala, Milan, in 1987.

Tancredi, an original ballet by Nureyev on contemporary themes to a score by Hans Werner Henze. Staged at the Vienna State Opera.

1967

Nutcracker, full-length. First performed by the Royal Swedish Ballet. Staged by the Royal Ballet in 1968, at La Scala, Milan, in 1969, for the Berlin Ballet in 1979, and for the Paris Opéra in 1984.

1972

The Sleeping Beauty, full-length, after Petipa. First performed by the National Ballet of Canada in 1972. Staged for London Festival Ballet in 1975, for the Vienna State Opera in 1980, the Paris Opéra in 1989, and the Berlin Ballet in 1991.

1977

Romeo and Juliet, full-length, choreography by Nureyev. First performed by London Festival Ballet in 1977. Staged at La Scala, Milan, in 1980, and for the Paris Opéra in 1984.

1979

Manfred, an original ballet based on Byron's poem, music by Tschaikovsky. Staged at Paris Opéra Ballet.

1982

The Tempest, an original work based on Shakespeare's play, music by Tschaikovsky. Staged at Royal Ballet in 1984.

1984

Bach Suite, an original work based on French court dance, developed in cooperation with Francine Lancelot.

1985

Washington Square, an original work based on the Henry James novel, music by Charles Ives.

1985

Cinderella, an original work, set in Hollywood of the 1920s, music by Prokofiev. First performed by the Paris Opéra. Staged in 1991 for the Naples Ballet.

1991

La Bayadère, abridged (minus the fourth and final act), after Petipa. First performed by Paris Opéra Ballet.

APPENDIX TWO

The Roles

1956

Diana and Acteon pas de deux, male solo, student performance, the Kirov ballet school.

1957

Nutcracker, the Nutcracker Prince, the Kirov Ballet.
Swan Lake, Act 1 pas de trois.

1958

Le Corsaire pas de deux, the Kirov Ballet (Moscow Competition and Kirov graduation performance).
Esmeralda, Diana and Acteon pas de deux, the Kirov Ballet (Moscow Competition and Kirov graduation performance).
Gayané, Kurdish dance, the Kirov Ballet (Moscow Competition).
The Red Poppy, pas de quatre, the Kirov Ballet.
Laurencia, Frondoso, the Kirov Ballet.
Valse Volonté, ensemble, the Kirov Ballet.

1959

The Sleeping Beauty, Bluebird pas de deux, the Kirov Ballet.
Raymonda, pas de quatre, the Kirov Ballet.
Gayané, Armen, the Kirov Ballet.
Muszkovsky Waltz, male lead, the Kirov Ballet.
Giselle, Albrecht, the Kirov Ballet.
Don Quichotte, Basilio, the Kirov Ballet.
La Bayadère, Solor, the Kirov Ballet.

1960

Flames of Paris, pas de deux, the Kirov Ballet.
Waltz, male lead, the Kirov Ballet.
The Sleeping Beauty, Prince Desire, the Kirov Ballet.
Swan Lake, Prince Siegfried, the Kirov Ballet.
Legend of Love, Ferkhad, the Kirov Ballet.
Taras Bulba, Cossack camp dance, the Kirov Ballet.

1961

Le spectre de la rose, the Rose, television broadcast, Frankfurt, Germany.
Poème tragique (solo), benefit performance for the Royal Academy of Dancing.
Toccata and Fugue, male lead, concert tour group with Arova, Bruhn, and Hightower.
Dances from Raymonda, male leads, concert tour group with Bruhn, et al.
Fantaisie, male lead, tour group with Bruhn et al.

1962

La fille mal gardée, Colas, Ballet de Marseille and American Ballet Theatre.
Flower Festival at Genzano, pas de deux, *The Bell Telephone Hour.*
Le Grand Pas Classique, pas de deux, Stuttgart Ballet.
Les Sylphides, male lead, the Royal Ballet.
Prince Igor (opera), Polovtsian Warrior, Ruth Page company for Chicago Opera and Chicago Opera Ballet.
The Merry Widow, Danilo, Ruth Page company with Chicago Opera Ballet.
Theme and Variations, male lead, American Ballet Theatre.

1963

Antigone, Eteocles, the Royal Ballet.
Marguerite and Armand, Armand, the Royal Ballet.
Petrushka, Petrushka, the Royal Ballet.
The Kingdom of the Shades from *La Bayadère* (staging by Nureyev), Solor, the Royal Ballet.
Laurencia (staging by Nureyev), pas de six, the Royal Ballet.
Diversions, male lead, the Royal Ballet.
Fantasie in C Minor, male lead, Royal Academy of Dancing gala.

1964

Swan Lake (new production staged by Nureyev), Prince Siegfried, the Vienna State Opera.
Raymonda (new version by Nureyev), Jean de Brienne, the Royal Ballet second company.
Images of Love, the Youth, the Royal Ballet.
Hamlet, Hamlet, the Royal Ballet.

1965

La Sylphide, James, the National Ballet of Canada.
Romeo and Juliet (MacMillan), Romeo, the Royal Ballet.

1966

The Sleeping Beauty (new production by Nureyev), Prince Desire, La Scala, Milan.
Don Quixote, Basilio, the Vienna State Opera.
Song of the Earth, the Messenger of Death, the Royal Ballet.
Tancredi (original choreography by Nureyev), Tancredi, Vienna State Opera.

1967

Apollo, Apollo, Vienna State Opera.
Paradise Lost, the male lead, the Royal Ballet.
Le jeune homme et la mort, the Young Man, French television broadcast.

1968

Monument for a Dead Boy, the Boy, Dutch National Ballet.
L'Estasi, male lead, La Scala, Milan.
Birthday Offering (new male variation), male lead, the Royal Ballet.
The Dream, Oberon, the Royal Ballet.
Jazz Calendar, Friday's Child, the Royal Ballet.

1969

Pelléas and Mélisande, Pelléas, the Royal Ballet.

1970

Les Rendez-vous, the Boy in Green, Ashton gala with the Royal Ballet.
Apparitions, the Poet, Ashton gala with the Royal Ballet.
Dances at a Gathering, the Boy in Brown, the Royal Ballet.
The Ropes of Time, the Traveler, the Royal Ballet.

1971

Big Bertha, male ensemble, *The Burt Bacharach Show* (television).
Le sacre du printemps (Béjart), the Chosen One, Ballet of the 20th Century.
Song of a Wayfarer, male lead, Ballet of the 20th Century.
Checkmate, the First Red Knight, the Royal Ballet.
Field Figures (replacement cast), principal dancer, the Royal Ballet.

1972

The Sleeping Beauty (new production by Nureyev), Prince Desire, the National Ballet of Canada.
The Moor's Pavane, Othello, National Ballet of Canada.
Aureole, male lead, Paul Taylor Dance Company.
Book of Beasts, Illuminations, Paul Taylor Dance Company.
Laborintus, male lead, the Royal Ballet.
Sideshow, male lead, the Royal Ballet.
Afternoon of a Faun (Robbins), the Boy, the Royal Ballet.

1973

Agon, Sarabande, the Royal Ballet.
The Prodigal Son, the Prodigal, the Royal Ballet.

1974

Tristan, Tristan, the Paris Opéra Ballet.
Manon, Des Grieux, the Royal Ballet.
Don Juan, Don Juan, the National Ballet of Canada.

1975

Coppélia, Franz, the National Ballet of Canada.
Moments, male lead, the Scottish Ballet.
The Lesson, the Teacher, the Scottish Ballet.
Sonate à trois, male lead, the Scottish Ballet.
Blown in a Gentle Wind, male lead, Dutch National Ballet.
Lucifer, Lucifer, the Martha Graham Dance Company.
Night Journey, Oedipus, the Martha Graham Dance Company.
Appalachian Spring, the Preacher, the Martha Graham Dance Company.
The Scarlet Letter, Reverend Dimmesdale, the Martha Graham Dance Company.

1976

Four Schumann Pieces, male lead, the National Ballet of Canada.

1977

Romeo and Juliet (new production by Nureyev), Romeo, London Festival Ballet.
Pierrot Lunaire, Pierrot Lunaire, the Royal Danish Ballet.
El Penitente, title role, the Martha Graham Dance Company.
Hamlet Prelude, Hamlet, gala in honor of Queen Elizabeth II with the Royal Ballet.
The Toreador, pas de deux, Nureyev and Friends.

1978

Schéhérazade, the Golden Slave, London Festival.
Konservatoriet, male lead, London Festival Ballet.
The Afternoon of a Faun (van Schayk), the Faun, Dutch National Ballet.
About a Dark Horse, male lead, Dutch National Ballet.
Vivace, solo, Nureyev and Friends.
The Canarsie Venus (originally, *The Brighton Venus*), the Gentleman, the
    Murray Louis Dance Company.

1979

Le Bourgeois Gentilhomme, Cléonte, New York City Opera.
The Afternoon of a Faun (after the Nijinsky original), the Faun, the Joffrey
    Ballet.
Ulysses, male lead, Dutch National Ballet.
Manfred (original choreography by Nureyev), Lord Byron, the Paris Opéra
    Ballet.

1980

The Idiot, Prince Myshkin, the Berlin Ballet.
Miss Julie, Jean, the Berlin Ballet.
Five Tangos, male lead, the Berlin Ballet.

1981

Marco Spada, Marco Spada, Rome Opera Ballet.

1982

The Tempest (new production by Nureyev), Prospero, the Royal Ballet.

1983

Notre-Dame de Paris, Quasimodo, the Ballet de Marseille.

1984

Phaedra's Dream, Hippolytus, the Martha Graham Dance Company.
Harlequin, or The Magician of Love, Harlequin, the Paris Opéra Ballet.
Le sacre du printemps: The Rehearsal (Taylor), male lead, the Paris Opéra
    Ballet.
Stravinsky Violin Concerto, First Aria, the Paris Opéra Ballet.
Romeo and Juliet, Mercutio, the Paris Opéra Ballet.
Bach Suite (original choreography by Nureyev and Francine Lancelot), solo,
    the Paris Opéra Ballet.

1985

Swan Lake (new production by Nureyev), Prince Siegfried and Von Rothbart, the Paris Opéra Ballet.
Washington Square (original choreography by Nureyev), Dr. Sloper, the Paris Opéra Ballet.
Nutcracker, Drosselmeyer, the Paris Opéra Ballet.

1986

La Dansomanie, Mr. Duléger, the Paris Opéra Ballet.
Cinderella, the Director, the Paris Opéra Ballet.

1987

Two Brothers, pas de deux, the Paris Opéra Ballet.

1988

Orpheus, Orpheus, the New York City Ballet.

1989

The Overcoat, Akaky Akakyevich, Maggio Musicale (Florence).

1990

Romeo and Juliet (MacMillan), Mercutio, the Royal Ballet.
Coppélia, Dr. Coppélius, Cleveland/San José Ballet.

1991

The Sleeping Beauty, Carabosse, the Berlin State Opera.
Christoforo, the Angel, Budapest State Opera.

NOTES

*Unless otherwise credited, the direct quotes in this book
are from interviews conducted by the author. Some in-
terviewees asked to remain anonymous.*

ONE: BORN ON A TRAIN

1. Geoffrey Hosking, *A History of the Soviet Union (Revised Edition)*,
p. 199.
2. Even Nureyev, in his brief 1963 autobiography *Nureyev*, misplaces the
city on the eastern side of the Urals.
3. Patricia Foy, *Ballet Review*, Winter 1991.
4. The Germans invaded Austria just five days before Nureyev was born.
5. Hosking, *A History of the Soviet Union*, p. 283.
6. Nureyev was also without two other Russian national traits noted by
Somerset Maugham on a 1917 visit to St. Petersburg, which had been
renamed Petrograd after the outbreak of World War I. Maugham observed
"a deep sense of masochism in Russians. . . . The Russian sets store on self-
abasement because it comes easily to him; he can accept humiliation because
to humiliate himself gives him a singular sensual gratification." Further,
"no one can make excursions into Russian life or Russian fiction without
noticing how great a place is taken by an acute sense of sin. Not only is the
Russian constantly telling you that he is a sinner, but apparently he feels it,
and he suffers from very lively pangs of remorse." W. Somerset Maugham,
A Writer's Notebook, New York, Penguin, 1984, pp. 145, 149–150.
7. Born Iosif Vissarionovich Djugashvili, the Great Moustache was cagier
about his literal physique, which included webbed feet and a foreshortened
arm right out of *Richard III*.
8. For a lucid but impassioned account of the hold Stalin still has on many
Russians, see Hedrick Smith, *The New Russians*, New York, Random
House, 1990, pp. 121–147.
9. Aleksandr Nekrich and Mikhail Heller, *Utopia in Power: The History of
the Soviet Union from 1917 to the Present*, New York, Summit, 1988,
p. 301.
10. John T. Lawrence, *A History of Russia*, New York, New American
Library, 1978, p. 283.
11. Alex de Jonge, *Stalin: And the Shaping of the Soviet Union*, New York,
Morrow, 1986, p. 273.
12. The most poignant, and cynically abused, martyr of the period, a boy

hero held up to the children of Nureyev's generation as an ideal and role model, was a thirteen-year-old from the Ural provinces named Pavlik Morozov. As a member of the Young Pioneers, Stalin's version of the Hitler Youth, Morozov turned in his own parents as traitors to the state. He and his younger brother were then murdered by their horrified "tsarist" grandfather. Perhaps apocryphal but wildly effective in galvanizing young minds well into the 1950s, Morozov's story became one of the most cherished legends of Stalin's Russia, his home village a shrine to the Stalinist youth of Nureyev's generation.

13. De Jonge, p. 274.

14. Nekrich and Heller, p. 307.

15. J. N. Westwood, *The Short Oxford History of the Modern World/ Endurance and Endeavor: Russian History (1812–1980)*, Oxford, Oxford University Press, 1973, p. 317.

16. Hosking, p. 506.

17. Walter Laqueur, *Stalin: The Glasnost Revelations*, New York, Macmillan, 1990, p. 123.

18. George de la Pena got the title role in the Hollywood film version of Vaslav Nijinsky's life that eluded Nureyev for a decade and created the role of a Russian defector in the Broadway musical comedy *Woman of the Year*. He was also a soloist with American Ballet Theatre during the box office heyday of the Soviet dance expatriates in the 1970s that had begun with Nureyev's move to the West.

19. Nureyev became an Austrian citizen in 1982. Until then his official status was that of a "stateless person."

20. *New York Post*, April 17, 1973, p. 37.

21. De Jonge, p. 140. Grisly contemporary accounts are cited: "We hear . . . that women cut the arms and legs off a human corpse and eat them. Children who die are not taken to the cemetery but kept for food."

22. Bashkir is almost identical with the language of the Volga district spoken by the family of Nureyev's mother, and *nurr* has the same meaning in both.

23. Hosking, p. 241.

24. Ibid., p. 445.

25. Alla Ivanovna Sizova was born in Leningrad one year after Nureyev. She graduated the Kirov ballet academy the same year as Nureyev and was his partner at their graduation performance. Celebrated for her Princess Aurora in *The Sleeping Beauty* with the Kirov, Sizova currently works as teacher and coach at the Universal Ballet School in Washington, DC.

TWO: "JUST A LITTLE TATAR BOY"

1. The most famous of the Imperial Russian ballerinas, Anna Pavlovna Pavlova was born in St. Petersburg in 1881 and died of pneumonia at The Hague in 1931. As a dancer and a diva, she was known for her musicality, the expressiveness of her line, and her temper. Her most famous roles generally were winged, such as Fokine's sylphs and *Dying Swan*, as well as assorted butterflies, fairy dolls, and autumn leaves.

2. By the "dance boom" of the late 1970s, Makarova and Baryshnikov were

reputed to be earning as much as ten thousand dollars a performance. Thanks at least in part to his Hollywood film hits *The Turning Point* in 1977 and *White Nights* in 1985, Baryshnikov is widely believed to have been the highest paid dancer in ballet history.

3. The highest estimate, $80 million, was made by *Vanity Fair* in March 1993.

4. Born in 1940, Makarova was the daughter of a comfortable Leningrad family. Despite the tragic cloud over his youth—his mother committed suicide when her son Misha was only twelve—Baryshnikov was born, in 1948, in the Latvian port city of Riga, with reasonable access to Leningrad.

5. Particularly in light of his son's future, Hamnet's choice of a life spent largely on the road is a telling bit of autobiography for a man whose family had kept to its tiny native village for generations.

6. Hedrick Smith, *The New Russians*, New York, Random House, 1990, p. 138.

7. John Percival, *Nureyev: Aspects of the Dancer*, New York, Popular Library, 1975, p. 10.

8. The spelling of the village's name also is given as Shuchia.

9. Chelyabinsk, now known as the city of Ozyorsk, is currently home to the Mayak nuclear processing plant. *New York Times*, September 2, 1994.

10. Rudolf Nureyev, *Nureyev: An Autobiography*, New York, Dutton, 1963, pp. 28–29.

11. Ibid., p. 31.

12. Nureyev remained areligious to the end of his life. "I don't believe in life after death," he said. His position, Nureyev wrote in his autobiography, began with the childhood discovery that the "the road to God was paved with food." His funeral service in Paris on January 12, 1993, was an entirely secular event. The standard dirges were replaced by Bach and Tschaikovsky, the standard liturgy by Pushkin and Byron. The only concession to religion was a private service attended by his closest family and friends and held a few days after the funeral according to the traditions of the White Russian cemetery at Sainte-Geneviève-des-Bois.

13. Ironically, Stalin had once been a seminarian.

14. The Soviet Union lost an estimated 20 million citizens to World War II.

15. Once again, the exact number depends upon who's telling the story. Nureyev's count in his autobiography is his uncle and one other family.

16. Nureyev, *Nureyev*, p. 32.

17. By the time Hamnet died of pneumonia in the mid-1960s, he and his son were no longer even on speaking terms. Nureyev's defection had been the last straw. Hamnet considered his son's move to the West the worst kind of betrayal, a rejection of all that his country had done for him. During the phone calls Nureyev occasionally managed to his mother after leaving the Soviet Union, Hamnet always refused to speak to him. He could only be heard coughing in the background.

18. Nureyev had no visual memory of his father before Hamnet's return from the war.

19. Nureyev, *Nureyev*, p. 32.

20. The exquisite French ballerina Ghislaine Thesmar, a friend and colleague of Nureyev from his first performances in the West, has described

photographs of Hamnet as a strikingly handsome man with powerful features and an arresting crown of thick black hair. His appearance in Nureyev family photographs, square-jawed and tight-lipped, is also right out of the state-sponsored art projecting the new Soviet male hero.

21. According to Nureyev, the legendary Russian basso Feodor Chaliapin made his professional debut at the Ufa Opera House in the final quarter of the nineteenth century, making the city one of the unexpected capitals of ballet history. Ufa not only produced Nureyev, but the celebrity status Chaliapin had achieved by the first decade of this century was directly responsible for the initial Paris seasons by Serge Diaghilev's Ballet Russe that introduced Western Europe to Russian ballet and rewrote the history of ballet in Europe and America.

22. The ballet academy from which Nureyev would eventually graduate was established by decree of the Empress Anna in 1738, ten years after ballet was introduced to the Romanov capital and three years after a resident company of Russian dancers had begun performing for the court. By the end of the nineteenth century, St. Petersburg had replaced Paris as the center of the ballet world and was producing the most famous dancers and choreographers in the world, including Kschessinskaya, Pavlova, Karsavina, Nijinsky, Fokine, Spessivtseva, Danilova, and Balanchine. From the 1920s until the *glasnost* era, the official name of the ballet academy attached to the company was the Leningrad State Academic Vaganova Choreographic Institute, renamed for Agrippina Vaganova (1879–1951), one of the last of the Imperial ballerinas but a woman who knew how to play ball with the Soviets from day one. The academy and theater are today once again known as the Maryinsky.

23. Of Bashkir origin, Zaituna Nazretdinova was a local celebrity throughout her two-decade career in Ufa. Even after his eye had become more discerning, Nureyev always remembered Nazretdinova as a capable, affecting dancer. She eventually performed *Song of the Crane* in London during a brief London season by the Bashkir Ballet in 1955. She received generally favorable, if understated, reviews, although a young critic named Clive Barnes noted her "deplorable makeup and generally unkempt appearance." *Dance and Dancers,* January 1956, p. 35.

24. The choreographers were Nina Anisimova and Khaliaf Safiullin. The ballet, sometimes known as *Crane Song,* had been premiered in Ufa in March 1944.

25. Nureyev, in fact, told many of his first interviewers that the ballet had been *Swan Lake.*

26. David K. Shipler, *Russia: Broken Idols, Solemn Dreams,* New York, Times Books, 1989, p. 164.

27. Ibid., p. 160.

28. Ibid.

29. Andrei Sinyavsky, *Soviet Civilization: A Cultural History,* Arcadia, Greenfield, WI, 1990, p. 144.

30. The school reports are all from *Ballet Review,* Winter 1993.

31. The same qualities were noted in the student Nijinsky's first ensemble performances with the Maryinsky company as a child.

32. "I think it was already then, at the end of the war, that I became poisoned, once and for all time, by praise." Nureyev, *Nureyev,* p. 40.

33. *Ballet Review*, Winter 1993.

34. "Between 1946 and 1950, inclusive, the [Soviet] nation built 18,500 schools seating 2,500,000 pupils, including premises for 1,300,000 pupils partially or wholly built on money contributed by the collective farms. In the first ten years after the war the country built or restored more than 30,000 educational establishments, with accommodation for 5,000,000." Dukes, p. 283.

35. Udeltsova outlived her most famous pupil by six months. She died in 1993, age 103, and reportedly maintained her high standard until her death. When Nureyev returned to the Kirov in 1989 as a guest performer in *La Sylphide*, Udeltsova was said to have been seriously disappointed by his performance. *Dance*, May 1990.

36. Foy documentary, *Nureyev*.

37. According to contemporary accounts, Vaitovitch was regarded particularly for the elevation of her jump, a performance quality she shared with Nureyev's major teacher at the Kirov academy, Alexander Pushkin. The height of his jump would be among Nureyev's first signatures.

THREE: THE WALKING CRISIS

1. Nureyev was born superstitious and died superstitious—only more so. Born on March 17, his defection waiting in the wings for June 17, 1961— although, as we shall see, that fact was actually gilding the lily—Nureyev considered seventeen his lucky number. To the end of his life, Nureyev would never seat thirteen people at a table.

2. Asaf Messerer (1903–92) was the Bolshoi's dominant male presence from the time he entered the Moscow company in 1921, until his retirement in 1954. He began teaching at the Bolshoi academy in 1942 and, by the time he left the stage a dozen years later, was the ranking Moscow ballet master of the next two decades. He also initiated a ballet dynasty that included his sister Sulamith, her son, Michael, and his niece, Maya Plisetskaya.

3. W. Somerset Maugham, *A Writer's Notebook*, New York, Penguin, 1984, p. 163.

4. Like the capital the new American nation would force out of the Potomac River wetlands a century later, the early history of St. Petersburg was plagued by marsh diseases such as typhus.

5. Nigel Gosling, *Leningrad*, New York, Dutton, 1965, p. 16.

6. The only government function he could not get away from Moscow was the holiest of ceremonies, the coronation of the tsar, where the Muscovite Orthodox Church drew the line.

7. Peter also initiated the Russian leaders' tradition of physical eccentricity that continued in Alexander III's bearlike proportions, his son Nicholas II's diminutive stature, Stalin's webbed feet, and Mikhail Gorbachev's birthmark. Peter was "six feet seven, 'scant of hair,' and terrified of black beetles." Gosling, p. 22.

8. Many a personal conflict has been ascribed to Peter's compulsive taste for the masculine. His private guard was required to wear towering headpieces—so that everyone was six feet seven.

The empresses also introduced luxury and license that would characterize the Romanov dynasty to its final days. Catherine, the great in many quarters, wrote, "I cannot go a day without love." George Brandes, *Impressions of Russia*, New York, Crowell, 1889, p. 22.

9. Designed in the 1760s by Quarenghi, the palace of the Yussupov family, whose lineage predated the Romanovs, also included a private theater that was a scale reproduction of the La Scala Opera House and even today retains his original gilt.

10. Despite a red-light illegitimacy well into the seventeenth century, dance became a special interest of the Romanov rulers very quickly. By the time the first Nicholas Romanov reached the throne, "the suppleness, stamina, imagination, and persistence of the Slavs" had begun a tradition that would continue until the second quarter of the twentieth century, producing "the greatest school, the greatest technicians and the greatest choreographers of traditional theatrical dancing." Lincoln Kirstein, *Dance: A Short History of Classic Theatrical Dancing*, Princeton, NJ, Princeton Books, 1987, pp. 227, 252.

11. The crown of the 1900 egg, celebrating the completion of the Trans-Siberian Railway, was lifted to reveal a miniature train encrusted with precious stones that crossed from one side to the other of a gilt-and-enamel map of the empire.

12. Galina Sergeyevna Ulanova was born in Romanov Petersburg in 1910. She trained as a child with her parents, who were both dancers, studied with Vaganova after the revolution, and joined the Leningrad company in 1928. In 1935, she joined the Bolshoi, and, by the time she created the role of Juliet in Leonid Lavrovsky's landmark staging of the Prokofiev *Romeo and Juliet* in 1940, was her nation's undisputed *assoluta*. Her stature was built on a unique combination of crowd-pleasing personal presence and, from all accounts, unsurpassed emotional and technical purity. She retired from the stage in 1962 and remains one of the Bolshoi's most treasured teachers and coaches.

13. Airport stories are a special corridor in the adult Nureyev's gallery of Great Moments in Pique, such as a legendary scene at Charles de Gaulle in the mid-1980s when Nureyev discovered the amount of taxes the unfortunate customs officials demanded he pay for a mass of Middle Eastern carpeting he'd acquired on tour. The French lost.

14. Rudolf Nureyev, *Nureyev*, New York, Dutton, 1963, p. 63. In his autobiography, Nureyev also remembers that his response came "with more aggression than was necessary."

15. Kirstein, *Dance*, p. 226.

16. Richard Buckle, *Nijinsky*, New York, Avon, 1971, p. 26.

17. Vakhtang Chaboukiani (1910–92) was the Kirov's leading male dancer throughout his ten years with the company beginning in 1931. The collision of syllables in Chaboukiani's name is a reasonable approximation of his dancing, pure punch and powerhouse effects. Like Nureyev, he tailored many roles to his specialties and was considered the prototype of the new Soviet ballet hero—athletic, powerful, given to physical heroics. His personal life kept him from sustained favor with the Soviet authorities. He was returned to his hometown of Tbilisi in Soviet Georgia in 1941 as director and choreographer of the local opera house. Finally, in 1977, after reports

of involvement in an arson attempt on the opera house, he was relegated to staging ice ballets in the Ukraine. He died there in 1992.

18. *Nureyev,* p. 65.

19. Nureyev once told a fellow student who also later made it to the West that one of the reasons their friendship had endured so many years was "because you are like me. You can smell where the trouble is."

20. The most effective account of the school's strict routine can be found in Tamara Karsavina's exhilarating autobiography, *Theatre Street,* particularly her description of the school's formidable headmistress, Varvara Ivanovna, a hushed, trailing figure of black serge and keys; more than a quarter century after leaving the school, Karsavina's "subconscious ear still heard the dread swish of Varvara Ivanova's skirts." (p. 128) In the first decades of this century, Varvara Ivanovna had her own bête noire, a fiery little orphan named Alexandra Danilova. "Varvara Ivanovna!" the sparkling *assoluta* of the Ballet Russe de Monte Carlo once recalled. "Zhe never liked me. Because I vas rich."

21. Nureyev's second long-term lover in the West, the American film producer Wallace Potts, told *Vanity Fair* that his first impressions of Nureyev offstage "broke my stereotype of dancers as ethereal. Both he and Margot could talk about physics, mathematics, philosophy, cosmology." *Vanity Fair,* March 1993.

22. David Daniel, "Nureyev Observed," *Christopher Street,* August 1976, p. 20.

23. The crown of the Imperial collars were the basis of the trademark insignia of a later company that would replace the Kirov as the ballet world's most influential troupe, the New York City Ballet founded by Maryinsky graduate Georgi Balanchivadze after he'd moved to the West and become George Balanchine. Buckle, *Nijinsky,* p. 13.

24. Daniel, *Christopher Street,* pp. 19–20.

25. Three years Nureyev's junior, Stefanschi returned to Romania after graduating the Kirov academy and was that country's leading danseur before emigrating to the West. He joined the National Ballet of Canada in 1971 as a principal dancer and works there today as the company's ballet master.

26. A surefire crowd rouser, a *jeté coupé manège* is a series of broad jumps punctuated by quick, flashing turns and always brings down the house.

27. The threat was not idle. Even today the KGB's Moscow offices are only a stone's throw from the Bolshoi Ballet's home theater.

28. Kitri's variation also involves the flashing fan of a Spanish coquette. *Vogue,* March 1993.

29. Daniel, *Christopher Street,* p. 21.

30. John Percival, *Nureyev: Aspects of the Dancer,* New York, Popular Library, 1975, p. 27.

31. *Ballet Review,* Winter 1993.

32. Equivalent today to ethnic and cultural slurs such as nigger, wop, kike, or faggot.

33. The enduring tradition was synopsized, and enshrined for posterity, by the acid-tongued character Sheila in Michael Bennett's *A Chorus Line:* "I knew the combination when I was in the front."

34. Nureyev, *Nureyev,* pp. 73–74.

35. Ibid., p. 45.

36. Balanchine was said to have held Pushkin in the same esteem.

37. Pushkin was the first contemporary writer to have his works translated to the ballet stage and by no less a figure than Charles-Louis Didelot, the fabled choreographer and pedagogue. Didelot's tenure as director of the Imperial Ballet in the first decade of the nineteenth century became the foundation of Imperial Russian ballet classicism. Since then, Shakespeare is the only other writer to have inspired as many choreographers.

38. Renamed with a frequency worthy of its hometown, the official St. Petersburg ballet company, known as the Maryinsky under the Romanovs before becoming the Kirov under Stalin before becoming the Maryinsky again under Gorbachev, was known in the 1920s as the State Academic Theater for Opera and Ballet.

39. *New York Times*, January 24, 1975.

40. Ibid.

41. Nureyev, *Nureyev*, p. 74.

42. It would reach its apotheosis in his partnership with Fonteyn.

43. And despite a legend—unconfirmed—that, since there were no real winners at the Moscow competition (the awarding of first, second, and third place citations would have encouraged a dangerous individualism), Nureyev felt obliged to treat the judges to that old Tatar moon and dropped the backside of his tights.

44. Elena Tchernichova interview, New York City, October 2, 1992.

FOUR: CENTER STAGE

1. Natalia Mikhailovna Dudinskaya was born in Romanov Russia in 1912. She graduated Vaganova's special "perfection" class for ballerinas in 1931 and was a leading light of the Kirov stage until her retirement more than thirty years later. During the 1950s, she and her husband, Konstantin Sergeyev, were the most powerful couple in Russian ballet. Dudinskaya's vast personal repertory included both the traditional standards, such as *Swan Lake* and *Giselle,* as well as contemporary works, such as Chaboukiani's *Laurencia,* Vainonen's *Flames of Paris,* and Fenster's *Taras Bulba.* Although always more than a stunning technician, Dudinskaya was celebrated throughout her career for her technical strength. The dynamism of her dancing had a powerful effect on Nureyev.

2. Rudolf Nureyev, *Nureyev*, New York, Dutton, 1963, p. 92.

3. In addition to his substitute performances during the main-stage company tour during the early months of 1958, Nureyev had also performed on the Kirov stage as a student supernumerary. Adding that "cast of thousands" touch, ballet students had been used to fill out the crowds in main-stage company productions since the days of the Romanovs.

4. Based on a Lope de Vega chronicle of a Spanish peasant uprising, *Laurencia* was choreographed by Chaboukiani in 1939. The lead male role, Frondoso, was designed as a showcase for his acrobatic specialties.

5. David Daniel, "Nureyev Observed," *Christopher Street*, August 1976, p. 21.

6. Five years older than Nureyev, Irina Alexandrovna Kolpakova was the

ascendant young Soviet ballerina of the middle to late 1950s and succeeded Dudinskaya as the Kirov's prima ballerina. She now works with American Ballet Theatre as one of the company's ballet mistresses and most valued coaches.

7. Through the 1880s, Zucchi was the ballerina who fired the imagination of the group of young aesthetes—Alexander Benois, Léon Bakst, et al.— who would soon gather around Serge Diaghilev and create the Ballets Russe.

8. Sergeyev, despite his unfortunate influence on Nureyev's early professional career, was, in fact, not the director of the Kirov during Nureyev's years in Leningrad. Sergeyev directed the troupe from 1951 until 1955, when Nureyev entered the Kirov academy, and then resumed his position from 1960 until 1970.

9. Nureyev's list of Soviet partners reads like a roll call of the major ballerinas during what is widely described as the Kirov's "golden age." Sizova was the only partner from his own generation. Beginning with Dudinskaya, Nureyev's Kirov ballerinas were the company's established names—i.e., women with some say on their choice of partners. Kolpakova expressed frustration at her first pairing with Nureyev in *Giselle;* she would have preferred to dance with her husband, Vladilen Semyonov. The performance changed her mind. In short order, her peers were lining up, including Ninel Kurgapkina, Olga Moiseyeva, Alla Osipenko, Xenia Ter-Stepanova, and Alla Shelest, Nureyev's personal favorite.

10. Known amongst Kirov dancers as "the monkey wig."

11. His staging of *The Sleeping Beauty* remains the basis of all contemporary versions of the Tschaikovsky/Petipa masterwork.

12. Specifically, Nureyev changed the *batterie*, or leg beats, near the finale of the ballet, replacing a diagonal series of *brisés* (traveling beats that flash to the front of the dancer's body) with a set of sixteen *entrechats six* (triple changes of feet performed in place) that even today are considered a standard measure of the male dance technique.

13. Irina Kolpakova interview, New York City, May 19, 1993.

14. The same decision about the same costume had been the spark that ignited Nijinsky's ejection from the same company.

15. Alla Sizova interview, Washington, DC, October 19, 1993.

16. A powerful influence on Balanchine's subsequent choreographic innovations in the West, Goleizovsky, a self-described traveler with a woman in every port, was never quite sure whether Alifimova was his daughter. "Is possible," he told a student peer of Nureyev.

17. "Personally," Nureyev wrote later, "I thought nothing [at the time] of flying from Leningrad to Moscow and back in a day whenever I heard that an interesting dancer was performing there." Nureyev, *Nureyev*, p. 104.

18. With one telling exception, a performance with Kurgapkina at a reunion of the surviving Soviet intelligentsia hosted by Khrushchev himself at a villa outside Moscow in June 1960. The event was a measure of Nureyev's de facto position among the new Soviet danseurs. Also in attendance were the composers Shostakovitch and Khachaturian, and the pianist Sviatoslav Richter, who performed the Rachmaninoff preludes.

19. Nureyev, *Nureyev*, p. 104.

20. A pseudonym.

FIVE: The Leap, or Enough Rope

1. A pseudonym for Nureyev's first long-term lover. See Chapter 4.
2. Yuri Vladimirovitch Soloviev was born near Leningrad in 1940. He entered the Kirov ballet school and graduated into the main company along with Nureyev in 1958. A gentle, blond stage presence with both power and poetry in his dancing, Soloviev was considered by many in Russia and in the West to be the superior dancer. He committed suicide at his private dacha on January 15, 1977.
3. Because the invitation was withdrawn, ballet audiences missed the opportunity for Ulanova and Dudinskaya, the regnant *assolutas* of, respectively, the Bolshoi and the Kirov, to perform on the same stage.
4. Raissa Stepanovna Struchkova was born in Moscow, studied at the Bolshoi school, and graduated into the company in 1944. Until her retirement in 1978, she remained a special favorite of Russian critics and audiences.
5. Despite Nureyev's defection, the company made its London and New York debuts, performing a full month in both cities, with two extra weeks added in New York. The American portion of the tour was cut short in the wake of local "better dead than red" protests. The troupe was back in Leningrad by the end of October.
6. John Percival, *Nureyev*, New York, Popular Library, 1977, p. 41.
7. The Modèrne has since become a Holiday Inn.
8. For the 1991 documentary *Nureyev* by Patricia Foy.
9. *Show Business Illustrated*, October 31, 1961.
10. A tactic the Russian ballet émigrés have been perfecting since the revolution and of which Makarova remains supreme mistress.
11. Clara Saint interview, Paris, June 10, 1993.
12. Pierre Lacotte interview, Paris, March 3, 1994.
13. Clara Saint interview, Paris, June 10, 1993.
14. Irina Kolpakova interview, New York City, May 19, 1993.
15. Stalin and his associates apparently could not even contemplate sex between women; to this day the Soviet criminal code does not even mention lesbians.
16. Frank Augustyn interview, Toronto, November 11, 1993.
17. Reenter the ghost of Nijinsky. The Champs-Elysées was also the theater in which the 1913 Stravinsky/Nijinsky *Rite of Spring* provoked a similar explosion.

SIX: The New Breed

1. *Weekend Review*, May 13, 1962.
2. John Percival, *Nureyev*, New York, Popular Library, 1975, p. 50.
3. *Ballet Review*, Spring 1975.
4. Ibid.
5. David Daniel interview, New York City, June 1, 1994.
6. Dame Ninette de Valois interview, London, June 17, 1993.
7. Martha Graham, *Blood Memory*, New York, Doubleday, 1991, p. 241.
8. Maria Tallchief interview, New York City, January 20, 1993.
9. John Wilson interview, New York City, January 25, 1994.
10. John Martin, *Saturday Review*, May 25, 1963.

11. *Time*, April 16, 1965.

12. Sonia Arova interview, New York City, February 15, 1994.

13. Volkova's influence continues to this day in her former student Stanley Williams, who is the ranking teacher of male dancing at the School of American Ballet in New York City. Nureyev was later a regular visitor to Williams's class and claimed that Williams gave him ten extra years as a dancer.

14. Peter Martins interview, New York City, February 23, 1994.

15. Ibid.

16. Anna Kisselgoff interview, New York City, February 17, 1994.

17. Elena Tchernichova interview, New York City, October 2, 1993.

18. Georgina Parkinson interview, New York City, January 28, 1994.

19. *Ballet Review,* Spring 1975.

20. Elena Tchernichova interview, New York City, October 2, 1993.

21. Sonia Arova interview, New York City, February 15, 1994.

22. *Ballet Review,* Spring 1975.

23. Peter Martins interview, New York City, February 23, 1994.

24. Heather Watts interview, New York City, May 31, 1993.

25. The pseudonym under which the critic Nigel Gosling and his wife, the ballerina Maude Lloyd, wrote about dancing.

26. Alexander Bland, *Observer of the Dance: 1958–1982*, Princeton, NJ, Princeton Books, 1986, p. 87.

27. Ibid.

28. Ninette de Valois interview, London, June 29, 1993.

SEVEN: THE LAST IMPERIAL BALLERINA

1. Fonteyn received the D.B.E. in 1959.

2. Margot Fonteyn, *Autobiography*, London, W. H. Allen, 1975, p. 214.

3. Ibid., p. 215.

4. Fonteyn and Nureyev documentary, *Fonteyn and Nureyev: The Perfect Partnership*, directed by Patricia Foy, 1985.

5. Margot Fonteyn documentary, *Margot Fonteyn*, 1989, produced and directed by Patricia Foy.

6. Arlene Croce, *After-Images*, New York, Knopf, 1977, p. 371.

7. Foy documentary, *Margot Fonteyn*.

8. Dame Ninette de Valois interview, London, June 29, 1994.

9. Foy, Fonteyn and Nureyev documentary, *Fonteyn and Nureyev: The Perfect Partnership*, directed by Patricia Foy.

10. Unimpressed, Balanchine described Fonteyn as having hands like spatulas.

11. Alexander Bland, *Observer of the Dance: 1958–1982*, Princeton, NJ, Princeton Books, 1986, p. 8.

12. Nadia Nerina interview, New York City, October 15, 1993.

13. Foy, Margot Fonteyn documentary, *Margot Fonteyn*.

14. *Time*, April 15, 1965.

15. Foy, Margot Fonteyn documentary, *Margot Fonteyn*.

16. John Wilson interview, New York City, January 25, 1994.

17. Martine van Hamel interview, New York City, February 25, 1994.

18. Sonia Arova interview, New York City, February 15, 1994.
19. Peter Martins interview, New York City, February 23, 1994.
20. Laura Young interview, Boston, November 7, 1993.
21. Ghislaine Thesmar interview, Paris, June 20, 1993.
22. *Nureyev*, Patricia Foy, director, 1991.
23. Foy, Margot Fonteyn documentary, *Margot Fonteyn*.
24. Ibid.
25. Fonteyn, *Autobiography*, p. 43.
26. Foy, Margot Fonteyn documentary, *Margot Fonteyn*.
27. Ninette de Valois interview, London, June 29, 1994.
28. *Time*, April 16, 1965.
29. *Ballet Review*, Summer 1993.
30. David Gillard, *Beryl Grey: A Biography*, London, W. H. Allen, 1977, p. 87.
31. Gillard also adds an interesting footnote: "Miss Sibley once told me that she was terrified when first asked to dance Chloë in *Daphnis and Chloë* —a role created for Fonteyn by Ashton in 1951. Fonteyn had made the part very much her own and Sibley had never seen it danced by anyone else. It was only when Ashton told her that, in the original story, Chloë was fair-haired [like Sibley] (not dark like Fonteyn) that she was able to separate the role from its creator and envision herself as the shepherdess." Gillard, *Beryl Grey*, p. 97.
32. Vancouver Ballet Society Tribute to Margot Fonteyn, Vancouver, May 1991.
33. Ibid.
34. *Ballet Review*, Summer 1993.
35. Foy documentary, *Margot Fonteyn*.
36. *The Daily Telegraph*, London, September 10, 1994. The placement of Arias's wounds seems to lend credence to the chauffeur version. The shots that left Arias paralyzed, concentrated in the lower back and buttocks, are suggestive of in flagrante delicto.
37. Heather Watts interview, New York City, May 31, 1993.
38. *The Daily Telegraph*, London, September 10, 1994.
39. *Vanity Fair*, March 1993.
40. Vancouver Ballet Society tribute to Margot Fonteyn, May 1991.
41. Fonteyn was not, however, a client of Hurok Concerts. Her association with Hurok was through his sponsorship of the Royal Ballet.
42. Nadia Nerina interview, London, October 15, 1993.

EIGHT: POP DANSEUR

1. *Time*, May 16, 1965.
2. Peter Martins, *Far from Denmark*, Boston, Little, Brown, 1982, p. 134.
3. Sheila Porter interview, New York City, November 12, 1993.
4. Merle Park interview, London, June 29, 1993.
5. Arlene Croce, *After-Images*, New York, Knopf, 1977, p. 113.
6. Jeremy Tunstall, "Stars, Status, Mobility," in *American Media and Mass Culture*, Donald Lazere, ed., p. 117.
7. Croce, *After-Images*, p. 91.

8. Peter Martins interview, New York City, February 23, 1994.
9. Edward P. Morgan, *The Sixties Experience: Hard Lessons about Modern America*, Philadelphia, Temple University Press, 1991, p. 44.
10. Ibid., p. 169.
11. Marshall McLuhan and Quentin Fiore, *The Medium Is the Massage*, New York, Touchstone, 1989, p. 88.
12. *San Francisco Examiner*, July 11, 1967.
13. John Wilson interview, New York City, January 25, 1994.
14. *National Observer*, September 27, 1965.
15. Gay Talese, *New York Times*, April 22, 1965.
16. *New York Times*, April 22, 1968.
17. Barbara Horgan interview, New York City, December 8, 1993.
18. Peter Martins interview, New York City, February 23, 1994.
19. Frank Augustyn interview, Toronto, November 3, 1993.

NINE: THE GREAT GAY MYTH: "I SLEPT WITH NUREYEV"

1. Martha Graham, *Blood Memory*, New York, Doubleday, 1991, p. 160.
2. *Newark Evening News*, December 29, 1962.
3. Unless it was a plot point, as in Antony Tudor's *Pillar of Fire*.
4. Eleanor d'Antuono interview, New York City, November 12, 1993.
5. *Ballet Review*, Spring 1979.
6. Lincoln Kirstein, *Dance: A Short History of Classic Theatrical Dancing*, Princeton, NJ, Princeton Books, 1987, p. 4.
7. Ibid., p.5.
8. Bob Colacello, *Vanity Fair*, March 1993.
9. Ibid.
10. Ibid.
11. Sonia Arova interview, New York City, February 15, 1994.
12. *Esquire*, March 1991.
13. Monique van Vooren interview, New York City, March 6, 1994.
14. Pseudonyms.
15. Kevin Gardner interview, Moscow, July 18, 1993.
16. James Toback interview, New York City, February 1, 1994.
17. Michael Callen interview, New York City, June 18, 1993.
18. Joel Rodham interview, June 12, 1994.
19. Paul Monette, *Becoming a Man: Half a Life Story*, Orlando, FL, Harcourt Brace, 1992, p. 4.
20. Monique van Vooren interview, New York City, March 6, 1994.
21. Lynn Barber, *The Independent on Sunday*, January 10, 1993.
22. *Geo*, June 27, 1983.
23. James Toback interview, New York City, February 1, 1994.

TEN: EVERYWHERE AT ONCE

1. The Sunday Review, *The Independent on Sunday*, January 10, 1993.
2. Nureyev's defection did not become public record in the former Soviet

Union until April 9, 1963. "Having betrayed Soviet art and his country," *Izvetsia* announced, "Nureyev [is now] decaying as a dancer. For some time he enjoyed scandalous popularity that could be explained by his vicious role of a turncoat." The article was accompanied by a scathing review of Nureyev's performances published in Paris one week before by Serge Lifar, the director of the Paris Opéra Ballet for more than thirty years who came within a hairsbreadth of summary execution after World War II on charges of collaboration (and who is buried not fifty feet from Nureyev in Sainte-Geneviève-des-Bois). Nureyev, Lifar wrote, was "unstable, hysterical, and vain. . . . He is simply a boy who stood against discipline, necessary in all art. This discipline is work, not whiskey at five o'clock in the morning. Now he betrays the whole world." *International Herald Tribune*, April 10, 1963; *New York Times*, April 10, 1963.

3. *Show Business Illustrated*, October 31, 1961.

4. *International Herald Tribune*, January 13, 1962.

5. Arlene Croce, *After-Images*, New York, Knopf, 1977, pp. 91–92.

6. *New York Post*, July 13, 1964.

7. The three Tschaikovsky/Petipa masterworks that are the basis of Imperial Russian classicism were first performed by Italian, not Russian, ballerinas—Carlotta Brianza in *The Sleeping Beauty*, Antonietta dell'Era in *Nutcracker*, and Pierina Legnani in *Swan Lake*.

8. In France, their quartet was known as *les quatres monstres sacrés*.

9. As a result of Nureyev's appearance in Athens, Sviatoslav Richter, the Soviet pianist whose performance at the Khrushchev soiree three years earlier so impressed Nureyev, canceled his three scheduled performances at the festival, which were to have included his appearance with the Vienna Philharmonic under Herbert von Karajan.

10. An irresistible razz at the Soviets and their vodka industry, the Suntory advertisement supplied Nureyev with the necessary cash for staging *Manfred* in Zurich that same year.

11. *The Observer*, January 10, 1993.

12. Georgina Parkinson interview, New York City, January 28, 1994.

13. Merle Park interview, London, June 29, 1993.

14. Antoinette Sibley interview, London, July 1, 1993.

15. Nadia Nerina interview, London, October 15, 1993.

16. *The Sunday Times Magazine*, London, January 31, 1993.

17. The only exception was the Russian-born ballerina, Violetta Elvin, who married British.

18. Interview with Antoinette Sibley, London, July 1, 1993.

19. Glen Tetley interview, New York City, January 27, 1993.

20. *Variety*, February 6, 1963.

21. Interview with Mavis Richardson, Thames Television, 1981.

22. Antoinette Sibley interview, London, July 1, 1993.

23. *Ballet Review*, Winter 1993.

24. David Blair (1932–76) was set to succeed Michael Somes as Fonteyn's resident partner when Nureyev arrived on the scene.

25. Thames Television interview, 1981.

26. Sonia Arova interview, New York City, February 15, 1993.

27. *Newsweek*, April 19, 1965.

28. Georgina Parkinson interview, New York City, January 28, 1994.

29. Ibid.

30. Nadia Nerina interview, London, October 15, 1993.

31. *Ballet Review*, Winter 1993.

32. Lynn Seymour interview, London, May 5, 1993.

33. Lynn, Seymour, *Lynn: The Autobiography of Lynn Seymour*, London, Grenada Publishing, 1984, p. 235.

34. Merle Park interview, London, June 29, 1993.

35. *Globe and Mail*, January 4, 1965.

36. Jerome Robbins interview, New York City, January 10, 1994.

37. *The Times Saturday Review*, London, March 30, 1991.

ELEVEN: THE NUREYEV INDUSTRY

1. *Vanity Fair*, March 1993.

2. *The Sunday Times* (London), January 10, 1993.

3. Nadia Nerina interview, London, October 15, 1993.

4. Sonia Arova interview, New York City, February 15, 1994.

5. Ibid.

6. For many years, Nureyev's legal counsel also included Jennette Thurnheer from Zurich. She is currently the director of the board supervising the Nureyev estate. The board is also based in Zurich.

7. Gordon volunteered his services to Nureyev, and their association was never official.

8. *The Spectator*, January 16, 1993.

9. Nureyev's apartment in the Dakota was sold in 1993 for an undisclosed sum, although another apartment in the building of approximately the same size and design was sold just before for an estimated $1.3 million.

10. *The Sunday Times* (London), January 10, 1993.

11. Ibid.

12. *The Spectator*, January 16, 1993.

13. Sonia Arova interview, New York City, February 15, 1994.

14. *The Spectator*, January 16, 1993.

15. Nadia Nerina interview, New York City, October 15, 1993.

16. *Dancemagazine*, March 1962.

17. The *New York Post*, November 10, 1963.

18. Estimates on the La Turbie villa vary from $50,000 to $80,000 to $150,000. Nureyev told Lee Radziwill in *Architectural Digest* in 1985 that he'd purchased the villa with money he made from his *Bell Telephone Hour* appearance with Tallchief, which seems unlikely in the extreme.

19. *Time*, March 29, 1968.

20. Sonia Arova interview, New York City, February 16, 1994.

21. John Wilson interview, New York City, January 25, 1994.

22. *This Week*, March 15, 1953.

23. John Wilson interview, New York City, January 25, 1994.

24. *New York Times*, August 8, 1975.

25. Seymour, *Lynn*, p. 238.

26. Bruhn recovered in time to dance his next scheduled performance two days later.

27. John Wilson interview, New York City, January 25, 1994.
28. John Gingritch interview, New York City, February 20, 1994.
29. *New York Times*, July 27, 1975.
30. Celia Franca interview, New York City, February 16, 1994.
31. Luis Falco died of AIDS shortly before Nureyev.
32. John Wilson interview, New York City, January 25, 1994.
33. *Variety*, February 1, 1978.
34. *New York Times*, February 1, 1976.

TWELVE: WHO'S AFRAID OF
MARTHA AND GEORGE?

1. Murray Louis, *Inside Dance*, New York, St. Martin's Press, 1981, p. 98.
2. Barely a year before Nureyev arrived in the West, a storm of controversy broke out over the landmark Ford Foundation grants given in support of American dance, which gave a lot of money to ballet and nada to the moderns. The fallout generated one of the great midnight rides in dance history —an early A.M. telephone call to Kirstein from Graham, well into her cups. Graham's opening salvo at Kirstein was a classic: "You are nothing but a common thief."
3. *Images of Love* was the first fully contemporary ballet created specifically for Nureyev. The cast also included Christopher Gable and Lynn Seymour. Seymour, *Lynn*, p. 236.
4. Ibid.
5. Rudi van Dantzig interview, New York City, February 17, 1994.
6. Ibid.
7. Ninette de Valois interview, London, June 30, 1993.
8. Nureyev did not perform *Field Figures* at its premiere on November 9, 1970. Nureyev took over the role originally made for Desmond Kelly. Glen Tetley interview, New York City, January 27, 1994.
9. Murray Louis interview, New York City, March 17, 1993.
10. Paul Taylor interview, New York City, January 31, 1994.
11. *Christopher Street*, August 1976.
12. Paul Taylor interview, New York City, January 30, 1993.
13. Gian Carlo Menotti founded the Spoleto festival.
14. Paul Taylor, *Private Domain*, New York, Knopf, 1987, p. 211.
15. Paul Taylor interview, New York City, January 31, 1994.
16. *Christopher Street*, August 1976.
17. *Dance*, July 1975.
18. Croce, *After-Images*, p. 162.
19. Don McDonagh, *Martha Graham: A Biography*, New York, Praeger, 1973, p. 289.
20. Christine Daikin interview, New York City, January 4, 1994.
21. Graham, *Blood Memory*, New York, Doubleday, 1991, pp. 242, 244.
22. Janet Eilber interview, New York City, January 11, 1994.
23. *New York Times*, June 15, 1975.
24. Janet Eilber interview, New York City, January 11, 1994.
25. Christine Daikin interview, New York City, January 4, 1994.
26. Janet Eilber interview, New York City, January 11, 1994.

27. Rudi van Dantzig interview, New York City, February 17, 1994.
28. Arlene Croce, *The New Yorker*, January 18, 1993.
29. Rudi van Dantzig interview, New York City, February 17, 1994.
30. Barbara Horgan interview, New York City, December 8, 1993.
31. Eleanor d'Antuono interview, New York City, November 12, 1993.
32. Barbara Horgan interview, New York City, December 8, 1993.
33. Croce, *After-Images*, p. 112.
34. Barbara Horgan interview, New York City, December 8, 1993.
35. Patricia McBride interview, New York City, March 10, 1994.
36. *Newsday*, April 8, 1989.

THIRTEEN: *VALENTINO* AND BEYOND

1. Richard Stites, *Russian Popular Culture: Entertainment and Society Since 1990*, New York, Cambridge University Press, 1992, p. 125.
2. Ibid., p.132.
3. Ibid.
4. Michael Canesi interview, Paris, June 21, 1993.
5. *The Sunday Times Magazine* (London), January 31, 1993.
6. *Variety*, May 20, 1964.
7. *Newsweek*, July 27, 1964.
8. *New York Times*, July 14, 1964.
9. *New York Times*, March 22, 1966.
10. The men who gave you James Bond.
11. Edward Albee interview, New York City, January 13, 1994.
12. *The Sunday Times* (London), April 30, 1972.
13. *Films and Filming*, September 1972.
14. The return engagement of *I Am a Dancer* raked in sixty thousand dollars after only three newspaper advertisements.
15. The film was coproduced by Nureyev, Robert Helpmann—the great Australian character dancer who performed the title role—and John Hargreaves, one of the producers of *I Am a Dancer*. Helpmann was also billed as codirector.
16. Judith Crist, *New York Magazine*, November 5, 1973.
17. Anna Kisselgoff, *New York Times*, March 11, 1973.
18. Heather Watts interview, New York City, May 19, 1993.
19. Nadia Nerina interview, London, October 15, 1993.
20. *The Sunday Times* (London), April 30, 1972.
21. James Toback interview, New York City, February 1, 1994.
22. Although he gave himself a full barre every day, frequently on that day's set, where the crew could be reminded that they were in the presence of something special.
23. Felicity Kendal interview, London, February 8, 1994.
24. Carol Kane interview, New York City, March 9, 1994.
25. The *Valentino* script was by Russell and John Byrum, although the screenwriting credit went to Russell and Mardik Martin.
26. Michelle Phillips interview, Los Angeles, February 10, 1994.
27. *New York Times*, November 10, 1977.
28. Ibid.

29. *Variety*, January 4, 1978.

30. The estimated total of ticket sales was $1.5 million, and the film was soon withdrawn from release.

31. *New York Times*, April 22, 1983.

32. *Variety*, April 20, 1983.

33. The last frame of *Exposed*, in fact, a tight, frozen close-up of Kinski, is an exact duplicate of Decae's fabled last shot of Jean-Pierre Léaud in *The Four Hundred Blows*.

34. James Toback interview, New York City, February 1, 1994.

35. Ibid.

36. Ibid.

37. *Variety*, December 20, 1972.

38. *GQ*, January 1983.

39. The duet is, in fact, from Mozart's *Don Giovanni*.

40. Performed by Royal Ballet soloist Graham Fletcher.

FOURTEEN: BACK TO PARIS

1. If Nureyev were to have been in Paris longer than a total of six months in a single year, he would have qualified as an official French resident, a status he did not want because it would have made his worldwide earnings taxable under French law. By remaining in Paris no more than six months a year, he was required to pay taxes only on money he earned in France.

2. Once again, however, the French were as astute in negotiation as Nureyev. His salary as a performer was set on a sliding scale: full pay for the performance of a full-length work, less for a shorter appearance on a repertory evening. The arrangement saved the Opéra a considerable amount of money by the last years of Nureyev's tenure with the company, when his number of performances decreased with his decreasing physical capacities and more frequent absences.

3. *New York Times*, October 23, 1983.

4. Patrice Bart interview, Paris, June 23, 1993.

5. Patricia Ruanne interview, New York City, May 10, 1993.

6. Thierry Fouquet interview, Paris, June 23, 1993.

7. Patrick Dupond interview, Paris, July 7, 1993.

8. Reprinted in *The Guardian*, June 30, 1985.

9. The Swan Queen and her sisters do not even appear until the second act.

10. Patrice Bart interview, Paris, June 23, 1993.

11. Antoinette Sibley interview, London, July 1, 1993.

12. Glen Tetley interview, New York City, January 27, 1994.

13. Lydia Sokolova, *Dancing for Diaghilev*, San Francisco, Mercury House, 1989, p. 24.

14. A promising, prominent young French dancer and choreographer.

15. Patrick Dupond interview, Paris, July 7, 1993.

16. Renault was one of the four male leads in the 1947 premiere of Balanchine's *Palais de cristal*, to Georges Bizet's only symphony, the ballet that is now known (and revered) the world over as *Symphony in C*.

17. For the definitive assessment of Béjart and his work, see Arlene Croce's

essay "The Follies Béjart" in her collection of criticism, *After-Images*, New York: Knopf, 1977, pp. 380–90.

18. The special irony, of course, is that Béjart had been forced to move on to Brussels because the Opéra refused to hire him as ballet director in Paris. An interesting side note to the Nureyev/Béjart standoff is that barely a year later the Théatre Royal de la Monnaie in Brussels, which had been home to the Béjart company, was in negotiation with the American Mark Morris Dance Group as a replacement for the Béjart troupe. It is entirely possible that Béjart, a man who kept his ear to the ground, already was aware of impending change when he attempted his coup at the Opéra.

19. *Philadelphia Inquirer*, March 27, 1986.

20. Thanks to the influx of Russian émigrés after the 1917 revolution, Paris also became the most important center for study in European ballet. The former Imperial ballerinas who opened their own studios in Paris included the greatest of the great, among them Olga Preobrajenska, Mathilde Kschessinskaya, and Lubov Egorova.

21. After three tense years, during which time Lifar more than once found himself handcuffed in a basement room in the company of angry guards with loaded revolvers, Lifar was acquitted after a public trial.

22. Edwin Denby, *Dance Writings*, New York, Knopf, 1986, p. 368.

23. Jerome Robbins interview, New York City, January 10, 1994.

24. Patricia Ruane interview, New York City, May 10, 1993.

25. The Opéra requires its women to retire at age forty, although the male dancers are allowed another five years.

26. Patrick Dupond interview, Paris, July 7, 1993.

27. Elisabeth Platel interview, Paris, June 19, 1993.

28. In a Nureyev-like move, Guillem left the Opéra in 1988 after a dispute over the number of her performances and is now an SRO attraction with the Royal Ballet. Nureyev's opinion of her eventually soured. "She doesn't bring light," Nureyev told *The Sunday Times Magazine* (London) in 1991. "We love her, admire her musicality . . . but she gives a selfish performance. Like Natalia Makarova. It is not a generous performance."

29. Elisabeth Platel interview, Paris, June 19, 1993.

30. Patrice Bart interview, Paris, June 23, 1993.

31. There was, in fact, no new contract. Nureyev's first contract simply remained operational for another three years.

FIFTEEN: "I Cannot Have AIDS"

1. Nureyev, the shaggy-haired danseur, became the first discernible bridge between the high-tone traditions of the Royal Opera House, Covent Garden, and the inspired underground of fresh young talent that produced the Beatles, the Rolling Stones, and low-budget film masterworks such as Tony Richardson's *Tom Jones* that put the tired British film industry back on the map.

2. Paul Monette, *Becoming a Man: Half a Life Story*, Orlando, FL, Harcourt Brace, 1992, p. 63.

3. According to Michael Callen's research for *Surviving AIDS*, which was

published in 1990, of the forty-eight people diagnosed with AIDS by January 1981, five were still alive; of the 191 people diagnosed with AIDS by January 1982, fifteen were still alive.

4. James Toback interview, New York City, February 1, 1994.

5. *Vanity Fair*, March 1993.

6. Patrick Dupond interview, Paris, July 7, 1993.

7. The interview Canesi gave to the Paris newspaper *Le Figaro* a week after Nureyev died was the first official announcement that the cause of Nureyev's death was AIDS-related complications. Despite Canesi's assertion that Nureyev had given him permission to do as he chose with the facts of Nureyev's illness after he was gone, Canesi was censured by the national organization of French doctors for violation of physician/patient confidentiality. He was subsequently forbidden to release any information that had not appeared in the *Figaro* interview, a condition of the interview he granted me for this book in Paris on June 21, 1993. Canesi would not specify the reason for Nureyev's first visit in 1983.

8. Reprinted in *The Guardian*, January 20, 1993.

9. According to Canesi, his estimate of the time frame for Nureyev's HIV infection was based on "certain biological items that he had at the time." Ten years later, Canesi's subsequent experience in working with AIDS patients, he says, has confirmed his initial diagnosis. Canesi interview, Paris, June 21, 1993.

10. Ibid.

11. Randy Shilts, *And the Band Played On: Politics, People, and the AIDS Epidemic*, New York, St. Martin's, 1987, pp. 475–76.

12. Canesi interview, Paris, June 21, 1993.

13. *Vanity Fair*, March 1993.

14. *The Guardian*, January 20, 1993.

15. Ibid.

16. *Vanity Fair*, March 1993.

17. *The Guardian*, January 20, 1993.

18. Paul Monette, *Borrowed Time*, pp. 2, 102.

19. Michael Callen, *Surviving AIDS*, New York, HarperCollins, 1990, p. 243.

20. Patrice Bart interview, Paris, June 23, 1993.

21. Rudi van Dantzig interview, New York City, February 17, 1994.

22. Paul Monette, *Borrowed Time*, p. 81.

23. *Newsweek*, January 18, 1993.

24. Paul Monette interview, February 11, 1994.

25. Canesi interview, Paris, June 21, 1993.

26. *Newsweek*, January 18, 1993.

27. Elisabeth Platel interview, Paris, June 19, 1993.

28. Michael Callen, *Surviving AIDS*, p. 183.

SIXTEEN: THE FAT LADY SINGS

1. *Esquire*, May 1991.

2. Anna Kisselgoff interview, New York City, February 17, 1994.

3. Nureyev received his Austrian passport in 1982. Until then he had been classified officially as a stateless person.

4. *Newsweek*, April 19, 1965.

5. *Dance Magazine*, May 1990.

6. *The Sunday Times Magazine* (London), January 31, 1993.

7. *The Sunday Times Magazine* (London), March 30, 1991.

8. *New York Times*, November 3, 1989.

9. Promotion to *étoile* status is the sole priority of the ballet director, but, according to the construct of the company, candidates for the highest rank in the Opéra hierarchy are required to work their way up through the ranks.

10. *Vanity Fair*, March 1993.

11. *New York Times*, November 2, 1989.

12. Ibid.

13. *Esquire*, March 1991.

14. Arlene Croce, *After-Images*, New York, Knopf, 1977, p. 111.

15. *The Daily Mail*, July 22, 1985.

16. *Le Figaro*, January 15, 1993.

17. Judith Mackrell, *The Independent*, July 31, 1993.

18. Antoinette Sibley interview, London, July 1, 1993.

19. Maria Tallchief interview, New York City, January 20, 1993.

20. Barbara Horgan interview, New York City, December 8, 1993.

21. Nadia Nerina interview, London, October 15, 1993.

22. *The Spectator*, January 16, 1993.

23. *The Sunday Times Magazine* (London), January 31, 1993.

24. Ibid.

25. London *Times*, May 8, 1991.

26. Nureyev had known Hubner since 1964 and referred to him as "Papa Hubner."

27. *The Observer*, May 21, 1991.

28. Charles Barker interview, New York City, February 11, 1994.

29. *The Sunday Times Magazine* (London), January 31, 1993.

30. *Le Figaro*, January 15, 1993.

31. Patricia Ruanne interview, New York City, May 10, 1993.

32. Ibid.

33. John Taras interview, New York City, June 7, 1993.

34. Charles Jude interview, Paris, June 17, 1993.

35. *Le Figaro*, January 15, 1993.

36. Michael Canesi interview, Paris, June 21, 1993.

37. Excepting his sister Rosa, Nureyev's relationship with his family had been strained for years. He regularly supplied them with money and the result was that they had become dependent on Nureyev's generosity rather than on trying to make their own way. On the visits that they made to their brother in the West, his sisters were clearly out of their element. On one visit to La Turbie, when Opéra was off on tour, they suddenly became frightened of their neighbors and broke up some of Nureyev's most expensive furniture to board up the windows. The incident was not atypical. When they came to Paris for the last visit, Nureyev's sisters reportedly were upset over changes Nureyev had made in his will during the last months of his life, such as the bequest for injured or disabled dancers. There

were reports of shouting matches in Nureyev's hospital room over the subject. He left his sisters $200,000 each and willed the same sum to each of his four nieces and nephews. The family currently is challenging the will and attempting to block the sale of Nureyev's personal effects. A countersuit has been filed by the legal representatives of Nureyev's estate.

38. *New York Times*, January 7, 1993.

SELECTED BIBLIOGRAPHY

DANCE

Bland, Alexander. *Observer of the Dance: 1958–1982*. London: Dance Books, Ltd., 1985.

Bremser, Martha, ed. *The International Dictionary of Ballet*. London: St. James Press, 1994.

Buckle, Richard. *Nijinsky*. New York: Simon & Schuster, 1971.

———. *Buckle at the Ballet*. New York: Atheneum, 1980.

Croce, Arlene. *After-Images*. New York: Knopf, 1977.

———. *Going to the Dance*. New York: Knopf, 1982.

———. *Sightlines*. New York: Knopf, 1987.

Denby, Edwin. *Dance Writings*. Robert Cornfield and William Mackay, eds. New York: Knopf, 1986.

Fonteyn, Margot. *Autobiography*. London: W.H. Allen, 1975.

Gillard, David. *Beryl Grey: A Biography*. London: W.H. Allen, 1977.

Graham, Martha. *Blood Memory: An Autobiography*. New York: Washington Square Press, 1991.

Haskell, Arnold, ed. *Ballet Annual/Ballet Decade*. New York: Macmillan, 1952.

Jowitt, Deborah. *The Dance in Mind*. Boston: David R. Godine, 1985.

———. *Time and the Dancing Image*. New York: William Morrow, 1988.

Karsavina, Tamara. *Theatre Street: The Reminiscences of Tamara Karsavina*. New York: E. P. Dutton, 1931.

Kirstein, Lincoln. *Dance: A Short History of Classic Theatrical Dancing*. New York: G. P. Putnam's Son, 1935.

Koegler, Horst, ed. *The Concise Oxford Dictionary of Ballet*, 2nd ed. Oxford: Oxford University Press, 1982.

Louis, Murray. *Inside Dance*. New York: St. Martin's Press, 1980.

Martins, Peter. *Far from Denmark*. Boston: Little, Brown, 1982.

McDonagh, Don. *Martha Graham: A Biography*. New York: Praeger, 1973.

Morley, Iris. *Soviet Ballet*. London: Collins Press, 1945.

Roslavleva, Natalia. *Era of the Russian Ballet*. London: Victor Gollancz, 1966.

Seymour, Lynn. *Lynn: The Autobiography of Lynn Seymour*. London: Granada Publishing, Ltd., 1984.

Slonimsky, Yuri. *The Soviet Ballet*. New York: Philosophical Library, 1947.

Smakov, Gennady. *The Great Russian Dancers*. New York: Knopf, 1984.

Sokolova, Lydia, with Richard Buckle, ed. *Dancing for Diaghilev: The Memoirs of Lydia Sokolova*. New York: Macmillan, 1961. Mercury House (reprint), 1989.

Swift, Mary Grace. *The Art of the Dance in the U.S.S.R.* Notre Dame: University of Notre Dame Press, 1968.

Taylor, Paul. *Private Domain*. New York: Knopf, 1987.

Tkachenko, T. *Soviet Dances*. Joan Lawson, ed. London: Imperial Society of Teachers of Dancing, 1964.

Walker, Katherine Sorley. *Ninette de Valois: Idealist Without Illusions*. London: Hamish Hamilton, 1987.

GENERAL

Andersen, Christopher. *Jagger Unauthorized*. New York: Dell, 1993.

Beatty, Bernard. *Don Juan and Other Poems: A Critical Study*. Harmondsworth, Middlesex, England: Penguin, 1987.

Blum, John Morton. *Years of Discord: American Politics and Society, 1961–1974*. New York: W.W. Norton, 1991.

Calder, Angus. *Byron*. Milton Keynes, England: Open University Press, 1987.

Fernandez, Ramon. *Molière: The Man Seen Through the Plays*. New York: Octagon, 1980.

Gitlin, Todd. *The Sixties: Years of Hope, Days of Rage*. New York: Bantam, 1987.

Howarth, W.D., and Merlin Thomas. *Molière: Stage and Study*. Oxford: Oxford University Press, 1973.

James, Henry. *Washington Square*. Oxford: Oxford University Press, 1982.

Lermontov, Mikhail. *A Hero of Our Time*. Paul Foote, trans. Harmondsworth, Middlesex, England: Penguin, 1966.

Maugham, W. Somerset. *A Writer's Notebook*. New York: Penguin, 1949.

McLuhan, Marshall, and Quentin Fiore. *The Medium Is the Massage*. New York: Simon & Schuster, 1967. Touchstone (reprint), 1989.

Morgan, Edward P. *The Sixties Experience: Hard Lessons About Modern America*. Philadelphia: Temple University Press, 1991.

Pushkin, Alexander. *Eugene Onegin*, Charles Johnson, trans. Harmondsworth, Middlesex, England: Penguin, 1977.

Raphael, Frederic. *Byron*. London: Little, Brown, 1992.

Stoker, Bram. *Dracula*. Harmondsworth, Middlesex, England: Penguin, 1979.

Twitchell, James B. *Carnival Culture: The Trashing of Taste in America*. New York: Columbia University Press, 1992.

Van Vooren, Monique. *Night Sanctuary*. New York: Simon & Schuster, 1981.

Nureyev

Bland, Alexander. *The Nureyev Image.* New York: Quadrangle/New York Times Books, 1976.

Nureyev, Rudolf. *Nureyev: An Autobiography with Pictures.* New York: E. P. Dutton, 1963.

Percival, John. *Nureyev: Aspects of the Dancer.* New York: G. P. Putnam's Sons, 1975.

Russia

Brandes, George. *Impressions of Russia: Life and Letters in Late Nineteenth Century Russia Viewed by a Distinguished Contemporary.* New York: Thomas Y. Crowell, 1889.

de Jonge, Alex. *Stalin and the Shaping of the Soviet Union.* New York: William Morrow, 1986.

Dukes, Paul. *A History of Russia: Medieval, Modern, Contemporary* (2nd ed.). Durham, N. Car., Duke University Press, 1990.

Gosling, Nigel. *Leningrad.* New York: E. P. Dutton, 1965.

Heller, Mikhail, and Aleksandr M. Nekrich. *Utopia in Power: The History of the Soviet Union from 1917 to the Present.* New York: Simon & Schuster, 1986.

Hosking, Geoffrey. *A History of the Soviet Union,* rev. ed. London: Fontana Press, 1990.

Klose, Kevin. *Russia and the Russians: Inside the Closed Society.* New York: W. W. Norton, 1984.

Laqueur, Walter. *Stalin: The Glasnost Revelation.* New York: Charles Scribner's Sons, 1990.

Lawrence, John. *A History of Russia,* 7th rev. ed. New York: Penguin, 1993.

Lee, Andrea. *Russian Journal.* New York: Random House, 1981.

Lieven, Dominic. *Nicholas II: Emperor of All the Russias.* London: John Murray, 1993.

Lincoln, W. Bruce. *The Romanovs: Autocrats of all the Russias.* New York: Dial Press, 1981.

Massie, Robert K. *Nicholas and Alexandra.* New York: Atheneum, 1967.

Shipler, David K. *Russia: Broken Idols, Solemn Dreams.* New York: Times Books, 1983.

Sinyavsky, Andrei. *Soviet Civilization: A Cultural History.* Boston: Little, Brown, 1990.

Smith, Hendrick. *The New Russians.* New York: Avon, 1990.

Stites, Richard. *Russian Popular Culture: Entertainment and Society Since 1900.* Cambridge: Cambridge University Press, 1992.

Teleshov, N. *A Writer Remembers: Reminiscences of Russian Literary Life.* London: Hutchinson, 1890.

Westwood, J. N. *The Short Oxford History of the Modern World/Endurance and Endeavor: Russian History 1812–1980* (2nd ed.). Oxford: Oxford University Press, 1973.

AIDS

Callen, Michael. *Surviving AIDS*. New York: HarperCollins, 1990.

Kramer, Larry. *Reports from the Holocaust*. New York: St. Martin's, 1981.

Monette, Paul. *Borrowed Time: An AIDS Memoir*. Orlando, FL: Harcourt Brace Jovanovich, 1988.

Preston, John, ed. *Personal Dispatches: Writers Confront AIDS*. New York: St. Martin's, 1988.

Shilts, Randy. *And the Band Played On: Politics, People, and the AIDS Epidemic*. New York: St. Martin's, 1987.

Sontag, Susan. *AIDS and Its Metaphors*. New York: Farrar, Straus and Giroux, 1989.

HOMOSEXUALITY

Monette, Paul. *Becoming a Man: Half a Life Story*. New York: HarperCollins, 1992.

Rich, Adrienne. *Bread, Blood, and Poetry: Selected Prose 1979–1985*. New York: W. W. Norton, 1986.

INDEX